The
Taliesin
Tradition

Emyr Humphreys was born in Prestatyn in 1919. An English-speaker, he learned Welsh after the burning of the bombing school on the Llyn peninsula in 1936, when his interest in Welsh culture was first awakened. He read History at Aberystwyth, and registered as a conscientious objector in 1939, and worked on farms in Pembrokeshire and north Wales as a result. Later in the war he served as a relief worker in the Middle East and Italy, and became an official of the Save the Children Fund under the U.N.

He later taught before joining the BBC as a drama producer in 1955. Ten years later he became a lecturer in Drama at UCNW Bangor, but resigned in 1972 to write full time. His first novel, *The Little Kingdom*, was published in 1946, and Humphreys went on to win the Somerset Maugham Prize in 1952, for *Hear and Forgive*, and the Hawthornden Prize in 1958, for *A Toy Epic*. He is the author of nineteen novels, four collections of poetry, a book of short stories and a miscellany of essays, stories and poems. He has also written and directed many television films in both Welsh and English.

Also by Emyr Humphreys from Seren

A Toy Epic
Outside the House of Baal
Unconditional Surrender
The Gift of a Daughter

The
Taliesin
Tradition

Emyr Humphreys

seren

seren is the book imprint of
Poetry Wales Press Ltd
38-40 Nolton Street, Bridgend, CF31 3BN
www.seren-books.com

© Emyr Humphreys, 1983, 1989, 2000
First published by Black Raven Press, 1983
This edition 2000

ISBN 1-85411-246-5

A CIP record for this title is available from
the British Library

Cover: Pentre Ifan photographed by Barry Needle

*The publisher works with the financial assistance of the
Arts Council of Wales*

Printed in Plantin by The Cromwell Press, Trowbridge

Contents

LIST OF PLATES

I Blant Ein Plant

ACKNOWLEDGEMENTS

'Do you remember 1926?' is from *Gwalia Deserta*, 'I lost my native language' is from 'I was born in Rhymney' in *Tonypandy and Other Poems*, and 'Ah, 1926, I will never forget you!' is from an unfinished poem in the Idris Davies material at the National Library of Wales, Aberystwyth. These are reproduced by kind permission of Ebenezer Morris on behalf of the Estate of the late Idris Davies.

Lines from David Jones's *In Parenthesis* are reproduced by kind permission of Faber and Faber Ltd.

The permission of the following to reproduce illustrations is gratefully acknowledged:
The Earl of Pembroke: plate 1 (a) and (c); The National Museum of Wales: plate 1 (b), plate 5 (a) and (b); National Museum of Wales (Welsh Folk Museum): plate 6; Laing Art Gallery, Newcastle and Tyne and Wear County Council Museums (photograph by courtesy of the Courtauld Institute of Art): plate 2 and cover; National Museum of American Art (formerly National Collection of Fine Arts), Smithsonian Institution, Washington D.C.: plate 3 (a) (b) and (c); The National Library of Wales: plate 4 (a) (b) and (c), plate 7 (b) and (c) (copyright photograph Ron Jones), plate 8 (a); Keystone Press Agency: plate 7 (a); BBC Hulton Picture Library: plate 8 (b).

Introduction

The continuing existence of a Welsh identity is in itself a remarkable historical fact. Whether it be described as the end-product of an inherently conservative temperament, or as a combination of incorrigible ignorance and stupidity, or as a triumph of the human spirit, its existence cannot be denied. At any time since the eleventh century, it could have disappeared, but for the determination of one generation or another that it should not. Had the Normans, for example, been allowed the untrammelled access to all the levers of spiritual and material power that they enjoyed in England, Wales would have become indistinguishable from Cumberland or Lancashire within a brief space of time.

The history of Wales, such as it is, is a history of unending resistance and unexpected survival. It is these qualities in all their surprising variety that give the story dignity and significance. They create the invisible and yet indissoluble bonds of attachment that bind a Welshman to his inheritance and test his character from the cradle to the grave. The reader will bear in mind of course that from the time of the failure of Owain Glyndŵr to establish a Welsh state, at the beginning of the fifteenth century, the unceasingly attractive alternative to being Welsh was to become English: and no one, least of all the English, could ever imagine a more desirable disguise or a more cherishable identity to adopt.

The Tudors set a fashion which was fatally easy to copy. The grandson of Owain Penmynydd became the founding father of 'Merrie England', so that any ambitious Welshman from that time forward could persuade himself that he had a stake in that country and the unquestioned right to enjoy the fruits of an Englishness that would continue to flourish on a basis first of sea power and mercantile capitalism and subsequently an unparalleled imperial and industrial expansion. In the nineteenth century the Liberal party in Wales made itself the bourgeois equivalent of the path to wealth and power in England that had first been laid down by the Tudor aristocracy. In the twentieth century this role was taken over by the Labour party. As the

1

century draws to a close and a crisis of identity becomes a central issue in the civilisation of the West, it seems an appropriate time to investigate how such an apparently unprofitable and unprestigious national identity as the Welsh managed to survive in the face of such overwhelming odds. However small the nation in question, there can be no denying the size and universality of the problem.

Any technique of historical analysis is in effect an exploration of a labyrinth. The thread which this book invites the reader to grasp is the unique phenomenon known as the Welsh poetic tradition. As he takes it in hand it is as well to remind him that nothing of comparable antiquity remains operational in the British Isles or for that matter in Europe: so that when a young Welsh poet today brings off the feat of a decent piece of verse in the strict metres, he is making his own individual contribution to an art form which stretches back in unbroken line to that moment in the sixth century when an already ancient art then took the momentous step of transferring itself from an oral to a written tradition. As Saunders Lewis put it in an essay written in the 1940s about a poem by a minor poet (Ioan Siencyn) of eighteenth-century Pembrokeshire, 'You cannot pluck a flower of song off a headland of Dyfed in the late eighteenth century without stirring a great northern star of the sixth century.' The great northern star of course is the first Taliesin who sang in Rheged, the lost Brythonic kingdom which is now south-west Scotland and Cumberland.

The Taliesinic tradition can be traced through the centuries. What is perhaps less conspicuous is the manner in which at all times it has contrived to be a major factor in the maintenance, stability, and continuity of the Welsh identity and the fragile concept of Welsh nationhood. Indeed it could be argued that this hidden force in Welsh life also served as a catalyst in the creation of the far more robust and aggressive phenomenon of English nationalism, and those changes in the mental and spiritual climate of Europe that gave rise to the dominant power structure of the nation state. But it is in the Welsh experience that we can see most clearly how a poetic tradition can inject into a native language an authority and power that is sufficient to breathe forms of life into the national being even when independent military and political power have long withered away.

From the middle of the sixteenth century, for example, there have always been powerful agencies among the Welsh themselves who urgently desired the demise of the ancient tongue and all 'Welsh particularities' on the grounds that they were impediments to the material and spiritual progress of their fellow countrymen. For its own good Wales should be totally incorporated into the realm of England. In the face of their machinations it seemed impossible that any national identity for the Welsh could be preserved. The very structure of the nation state consolidated by the Tudor dynasty presented the aristocratic Welsh with an insoluble dilemma: how were they to get on in the new order, which seemed in so many ways to be created for their special benefit, and still be loyal to that ancient identity that had made the Tudor triumph possible? In any regime, and indeed for any class, minority status presents the continuing threat of statutory inferiority. The Welsh aristocracy solved their problem by polishing their pedigrees and becoming anglicised as quickly as possible. Thus the sense of Welsh nationhood, which has persisted stubbornly down to the present day, has done so without the exercise of military or political power and without any indigenous control of the economic base.

However, the Welsh experience prefigures in several essentials what is in effect now the position of most European nations, even the great ones like England, Germany and France. Their position in relation to each other, their inter-national bodies and the guiding power of the United States, bears some resemblance, especially in its cultural and even spiritual aspects, to the position of Wales in relation to the greatness of England over four centuries. Under such conditions, what is the value of a distinct identity? Why should England, for example, resist the massive historic forces that would transform it into an off-shore platform of an American culture vibrating with diverse and exciting forms?

Among the Welsh the Taliesinic tradition was always more than a conservative expression of poetic art. Its more elusive and perhaps ultimately more profound function was to serve as a crucible of myth. The manufacture and proliferation of myth must always be a major creative activity among a people with unnaturally high expectations reduced by historic necessity, or at least history, forced into what is often described as a marginal condition. In fact this marginal condition is now the essence of the human condition, with or without material security: we can bear even less than a little reality when it hovers over our heads in the shape of a nuclear missile. In Wales history and myth have always mingled and both have been of equal importance in the struggle for survival. If anyone doubts this, he has only to visit the memorial erected to Aneurin Bevan on the hillside above Ebbw Vale. It stands like a mysterious megalith, halfway between the Preseli and Stonehenge, already hung about with mist and myth and still not twenty years old.

A few years ago the present writer was faced with an unexpected question. He had attended and enjoyed a lecture on the poetry of Dylan Thomas by a distinguished English critic. The substance of the lecture dealt in some depth with the relation between the poetry and the poet's character, including the trauma of his birth and upbringing. In the queue for coffee, this lecturer suddenly put his unexpected question. The Englishness of it was both arrogant and touching. 'Tell me, how long have the Welsh considered themselves a nation?'

One never has the appropriate answer ready. My answer was lame. 'Since about the fifth century,' was what I said. But my answer should have been at least as elaborate as the contents of this book. And since Dylan Thomas was the subject of his lecture I should have brought in some reference to understanding the Welsh character. Even when the poet writes in English, you cannot pluck a flower in Cwmdonkin Park without disturbing a great northern star. Beyond durability and versatility, the Taliesinic tradition has one great quality to commend it: the secret of creative survival.

Taliesin the shape-shifter takes many forms. Dylan Thomas's great-uncle was a noted Welsh poet in his day. His name was Gwilym Marles and his poetic effusions bore a distinct resemblance to the muse of the Reverend Eli Jenkins. He was more important as a Unitarian minister of a small church in Cardiganshire which faced persistent persecution, and as an advocate of democratic and religious liberty. Taliesin in his later manifestation seems to have had a particular affection for this little congregation. The rule-book of the Welsh Unitarians was drawn up by no less a Taliesinic spirit than Iolo Morganwg, the late eighteenth-century universal genius of Glamorgan, literary forger and inventor of the *Gorsedd* of Druids and much of the pomp and circumstance of the modern eisteddfod. The rule-book was taken to Wisconsin, along with the druidic lore, by Richard Lloyd Jones, an earlier pastor of the Cardiganshire Unitarian flock of Gwilym Marles. He and his sons brought up the young Frank Lloyd Wright who, in the fullness of time created his own Taliesin, West and East.

No doubt the question could be reformulated. 'How long will the Welsh continue to consider themselves a nation?' If the experience of history is anything to go by – and if it isn't, then it can hardly be said to have served its purpose – the short answer must be, 'As long as the spirit of Taliesin continues to function as the tutelar spirit of the place.' There are of course less dithyrambic ways of putting it. All historical writing is an extension of a point of view, which is itself fixed in its own present. The only satisfactory test of its validity is the extent to which it can be sustained in the course of a prolonged look at the past. It is always the past rather than the present that offers the best hope for a future.

1   The Gift of Taliesin

Early in the seventeenth century a Glamorgan poet named Meurig Dafydd, a skilled practitioner of the art of the strict metres, called at Old Beaupre, a country house in the Vale of Glamorgan, to pay his respects to the squire in the traditional manner. An account of the visit has been preserved among the manuscripts of one of the squire's neighbours, John Stradling of St. Donats. The Stradling family had themselves been patrons of the poets. They were of Swiss origin and had come to Wales in the retinue of Edward I during his wars against Llywelyn. They were established at St. Donats early in the fourteenth century and from that time onwards, by marriage and by the patronage of the bards, they had insinuated themselves towards the centre of Welsh mediaeval life. This John Stradling however was an English relative. Although he had some pretensions to being a man of letters himself, it is evident from the way in which he records the following anecdote that he knew very little about Welsh poetry and was out of sympathy with what was left of its traditional practice.

> This bard resorting a brode to gentlemens howses in the loytringe time betweene Christmas and Candlemas to singe songes and receave rewardes, comminge to Bewper hee presented the good ould squier with a cowydh, odle or englyn (I knowe not whither) containinge partelie the praises of the gentleman, and partelie the pettygrees and matches of his auncesters. The gentleman havinge perused the rhyme, prepared in his hand a noble for a reward and called the poet who came with a good will; of whom he demaunded whether he had reserved to himself any copie of that rhyme; no by my fayth (sayd the rhymer) but I hope to take a copie of that which I delivered to you: Then replyed the gentleman, hould, here ys thy fee, and by my honestie I swere yf there bee no copie of this extante, none shall there ever bee, and therewith put it sure enough into the fier.

Meurig Dafydd, whatever the quality of the eulogy he had written, represented a bardic tradition which stretched back in unbroken line to the sixth century and the imposing figure of Taliesin; and before that into untold centuries of oral tradition. The function of praise poetry in

5

the Celtic world was to celebrate and sustain the social order. In the Welsh context, from the very beginning, this also involved the poet as the voice of resistance, the tireless mouthpiece of the endless process of defending a realm under siege. The terms of reference were laid down clearly in the first utterance of Taliesin in praise of his master the king Urien Rheged: 'Defender of Rheged, Lord of my Praises, your country's anchor . . . When you attack the Angles have no answer . . . You are the bridge from the past to the future, the best of your breed, the head of your race.'

The old squire's action was more than a calculated insult. A great deal more than a few lines of alliterative poetry was being thrown away. His gesture was a symbol. An entire class was relinquishing responsibilities that in former times had held the Welsh cultural and social fabric together. An aristocratic tradition of more than a thousand years duration was being tossed 'into the fier'.

When Taliesin sang, two hundred years had gone by since the end of effective Roman rule in Britain. Only the memory of a former glory lingered, and nowhere more vividly than in the country between the two Roman walls in what is now southern Scotland. The breathing space gained by a shadowy military genius who came to be known as Arthur had long since come to an end. By Taliesin's day the most active point of resistance to the renewed barbarian incursions was among the kingdoms of the Old North. It was thither that Taliesin travelled from his native Powys to sing the praise of the most successful Brythonic leader on the most active battle-front. Rheged, the kingdom that included south-west Scotland and Cumberland, was the leader of a Brythonic confederacy successfully withstanding onslaughts of savage enemies on all sides: Picts from the north, Angles to the east and south, and Irish Goidels, later to be called Scots, from the west. The successes of Urien were noised abroad throughout a Brythonic world that extended from Edinburgh in the north down the western side of Britain to Devon in the south. Here was a leader who played to win. At last, a grey-haired warrior, he had Deodoric the king of the Angles of Northumbria cornered on Lindisfarne. On the verge of triumph his confederacy of British princes fell apart. It seems that his own overbearing nature got the better of him. A jealous ally deserted him at the crucial moment, leaving him to taste death and defeat in what should have been the moment of victory. Urien had been as bold and impetuous as Arthur.

The ideal of the Brythonic warrior aristocrat was perfectly delineated in the work of Taliesin's contemporary Aneirin, the poet of the people and the land of Gododdin, whose capital was Edinburgh. Here the ruler, Mynyddog, trained and entertained a select band of three hundred heroes, drawn from all over the Brythonic world, for the ritual length of one year. They had pledged themselves to their sovereign by drinking his mead and thence forward nothing would deter them. The war-band prepared for a lightning attack on a stronghold that was now deep in the heart of enemy territory. They were doomed to destruction. By the end of the sixth century the long-range mobile tactics that had made Arthur famous no longer worked. A massive demographic swing could not be held up by a handful of horsemen. Nevertheless they could not turn back. The code of honour that they practised demanded their lives 'in payment for their mead'.

In Aneirin's epic poem *Y Gododdin* we come close to the spirit of the age of the original Arthur. He must have been the leader of just such a war-band. His great accomplishment was adapting such loyalty and fidelity to stemming the inexorable advance of the Anglo-Saxons. His tactics held up their occupation of the depleted and demoralised lowlands long enough to give the Celtic kingdoms time to emerge from the sub-Roman twilight.

> The men who went to Catraeth with the dawn allowed their spirit to shorten their lives. They drank their mead. It was yellow, it was sweet, it was the last snare. For one year the musicians were merry. Now their swords are red – they need not be cleaned . . .

> The men who went to Catraeth were an eager force, fresh mead was their drink, it became their poison. Three hundred disciplined for attack; and after the tumult there was silence. Though they had been to their churches to do penance, the tale must be told, they were felled by death.

One by one the courts of the Old North in which poets like Taliesin and Aneirin sang disappeared. Aneirin's Gododdin went first, absorbed into the power of Northumbria which became the first great English kingdom. Then Elmet went. Taliesin had sung there too, much to Urien's displeasure. When the remnants of the ruling British aristocracy retreated to Strathclyde and Rheged, they took their singers with them and the concepts that they celebrated: the ruler as dedicated defender of the Christian society under siege, and his knights living by a code of loyalty and self-sacrifice in which honour took precedence over worldly well-being or self-interest or mere prudent common sense. History shows clearly enough that they did not always live up to such high standards. The Celtic tradition of sudden quarrels and internecine warfare would have been sufficient to see to that. But the ideal was there and it was the first business of the professional poet to exercise his art in its celebration.

This was not the only literary activity in the British world of the sixth century. The church was an active force, and its leaders were recruited from the same families that sustained the network of little kingdoms stretching all over Celtic Britain. Judging by the writing of the angry monk Gildas, it looked with some disfavour on the activities of the praise poets. Gildas's book, on what he called *The Ruin of Britain*, was written in the period of comparative calm before the second wave of Anglo-Saxon advance which created the crisis that Taliesin and Aneirin had to face. His pattern was the prophetic books of the Old Testament, in particular Jeremiah, and he addressed the secular and religious leadership of the British people as if they were 'the lost sheep of the house of Israel'. They had fallen from the grace which had gone with the amplitude of Romano-Christian civilisation. Gildas looked back and saw the past through a haze of golden glory. It was the present on which he poured his anger. His explanation for historical catastrophe was the anger of a jealous God. The Romano-British were being punished for their innumerable shortcomings. Every calamity could be attributed to some defect in the national character. Gildas treated the praise poets as if he himself were Elijah and they were the prophets of Baal invoking some unknown Celtic deity in their extravagant eulogies. He takes particular exception to the poets of Maelgwn Gwynedd, the Dragon of the Island, with his court at Deganwy in Gwynedd. Maelgwn was singled out because he was a great man who could not make his mind up whether to become a humble hermit or a power-driven imperial sinner.

> What shall I say of you, Dragon of the Island, overthrower of tyrants, you are last on my list but first in evil, mightier than most in power, but also in malice, more liberal in giving and more given to sin, strong in arms but stronger still in that which destroys an immortal soul, Maglocunnus!

Maelgwn was able to sit and dream in his citadel which overlooked mythical cities under the sea. He had probably never seen a Saxon and he knew a great deal about the imperial habits of Roman emperors. And as he dreamed, Maelgwn could listen to his bards. Gildas describes their efforts and in so doing gives the earliest known portrait of Welsh poets in action.

> What you listen to, when your attention is caught, is not the praise of God from the sweet voices of Christ's recruits rehearsing the melodious music of the Church, but vain and empty praises of yourself from the mouths of a pack of scoundrels bawling out like drunken revellers, their lies and foaming phlegm spattering everyone within reach.

Gildas wrote in Latin and the bards sang in late Brythonic or the first utterance of early Welsh. The British aristocracy was making a fateful selection of the remnants of *Romanitas* and an heroic way of life, emerging like a characteristic hero in a Celtic tale from a prolonged sojourn in the Underworld. These were welded together by the exigencies of the British experience of the great movement of peoples that was transforming the face of Europe. Because he wrote in Latin it was Gildas's version of events which prevailed and came to dominate the thinking of both Briton and Saxon with the passage of time. The Venerable Bede, writing about 735 AD, relied completely on Gildas for his account of the history of Britain before and during the Saxon invasions. He makes skilful use of this material. He seizes on the testimony of a British monk concerning the sinfulness of the Britons and then proceeds to demonstrate how the favour of the God of battles was transferred from the sin-stained decadent natives to the virtuous and victorious heathens.

On the British who were to become Welsh, Gildas's diatribe had a different effect. When it listens to prophetic messages, the human ear is highly selective and in the case of large scale societies which look upon themselves as nations, the tendency to listen only to those parts the collective ear wishes to hear is even more pronounced. The Cambro-British seized on the pseudo-history as proof positive that the whole of the isle of Britain once belonged to them. The notion of this lost paradise and the treachery by which it had been stolen from them took firm root in the Cymric imagination and provided a new source of intense fuel for the engines of praise poetry. Well on into the middle ages a prince of some small kingdom in Wales could be addressed as the legitimate ruler of the whole island, with the praise poet embellishing a surprisingly accurate pedigree to prove it. Unfortunately with this euphoric gift went a sense of guilt which sank down into the depth of the collective unconscious. If they had been turned out of paradise, providence must have had a good reason. It was not difficult to equate the loss of Britain with the fall of man. Thus, among the people of this nation, a prince of the ninth century or a peasant of the nineteenth could ask with equal urgency and desperation, 'For what new sin of the spirit am I now being punished?'

Modern archaeology and a scientific reappraisal of ancient genealogies both bring some relief to the beleaguered Cymric conscience. The Angles and Saxons were firmly established on the soil of eastern lowland Britain before the departure of the Roman legions. In the fourth and fifth centuries the greater menace which threatened the British homeland came from the west and from the north. Irish settlements and petty kingdoms came into being from Cornwall to the west of Scotland. Even Gildas found the space to denounce Maximus Magnus for denuding the west of its military protection in order to pursue his imperial adventures on the continent. The long struggle between Briton and Saxon is best understood as a contest for the supreme authority left vacant by the departure of a Roman power that had been obliged to raise both of them to comparable positions of semi-independence: the Britons at their strongest and most independent in the highland zone, the Angles and the Saxons firmly established on the eastern side of the lowland zone. The Celtic aristocracy of the highland west could never at any time have possessed any of the provinces of the plain.

Nevertheless there were lost kingdoms. A British heroic age had occurred between the departure of the Romans and the establishment of the Anglo-Saxon hegemony. The Saxons were bound to occupy the lowland zone because they had an inexhaustible reservoir of land-hungry farming folk ready to migrate across the North Sea. The Britons had no such reserves and they were fighting on two fronts. Moreover the decay of Roman order and Celtic resurgence created discord both in their psychology and their social organisation. Merely to be Christian in these circumstances was an unhelpful inhibition. Heathen invaders, like the Vikings who were to spread destruction three centuries later, were never burdened with too many forms of scruple or conscience. The heroic age of the lost kingdoms coincided with the age of the Celtic saints. While the proto-Arthurian warriors held the advance of the pagans in check, their dedicated relatives wove an empire of the spirit around the waterways of the western seas, and in this process Wales occupied a pivotal position. Place names and the ancient dedications of churches bear witness to their activity. The centre of their world was the sea.

Towards the end of the eighth century a king arose in England determined to emulate his great contemporary on the continent, Charlemagne the sole king of the Franks and Holy Roman Emperor. This was Offa of Mercia who restored order in Northumbria and East Anglia when they were sinking into what he might well have considered Celtic-British anarchy: and in the same spirit of tidiness put up his celebrated Dyke to contain the excesses and pretensions of the petty kings of the mountainous west. In doing this he must have annexed a large portion of what had been a greater kingdom of Powys, including Shrewsbury, its former capital. Thus he increased the ghostly ranks of lost kingdoms and intensified a complex which the Welsh had already developed in this respect. The Dyke was a political and psychological calamity. It demonstrated that Gildas's worst fears had been realised. The loss of Britain became a feature of the landscape that no amount of bardic eloquence could disturb. Beyond it stretched the interminable great plain of Europe as far as the Urals, swarming with peoples hungry for good land and a temperate climate, and totally lacking in respect for the exalted lineage of Cambro-British princes.

Thus the mountainous peninsula of Wales, surrounded on three sides by the sea and marked off by the Dyke on the east, took on the nature of a fortress. For five centuries the Welsh were at full stretch defending a great deal more than any Ordnance Survey map could reveal. Under siege conditions the Welsh psyche developed an intense awareness of its own identity and cultural responsibilities. All the traditions of the Old North and the lost kingdoms were in their special care. The renown of the men of the north had been celebrated so effectively that in Wales it became the custom to refer to Taliesin as 'the Chief of Poets' (*Taliesin Pen Beirdd*). The Welsh saw themselves as the Israelites of old, the remnant of a more glorious past celebrated by a continuing poetic tradition which kept them buoyant and confident and filled with an unquenchable expectation of a promised land.

This loose confederation of little kingdoms was never a nation state. It resembled more closely a desirable Welsh universe to be defended whenever the occasion arose by a warrior aristocracy which kept itself in training with the traditional sport of limited internecine warfare. Constant military and naval pressure on every side gave equal opportunities for the acquisition of renown and glory, the necessary raw material for a lively poetic tradition. All this might have gone on for ever, had not the black pagans of Scandinavia been transformed in a matter of three generations into that reincarnation of Roman power seeking to dominate the whole of Western Europe with their unique combination of military and ecclesiastical might, the Normans.

After their conquest of England, the Normans had swept into Wales and at first it seemed as if nothing could withstand them. It was some time before the mountain princes rallied. But rally they did. As had been the case with all previous invasions, the habit of resistance triumphed. In his *Itinerary Through Wales* Giraldus Cambrensis, a Norman prelate who was one quarter Welsh, gives us a vivid glimpse of the native character at the end of the twelfth century:

> They pay no attention to commerce, shipping or industry, and their only preoccupation is military training. They are passionately devoted to their freedom and to the defence of their country: for these they fight, for these they suffer hardships, for these they will take up their weapons and willingly sacrifice their lives. They esteem it a disgrace to die in bed but an honour to be killed in battle.

For two centuries, chiefly under the leadership of the house of Gwynedd, the Welsh were able to preserve an essential independence in the face of the might of the Normans. It was this resistance that gave their culture and traditions a peculiar glamour in the eyes of mediaeval Europe.

2 Prince and Poet

The confrontation between the Normans and the Welsh was epic making. From the Pyrenees to the Perfeddwlad* the machinery of myth worked away at frontier encounters to feed the mediaeval imagination as effectively as Hollywood has supplied this necessary substance for our own time. The size of the operations in the field of reality bear little relation to the magnitude of the myth. All the same when Gruffudd ap Cynan returned from Ireland in 1081 to claim the throne of Gwynedd, the impact on the making of myth was greater than the arrival of William of Normandy on the shores of Sussex fifteen years earlier. Gruffudd, like William, had Viking blood and it was with the aid of a Viking fleet from his mother's Scandinavian Dublin that he turned the Norman tide and re-established the authority of the House of Cunedda – Cunedda Wledig, that Romano-British official from north of Hadrian's Wall who established the only ruling dynasty in Britain stemming directly from Roman Britain.

The surge of creative energy released by the fight for independence was aware of this illustrious genealogical fact and interpreted it to enlarge its own social and political influence. Since this release was also a resurgence of what we now recognise as the underlying Celticity of Europe, it is appropriate to distinguish between three categories of early mediaeval Welsh literary creation. It was the compositions in Latin which drew the widest attention, and most conspicuously the work of Geoffrey of Monmouth. Geoffrey picked up the worn mantles of Gildas and Nennius and incorporated them in his own more elaborate and colourful cloak. His monumental and mythic *History of the Kings of Britain* became the most influential pseudo-history ever written and on no people did it have a more lasting effect than on the Cambro-British themselves.

In the eyes of the Welsh, Geoffrey's book overshadowed their native prose masterpieces for centuries. It is only since the nineteenth century that they came to recognise the prose tales of the *Mabinogion* collection

* Literally either 'the middle earth' or 'entrail country', and now placid Denbighshire.

among the finest sustained artistic creations in their language. This single fact is in itself a clear indication of the lasting relationship between the activity we now call 'literary criticism' and political awareness. For the Welsh to distinguish between myth and history has always been a difficult exercise. This may be inevitable among a gifted and sensitive people, apparently condemned by historical materialism to a permanently marginal existence. In order to be coaxed into action they need to be offered a world. Nothing less could persuade them to stir out of the cocoon of their comfortable illusions. It is for this very reason that they are obliged to develop and continually assert their critical faculty: in order to avoid the fate of the folk hero who falls into the dangerous slumber, or captivity in the house of crystal, or any of the many forms of Celtic fool's paradise. Fiction can of course catch closer glimpses of ultimate truth than mere recorded fact, but it can only do so when both the maker and the society he serves are sufficiently wide awake to make the elementary distinction. In the case of the mediaeval and for that matter the modern Welsh, it was and is always exaggerated expectations that led and lead them down the broad avenues towards extinction or assimilation. In the Cymric world, from the thirteenth to the nineteenth century, this was the chief reason why the false history of Geoffrey took precedence over the truth-bearing fiction of the romances of the *Mabinogion*.

However during the two centuries of armed struggle the aristocratic order of court poets used their special relationship with the prince to make sure that the greatest prestige of all belonged to their poetry. In form and in content and in function they made certain that it could not be otherwise. They were known as the *gogynfeirdd* (literally 'the almost first poets'), and their extreme deference to the *cynfeirdd* (the first poets), to the tradition of Taliesin and Aneirin, served in fact to reinforce their privileged position and their pre-eminence. They cultivated archaic language and made subtle developments in the time-honoured panegyric and elegiac forms. One of the greatest, Cynddelw Brydydd Mawr (Cynddelw the great poet), schooled himself to use the already ancient vocabulary of Aneirin and Taliesin in an act of homage and regeneration. In the thirteenth century Dafydd Benfras, the court poet of Llywelyn the Great, invoked the *hen gerdd* (old song) in the manner of a classical poet invoking the muse: 'May God endow me with the complete muse, the forceful urge of Myrddin [Merlin] let me render praise as Aneirin did, the day he sang *Y Gododdin.*' Not only in form but also in content they re-enacted the drama of the Old North. They saw the struggle of the independent princes of Wales as an 'action replay' of the sixth-century struggles of the Britons of the Old North. As consciously as any twentieth-century scholar, they were intent on recapturing the British Heroic Age and they were prepared to carve history as well as metrical systems out of their own flesh. At the very beginning Meilyr Brydydd's elegy to Gruffudd ap Cynan is a war-song in the spirit of *Y Gododdin*. Gruffudd only ruled over little Gwynedd but he was addressed as Lord of Britain, his battles were for Christendom and the cathedral-building Normans were dismissed as pagan Bryneich (proto-Northumbrians). Cynddelw constructed his portrait of Gruffudd's son, Owain Gwynedd, on the traditional design of Taliesin's master portrait of another Owain, also the son of an illustrious father, Owain ab Urien Rheged, the ideal Brythonic ruler.

These poets were privileged. Their status was legally recognised. As in Ireland, there were bardic dynasties and these held land by virtue of their poetic practice. There were systems of bardic apprenticeships which could overcome any temporary gap in the transmission of poetic gift. While the geographical distribution of the thirty-one poets whose work has survived in only two known manuscript collections reflects the demand for their services. Eighteen of the surviving *gogynfeirdd* belonged to Gwynedd, nine to Powys, one came from the old kingdom of Brycheiniog (Brecon) and three from what is now Dyfed. Gwynedd led the patriotic struggle and therefore had the most pressing need of this militant bardic order. When Cynddelw transferred his allegiance from Powys to Gwynedd he did so in conscious imitation of the first Taliesin's removal from Powys to Rheged.

There were prince-poets among the *gogynfeirdd*. The two outstanding were Owain Gwynedd's natural son, Hywel ap Owain Gwynedd (d. 1170) and his more strictly royal relative Owain Cyfeiliog of Powys (d. 1197). Hywel's love poetry is the earliest surviving illustration in Welsh of the Celtic inclination to equate love of native land with the love of woman. His *Gorhoffedd*, an amalgam of personal boast, exultant love and attachment to place could still be quoted by a twentieth-century politician looking for votes in the same constituency.

> I love her foreshore and her mountains, her castle near the woods and her cultivated land, her water meadows, her valleys and her fountains, her white seagulls and gracious women . . . I love her armed men, their trained stallions, her woodland, her heroes and their homes. I love the small clover on her pastures where I was honoured with a certain joy. I love all her *broydd** to which my valour entitles me, all the wide wasteland and the wealth that hides there.

As a warrior poet of the royal house, Hywel could exercise greater freedom in his choice of subject matter, just as he could pursue a condottieri-like career in the south outside his hereditary territory. Unfortunately only eight of his poems survive. He himself met his end in characteristic Celtic fashion: in battle with his foster-brothers against

* *bro*, plural *broydd*, native haunt, a place to which a special allegiance is owed. The twentieth-century politician was Lloyd George.

his own half-brothers, he fell at Pentraeth in Anglesey with a spear sticking out of his chest.

Owain died more decorously in the monastery of Strata Marcella, having handed over the government of his part of Powys to his son. As a statesman he pursued the quieter policy of friendship with the English crown. Gerald Cambrensis referred to him as 'one of the three princes in Wales conspicuous for the justice, wisdom and moderation of their rule'. But there was another aspect to his career and it was this he chose to celebrate in his *Hirlas Owain* (Owain's Drinking Horn). It is addressed to the heroes of a successful raid over the border that, like the poem itself, was conceived in direct imitation of *Y Gododdin*. But now the objective was not distant Catraeth (Catterick in Yorkshire), but the land beyond the Long Mynd in Shropshire. The cup-bearer at the feast is ordered to serve each hero generously in token of his valour in the expedition made the previous night to rescue a comrade taken prisoner. The prince knew his *Gododdin* and so did his boon companions. The honour paid to them with the long blue drinking-horn was that much greater because of the deliberate echo of what took place in the Court of Mynyddog Mwynfawr in Edinburgh more than five centuries before: 'Cupbearer, fill with satisfaction that horn in Rhys's hand, as he sits in the court of his gift-giver and lord.'

The profound homage paid by all the *gogynfeirdd* to their illustrious predecessors should not obscure the extent of their own sophisticated originality. The training of a poet in a bardic school gave him the artistic muscle necessary to create variety inside the confines of a rigid tradition. These poets extended the range of praise poetry far beyond the bounds of the heroic mould. While it is true that, like most mediaeval artists, the impersonal 'contributory' function of their art absorbed their individuality to the point of anonymity, their sonorous names still give out to the Welsh ear something of the quality of the music they created: Meilyr, Gwalchmai, Dafydd Benfras, Prydydd y Moch, Elidir Sais, Gwilym Ryfel, Llygad Gŵr. Every one of them has left subtle extensions of praise poetry to include religion and love as well as princely panegyric odes and elegies. Cynddelw Brydydd Mawr earned the respect implicit in his title during forty years unbroken practice of his profession. Half a century ago when academic research in this field was still at an early stage, Saunders Lewis ventured on a brief character sketch of this outstanding figure, based on what he was able to glean from his work.

Unlike many of the poets of his day, Cynddelw was not the son of a poet and there was some resentment at his presumption in taking up the poet's calling. But he was brave, with a reputation as a good soldier and with something of the same aggressive attitude in bardic session, argumentative, competitive, challenging, daring, prepared to hold his own and conquer. He was handsome, conscious of his own strength, born with a masterful temperament and not prepared to swallow a boast. 'Silence you poets, and listen to a poet!' As he matured his masterful manner channelled itself into technical mastery. He was acknowledged as a master, the head of his profession, the chief exponent and teacher of his day. When the political leadership shifted from Powys to Gwynedd it was natural that he should move with it . . . He enjoyed a season at the court of the Lord Rhys in the South, but he disliked travelling. As he grew older a new tenderness came into his song . . . He loved three things above all, his family, Powys where he was born and his profession.

But it is in a masterpiece by one of the lesser figures, Gruffydd ab yr Ynad Coch (Gruffydd son of the Red Judge), that the music of the tradition comes closest to touching our modern sensibilities. In this elegy for the death of Llywelyn, the fall of the house of Gwynedd, the end of the struggle for independence, becomes a catastrophe of cosmic proportions. Through the controlled structures of this poem of over a hundred lines, where the final rhyme and sound correspondences recur like the bass notes of a great *Dies Irae*, the poet's vision and anguish cry out with elemental power:

> *Oer calon dan fron o fraw . . .*
>
> Heart frozen under a breast of fear, under sadness for the fall of our oak door, our dear defender . . . Can you not see the path of the wind and the rain? Can you not see the oak trees clashing together? Can you not see the sea scourge the land? . . . the truth arming itself . . . the sun loose in the sky . . . the stars fallen? . . .
>
> Much blood soaks to the feet, there are many widows, many cries, many sons without fathers. Many burnt out homesteads in the track of havoc and lands laid waste by long pillage. Many pitiful cries, as once at Camlan.

Camlan, Arthur's last battle, was the point of reference. Llywelyn wore Arthur's crown. Now it was lost. It seemed the end of the old order, the end of an old song. Even the stoical monk writing *Brut y Brenhinedd* (The Chronicle of the Princes) could not repress his emotion. After writing opposite December 11th, 1282, that Prince Llywelyn had been killed on that day, he adds, 'Then were all the Welsh cast down to the ground.'

The skull of Saint David went with the Crown of Arthur to Westminster as part of the loot. The Prince's severed head, crowned with ivy, was carried on the end of a pole through the city in derisory fulfilment of a Merlin prophecy that a Welsh king would ride crowned through London. Myths, pretensions, age-old claims and particularities were being finally exterminated.

The court poets took pride of place, but they were only part of the cultural apparatus that served the world of the Welsh princes. *The Triads of the Isle of Britain* give us some inkling of the vast repertoire of the *cyfarwydd*, the professional story-tellers. Unlike the classical model, in most Celtic cultures, narrative was what we would call a prose function, whereas poetry was reserved for forms of celebration. (This, briefly, is why we must look to non-metrical composition for the Welsh epic.) The musicians were sufficiently exalted to raise occasional demarcation problems between them and the jealously guarded privileges of the poets. Then there were the *clêr*, the lower order of poets who dealt with everyday themes and satire and entertained the ladies and the multitude. The political collapse brought down a carefully balanced hierarchy of artistic creation.

What could be salvaged from the wreckage? It was a dark period and literary historians suggest a forty year period of stylistic confusion reflecting a society undergoing profound changes in its structure. Quite apart from political changes, the early fourteenth century was a time of plagues, in particular the horrific Black Death. There are examples of the high art of the *gogynfeirdd* engaged in the composition of elegies for putrefying young women instead of men in battle. The English kings built towns in the shadow of their castles and in the towns markets were established under alien control. Culture conflicts of extraordinary complexity must have occurred. In the countryside leadership remained in the hands of native families, aristocratic warriors still nursing their pedigrees but relieved of the heroic but materially unprofitable role of defending tattered frontiers. Such a condition of affairs was not entirely uncongenial to the more ancient Celtic social order that had always been inclined to political anarchy and unlimited local independence.

The Church was also a rock and a refuge in this time of trouble. The Cistercians in particular were generous patrons of native art. They owed a debt of gratitude for all the encouragement the princes had given them in the twelfth century to settle and build their oases of monastic peace in a troubled country and they paid it in full. The Franciscans too had been made welcome. It was a Franciscan friar who wrote the first surviving nativity poem in Welsh in a complex metre derived from the *gogynfeirdd*, but full of the naive tenderness of an Italian '*trecento* painting.

Mab a'n rhodded . . .

A son is given, born of goodness, son to save us, bearing privilege and gifts . . . giant great but small, strong deliverer, white and weak . . .

Churchmen also wrote the first treatises on Welsh poetic art in the thirteenth century. It was they who had the strongest inclination to codify the ideal, give it philosophical justification, and draw up rules that were to have a permanent and powerful effect on the poetic function up to the decline of the bardic order at the end of the sixteenth century.

The poets could turn to the church and to the noble families for patronage and protection. The lordly styles of the *gogynfeirdd* persisted well into the fourteenth century under the new dispensation. But many of the old restraints were gone. There were more contacts with a wider world. The embattled north was at last able to adopt the more relaxed life style of the south: and it was appropriate that the new song, when it came, should come from the south, from the offspring of a noble family that had taken office under the English crown. Dafydd ap Gwilym's uncle was Constable of Newcastle Emlyn and took an oath of allegiance to the Black Prince in 1343. Dafydd's best known patron was Ifor Hael (Ifor the Generous) whose court was at Bassaleg, then in Glamorgan but now in Gwent. One of the notable features of Dafydd's work is his lack of interest both in politics and the hard fact of English rule. For his characteristic subject matter he retreats into his own version of the pursuit of love and his stalking ground is a realistic rural Arcadia half way between Provence and the Forest of Arden.

Dafydd is usually described as the greatest poet in the Welsh language. Of his greatness there can be no doubt, but to call him 'the greatest' is to place an emphasis on uniqueness and individuality which is foreign to the Welsh poetic tradition. Paradoxically for a Celtic people fully endowed with the competitive spirit and an innate inclination to 'showing off', during the centuries of poetic pre-eminence the value of a poet was measured by the extent of his contribution to the great tradition. During Dafydd's lifetime there were at least five poets who were his peers. These all came from different parts of the north. With one of them, Gruffydd Grug, he engaged in a running poetic battle which brought into the mainstream of strict metre poetry a degree of humour and satire that the *gogynfeirdd* would have considered far beneath the grand business of poetic composition.

Confident as they were of their own powers, these first *cywyddwyr* were even more conscious of their professional obligation and their social role. They sang so that others could sing after them. Like the architects of the great mediaeval cathedrals, these carpenters of song initiated great designs that would never be completed in their lifetime. What they created was poetic capital for future development and the great body of three centuries' work in the strict metres is their enduring monument. There is nothing quite comparable in the whole of European literature.

And yet Dafydd is unique. There is a sense in which he had to be in order to break the rigid mould of court poetry. He was not alone in creating the *cywydd* form, based on lines of seven syllables woven together by the intricate systems of alliteration and internal rhyme known as *cynghanedd*. But he exploited it and popularised it in much the same way as Petrarch propagated the sonnet in fourteenth-century Italy. Dafydd, too, was the poet who was 'most poet'. The *cywydd* was a considerably more intricate and difficult form to master than the sonnet. There are, for example, four main divisions of *cynghanedd* and they have to be manipulated with the skill of a trained musician before the poet can hope to display his qualities. Dafydd and his colleagues snatched the form out of the stern jaws of the *gogynfeirdd*, and their successors contrived to make it even stricter, partly to safeguard the privileges of their profession, but also in order to provide in the exercise of high culture that law-giving unity that was absent from the social and political life of their time.

Although the form was intricate, the language was no longer archaic or specialised. When he chose Dafydd could use dialogue and engage in forms of light-hearted banter with the subjects of his new version of praise poetry. In 'A Celebration of Summer' he addresses the season as the guardian of the forest, anointing the trees, as a cauldron of rebirth, as the ointment of increase, the foster-father and prophet of the highway, the architect of the fair earth and so on until the summer is obliged to turn on him, telling him to shut up. He is in fact only a prince doing his job and carrying out his seasonal function after which he will return to the Underworld to keep himself warm until the following spring. Just as life had become less of an awesome ritual, Dafydd was able to use everyday speech to capture the wonder of spontaneous experience as if it had never happened before. His prolific love poems are no more than an excuse for this delightful exercise and often it appears as though the exercise is all. And yet it isn't. Never was the celebrated remark of Robert Frost more true than in the case of Dafydd, and indeed of the long line of his successors: poetry is the bit that gets lost in translation. But the most superficial examination of any of his *dyfalu*, for example, demonstrates his inexhaustible zest and powers of invention. (*Dyfalu* could be described as a cadenza-like sequence of swift metaphors and lightning comparisons.) He addresses a seagull in order to coax it into carrying a message to his besieged beloved.

> One colour with snow or the white moon, unsmutched in your bright beauty, a piece of the sun, a steel glove at sea, and yet swift and proud and light on the wave, fish fed, foam footed . . . lily of the sea, contemplative of the wave, like a written page, speak for me.

Cynghanedd is uncomfortable in English so that there is no way of reproducing adequately the succinct ease and musical eloquence of Dafydd's verse. But there are two poets in English who show something of his influence: Gerard Manley Hopkins and Dylan Thomas. Poems like 'The Windhover' or 'Fern Hill' reproduce very closely that overwhelming and yet disciplined delight in living and the margin of miracle attached to everyday experience that is the hallmark of the great body of work associated with Dafydd ap Gwilym's name.

In Sir Thomas Parry's *History of Welsh Literature* there is a list of thirty-four of the major poets who succeeded Dafydd and his contemporaries. They stretch from Iolo Goch (c. 1340–98), who sang to the young lord Owain Glyndŵr, down to Archdeacon Edmund Prys (1544–1623) who, like Dafydd himself, took to more colloquial language and simpler verse forms in order to reach a wider audience. They were no more than the most conspicuous figures in a noble army of poets who maintained a level of civilised living and a network of cultural unity for a nation otherwise submerged in aristocratic anarchy. When he talked to the seagull, just like a *gogynfardd*, Dafydd brought up Taliesin and Myrddin, those stalwarts of Cymric consciousness. But he did so in order to bring out more light-hearted aspects of their survival tactics and shape-shifting activities.

> I can tell you bird, I love that girl, God help me, with complete intensity. Merlin with his lively flattering lips, nor Taliesin himself, ever loved anything more beautiful.

3   Alternative Heroes

While the poets of the strict metres mourned the death of Llywelyn ap Gruffydd in terms of Arthur's last battle at Camlan, a totally different and highly durable Arthur had already been manufactured, as it were for the export market. Arthur, the supreme hero of the Britons, good-luck mascot of the house of Tudor, was more the creation of the imagination and politic acumen of Geoffrey of Monmouth than an accurate replica of any fifth- or sixth-century original. Geoffrey, born about 1100, was an ambitious cleric of Breton origin brought up in Gwent. His work was a product of the second phase of the Norman invasion of Wales. He understood that the Welsh imagination was a mythological factory working overtime. All he needed to do was to package its surplus production for the widest possible distribution.

Both the Anglo-Saxons and the Normans already had their chronicles. What they could never have were credible links with classical antiquity, early Christianity, and Roman civilisation and the royal pedigrees necessary to prove them. The Normans mattered most in Geoffrey's world. They were rich, powerful and pious: but they were *nouveaux riches*. By force of arms they had blundered into the limelight and what they needed most of all were the trappings of legitimacy to hide their naked savagery, to justify their forceful ways in the eyes of the world and even in the eyes of God. Geoffrey saw his chance. His *Historia* would be a synthesis of the art of the storyteller and the gravity of the chronicler, offering the ruling power an inspirational account of the great island of Britain they had conquered. *Historia Regum Britanniae*, the *History of the Kings of Britain*, begins in Troy with Brutus, the founder of the British race, and continues to unfold two thousand years of colourful history, ending in the seventh century with the Anglo-Saxon occupation of most of England. Geoffrey drew heavily on Gildas and the historical miscellany assembled by the eighth-century monk Nennius. It was in Nennius's book that he picked up the clues to his characterisation of some of his most important dramatis personae. But most of all he drew on his own imagination.

His crowning achievement both as an imaginative writer and as a

propagandist for the idea of British supremacy in the political world
was the creation of the figure of Arthur as the ideal mediaeval king.
Before he comes to Arthur he has already established a line of British
kings more illustrious than any other in Europe. Two of them had been
Emperors of Rome and everything they did established a precedent for
the glory that was to come. Geoffrey devoted a whole book to his
elaboration of the story of Arthur. This was in itself a masterstroke.
Without this glamorous figure it is doubtful whether his eccentric
version of history would ever have gained its amazingly wide currency.
Soon after Geoffrey's death we find an enthusiastic scribe writing
in the language of the rave reviewer: 'Where is the place within
the bounds of Christendom to which the winged praise of Arthur
the Briton was not extended? . . . The people of the East speak of
him as do those of the West, though separated by the width of the
whole earth.' Geoffrey found Arthur a hero of Welsh legend, a
Celtic warrior-king with more than a touch of the supernatural about him, a half-divine character celebrated by
storytellers and poets throughout the Celtic lands. He left him
a mediaeval king-emperor, an 'historical' figure, the leader of the
past glory of the Britons and a model of military leader capable of
outshining Alexander, Caesar, and Charlemagne. The Arthurian
theme had been transformed from Welsh saga and Celtic story-cycle
into solid history, stamped with the Latin seal of authority of church
and state. Geoffrey was a bishop writing to please the most powerful
royal house in Western Europe, but he sang the song the mountain
princes wanted to hear. It confirmed their glorious ancestry, it built an
historic bridge between their Heroic Age and the Age of Chivalry, it
promised the world and God's blessing to the victor; it gave a new
dimension to the most cherished pastime of a warrior aristocracy – the
struggle for power.

The essential ingredient to replace supernatural prowess was an
unique combination of virtue and courage. It was this above all that
made Arthur the pattern of a Christian monarch. In Geoffrey's story a
fifteen-year-old youth, already noted for his physical strength, courage
and liberality, is consecrated king. He wishes to show even more
generosity towards his followers and therefore makes war against the
Saxons in order to seize their wealth. He routs them completely with
some judicious help from Geoffrey's ancestral Brittany. Then he settles
the Picts and Scots and the Irish and, having asserted his authority over
these islands, like a Norman in reverse, or as future English kings were
destined to do, he turned his attention to France. After a thrilling single
combat against Frolo the king, and polishing off a few giants on the
way, Arthur becomes master of France. This disturbs the emperor of
Rome and Arthur is obliged, in the style of Alexander, to take on the
biggest opposition available. He defeats the emperor, but in the

moment of victory, like Urien Rheged and many another Celtic king, he learns of treachery at home. The last battle was at Camlan, 'the hardest battle ever fought in the island of Britain, either before or after that time'. This was the ultimate in internecine strife. 'The most worthy King Arthur was mortally wounded and was borne thence to the island of Avalon to be healed of his wounds.'

To achieve his transformation of the figure of Arthur, an act of literary alchemy of the most subtle kind, Geoffrey had been obliged to seek the assistance of a Welsh poetic prophet who could also boast of supernatural powers. Before he published his great work he issued what amounted to a brief prospectus which he called *Prophetiae Merlini*, the *Prophecies of Merlin*. Among the Welsh, Myrddin had long been a prophetic poet of equal status with Taliesin. He too came originally from the Old North. Geoffrey found it necessary to change Myrddin to Merlin because he feared the Welsh name would sound too much like *merde* to Francophone ears. In Geoffrey's book it was Merlin's wisdom and skill which brought the great stones from Ireland to Stonehenge to perform their petrified giant's dance as a memorial to the British chieftains who had been murdered by Hengist and the Treachery of the Long Knives. Hardly less spectacular and with more far-reaching historical consequences, Geoffrey also made Merlin the stage manager of the conception of King Arthur. Arthur's mother had to be royal and the most beautiful woman in the whole of Britain. His father had to be a British king with strong Roman connections. Geoffrey solved his novelistic problem by making the king fall in love with the wife of the Duke of Cornwall. He employs Merlin, who has degenerated from being a prophetic poet to the status of a wizard, to shift the king's shape, convert him for one night into the duke's double, in order to allow him to penetrate his fortress and his wife with impunity. There would have been no Arthur of the new model without Merlin and the fate of these two figures would continue to be linked in their influence on historical reality.

Geoffrey had little sympathy for the beleaguered Welsh. They were no more than a bunch of unreliable mountain fighters, unworthy of their noble ancestors. Twelve years after he completed his *Historia*, he composed a narrative poem about the original Myrddin which suggested that his attitude had mellowed a little. Needless to say this poem did not gain anything like the popularity of the earlier work which has some claim to being the first European bestseller. What Geoffrey could never have foreseen was the electrifying effect his *Historia* would have on the Welsh. Before the end of the thirteenth century at least three translations into Welsh were made.

In Wales, long before Geoffrey's day the figure of Arthur, by the sheer gravitational pull of popularity, had drawn into its orbit story cycles from older mythology, semi-historical material from other parts of Britain and themes from international folklore. Nothing illustrates more vividly the highly developed national consciousness of the Welsh and the Irish of this period than the free circulation of vast bodies of oral literature over all the territories where the national languages were spoken. Once again this demonstrates the striking continuity of the Celtic tradition: its ability to sustain an overriding cultural unity in spite of habits of political anarchy and over-indulgence in the doubtful pleasures of internecine warfare. The chief agents of this unity were professional storytellers, poets, the bardic tradition, the church and men of learning. When the Norman invasions came they seemed to reassert the ancient polarity between the Roman and the Celtic outlook on life, and this fundamental difference is sharply reflected in Geoffrey's treatment of his Welsh source material when it is compared to the first four stories of the collection known in English as *The Mabinogion*.

Pedair Cainc y Mabinogi (The Four Branches of the Mabinogi) is generally believed to be the work of a monk writing somewhere in Dyfed, either in the period immediately before the Norman onslaught or in loving recollection of such a blessed cultural breathing space. The stories inhabit an exclusively Celtic world. Mention of Saxons, let alone Normans, is conspicuously absent. It seems also a conscious act on the part of the author that there should be no mention of Arthur. (Arthur figures prominently enough in *Culhwch ac Olwen*, a longer tale in the same collection which belongs to an even earlier period.) Just as much as Geoffrey of Monmouth, this anonymous author wishes his writing to be a comment on life. But he chooses a totally different mode of operation. Instead of neutralising the supernatural element in his material he embraces it, until it becomes a fully integrated part of the narrative. Geoffrey is a proto-novelist posing as an historian. He is absorbed in the rise and fall of empires and the pomp and circumstance that must attend the lives of the great men who govern them. He is dazzled by the prospect of worldly success and the inexorable movement of the great wheel of fortune. The vast oral tradition of the Welsh, their myths, folklore and poetry, are treasures heaped in a cave which he comes to plunder for decorative material that will give his history a touch of colour and the fascination of romance.

Superficially the aim of the author of the *Pedair Cainc* would appear to be far more modest. Because the confines of his world include the depth of experience that accompanies the supernatural, he is content to occupy a limited space. The first of his heroes, Pwyll, Prince of Dyfed, goes hunting in Cwm Cuch, which to this day is small enough to pass unnoticed by visitors to Pembrokeshire; but it is large enough for him to encounter the king of the Underworld and exchange kingdoms with him for one whole year. An earlier version of the tale probably related how this circumstance allowed the king of the Underworld to sleep with

Rhiannon and thus father the hero Pryderi. This would also conform with a popular theme of primitive folklore. But the author of the *Pedair Cainc* follows the fortunes of Pwyll in the Otherworld in order to illustrate a subtle extension to the nature of the hero. Courage and fidelity were as essential as ever. To these Pwyll adds, in the name of friendship, loyalty and fidelity, a prolonged act of chastity. The task imposed upon him involves sleeping with the beautiful queen. He refrains from intercourse with her as an act of fidelity to the king whose place he has taken. The discipline of the trained warrior, the story implies, can be extended into the most intimate area of the ceremony of living. This adaptation of a Celtic motif is in strong contrast to the way Geoffrey uses shape-shifting to manipulate the conception of Arthur.

In the *Pedair Cainc*, the hero's field of endeavour, by an act of levitation which at this distance in time appears one of the most mysterious aspects of the storyteller's art, is elevated into a zone of experience miraculously suspended between myth and reality. But the heroes are still called upon to cope with crises great and small which lie strictly in parallel with problems faced by the society for whom they were composed in the first place. The *Pedair Cainc* focus our attention on figures that are recognisably human and yet free of the constrictions of a specific historic process. These heroes could never set out to conquer Europe, because no such place existed on the map of their experience. And yet such is the artistry of the author, and the power of his imagination, that we become conscious as we read that in spite of the particularity of these shadowy kingdoms, the *Pedair Cainc* belong to that rare category of literature capable of presenting a vision of the human condition which is valid for all time. Unlike Geoffrey's pseudo-history, they are not weighed down with the heavy chains of mediaeval time and place.

Great works of art are rarely put together by accident. These dramatic tales have a timeless element, but they were written for an audience well acquainted with the repertoire. There was, for example, a story about Pwyll and Pryderi leading an expedition to Annwn (the Underworld or the Otherworld) in order to capture its chief treasure, the cauldron of rebirth, or resuscitation. A poem of considerable antiquity known as *Preiddiau Annwfn* (The Spoils of Annwfn) deals with a similar raid, but led on that occasion by Arthur. This obscure poem has a refrain: '*Nam saith ni ddyriaith*' ('Only seven came back'), which would seem to be echoed in the ending of the tragic second story in the *Pedair Cainc*, *Branwen Ferch Llŷr* (Branwen the daughter of Lear) where only seven warriors returned from the ill-fated expedition to Ireland, which also involved a cauldron of rebirth. The contemporary audience must have been well aware of the symphonic correspondences both between incidents and betweeen variant versions. In this case they would also have been alive to the military value of a utensil that could be used for recycling dead soldiers. A people at the wrong end of an historic sequence of demographic swings would know just how much value, ironic or otherwise, to attach to such a conception. On the less sophisticated level, the emergence from a cauldron of resuscitation of armed men who have only lost the power of speech, would be an eleventh-century equivalent of the science-fiction robots that wander across the twentieth-century screens.

In the second story the arranged marriage between Branwen of Wales and Matholwch, the king of Ireland, would have been from a political point of view a very satisfactory arrangement. It becomes a curse instead of a blessing principally because of the ungovernable behaviour of her half-brother Efnisien. He is just as heroic a personality as his brother Nisien, although he is given to scowling as much as his brother is given to smiling. He possesses that essential heroic age ferocity which was the basic Arthurian ingredient. But he was incapable of controlling his supply of vital heroic passion. Because of Efnisien's brutal and calculated insults, Branwen is ill-treated by the Irish and the great Brân himself leads an expedition to rescue her and avenge the insult. She attempts to bring peace but Efnisien thirsts for battle. The dynamic lust that is necessary for success in battle is also the dangerous volatile element that the character of Efnisien transforms into incestuous passion and destructive jealousy and the ruin of two islands. He takes her child, the heir to the Irish throne, and throws him into the fire. Ireland is laid waste, the cauldron of resuscitation is destroyed and only seven return: 'Nam saith ni ddyriaith.'

At many points the Pedair Cainc can be understood as civilised and sensitive comment on the nature of the heroic ideal and the problem of cruelty. The heroic virtues had to be celebrated by the poetic tradition for the simple reason that it was necessary to reactivate them each time the fragile integrity of the Welsh world was threatened. Always in the immediate future another and greater effort would more than likely be called for. The formal poetry of the twelfth and thirteenth centuries abounded with echoes of the classic encounters of the sixth century not merely because of the inherent conservatism of the Celtic tradition. It was the reality of the situation which also recurred. The Welsh ruling houses had to be fierce because the outside world insisted on regarding them as no more than squatters holding a frontier territory with many attractions to adventurers from all over Western Europe. When Henry II, the most powerful monarch of his time and never a paragon of public or private virtue, arrived on the Welsh scene, he soon revealed a hand as hot and as hasty as Efnisien's. He had martyred Thomas Becket, kept his wife in prison, attacked his sons and his brothers. Now, when his great army got bogged down on the Berwyn mountains, he put out the eyes of the sons of Owain Gwynedd, his hostages, even though their brother Dafydd was married to his half-sister, Emma of

Anjou. Being blinded and castrated was the common fate of Henry's hostages.

The dramatic narrative of the third story of the *Pedair Cainc* offers a distinct and almost revolutionary pattern for a new type of hero. It begins among the survivors. Two of the seven who return from the disastrous Irish expedition, Pryderi and Manawydan, feel like strangers in the country to which they have returned after a super-naturally long absence. They are both heroes, Pryderi young and still eager for more adventure, Manawydan middle-aged, weary of slaughter and searching for some viable alternative to the unending cycle of violence. He is the rightful heir to the throne of the Island of the Mighty. But since the *Triads* have already categorised him as one of the Three Ungrasping Princes of the Isle of Britain, the storyteller is able to seize upon the vatic authority of this description and make it the principal motif of his story.

Pryderi sees his veteran companion as the ideal second husband for his widowed mother, Rhiannon. Manawydan has no desire to go campaigning for the throne that is rightfully his, and once he sees Rhiannon he is captivated by her youthful zest, her wit, her confident charm. With the art of a poetic dramatist, the author makes us sense the immediate attraction between cautious and unassuming Manawydan and the redoubtable heroine of the first branch of the *Mabinogi*. Pryderi is married to a well-born young woman, Cigfa, and the four of them settle down to enjoy an idyllic existence in Dyfed. Since this was the native province of the storyteller, he leaves us in no doubt that in all the world it was the most perfect place to be.

Pryderi, being young and a hero in the true Arthurian mould with a fate still to fulfil, is the first to grow restless. He wants to pay homage to Caswallon, the king of the new Britain. The audience could interpret this as an indication of the first stirring among the Welsh ruling class towards a form of feudalisation. Caswallon sits in the White Tower in London as a shadowy stand-in for Arthur. With easy skill the story-teller steers his audience's attention back to contemplation of Celtic legend. Pryderi cannot resist one evening leading a party out of doors to visit that same mysterious mound and throne of magic where his impatient father, Pwyll, had once sat. It is as if he wishes to return to the original Celtic heroic mould, to demand a wound or a wonder. The hero insists that he be put to the test and the storyteller must now provide his own instructive and diverting variation on the theme.

When the wonder comes, it is, as usual, rather more than what was bargained for – sudden thunder and impenetrable mist.

> And after the mist, everywhere was light. And when they looked in the direction where they had seen flocks and herds and dwelling places, they now saw no living thing, no house, no animal, no smoke, no fire, no man,

no inhabited dwelling, only the deserted rooms of the court, without man or beast living in them: their companions too were lost, vanished without a sign, leaving the four alone.

'O Lord God,' said Manawydan. 'Where are our retainers? And the men that were with us? Let us try and find them.'

They came to the great hall and saw no one. They searched the rooms and the sleeping quarters and found no one. In the mead cellar and in the kitchen they looked and found only desolation.

At first they make the best of it. There is a certain excitement being survivors in an empty world. There are wild beasts still and wild honey. But they grow tired of this isolated existence. It is Manawydan who suggests that they should go to an English town and take up a trade. With practised ease the storyteller propels his protagonists from an enchanted wilderness to the reality of the new urban life; from a Celtic desert to the mediaeval town life of a commercial England beginning to thrive and the new concepts of law and order imposed by a Caswallon who stands in now, not so much for Arthur, as for the practical peace of the Plantagenets.

First they take up saddle-making. They do it so well that the local saddlers conspire to kill them. Pryderi is all for killing the conspirators there and then. But Manawydan counsels caution. They move to another town to take up making shields. The same situation arises. Again their competitors conspire to kill them. How are honest craftsmen to cope with the twilight zone between protection rackets and incipient trades-unionism? Manawydan's answer is to respect the law and back down. Pryderi, as usual, is all for confrontation and a quick kill. They move to another town and become shoemakers. From saddles to shields, and from shields to shoes. Cymric heroes have become craftsmen in anonymous yet exotic English towns. The situation must have been a source of much amusement among a noble audience, happily unaware of any prophetic undertone to the material, but well acquainted with another tale where the great Caswallon himself put on the guise of a cobbler in order to follow his beloved Ffleur to Rome: which itself was a narrative inversion of the *Dream of Macsen Wledig*, a tale of an emperor who dreamt of a Welsh Helen seated on a golden throne in a castle in Gwynedd. (Ffleur was mistress of 'Julius Caesar'!)

Manawydan's counsel prevails:

'We shall take up shoemaking. At least shoemakers will never have the stomach to forbid us to practise or to try to kill us.'

'But I don't know the first thing about shoemaking,' Pryderi said.

'I do,' said Manawydan. 'And I shall teach you how to stitch.'

Again they are too successful. They become famous as the Golden Shoemakers and all the cobblers are up in arms, planning to kill them.

'Why should we put up with such nonsense from a bunch of thieving serfs?' said Pryderi. 'Let's kill the lot of them.'

No doubt the majority of listeners identified with Pryderi. He was the traditional hero. They would be mystified and quietly intrigued by Manawydan's behaviour. Could it possibly be that the brother of the great Bendigeidfran was going to turn out to be a coward?

'No,' said Manawydan, 'we won't fight with them. And we won't stay in Lloegr [England] any longer. Let us return to Dyfed and see how things stand.'

Things stood pretty much the same. When the customary year has gone by, Pryderi and Manawydan go hunting. It is now they encounter the shining white boar that leads them to a vast and lofty fortress they have never seen before. The boar and the hounds disappear inside. Pryderi is all for going after them.

'In truth,' Manawydan said, 'you would be ill advised to do so. We never saw a fort in this place before. And if you take my advice you will not go inside it. Whoever placed a spell on this land, caused this castle to appear.'
'It is not my intention to lose those dogs,' Pryderi said.

Inside the fortress he finds nothing living only a fountain and a golden bowl with chains extending upwards out of sight. As soon as he grasps the golden bowl his hands stick to it, and his feet stick to the slab on which he stands, and his tongue to the roof of his mouth. He cannot utter a word. Manawydan waits outside until nightfall and then returns home. Rhiannon chides him for deserting her son. And in her usual positive way she rushes off to the fort to rescue Pryderi. Once inside she too grasps the bowl and cannot move. The same peal of thunder rolls, the mist falls, the fortress vanishes and the mother and son with it. Thus Manawydan is left alone with Cigfa. She breaks into ululating lamentation, apparently more nervous of Manawydan's possible sexual advances than distressed by the disappearance of her husband and mother-in-law. In a speech of great dignity which is also an eloquent plea for gentleness and gracious behaviour Manawydan manages to reassure her. His capacity for hunting has been undermined by the loss of the dogs and he proposes that they should return to shoemaking in England to keep themselves alive. With certain snobbish reservations, Cigfa agrees.
After a year of prosperous trading they run into the same old trouble.

Cigfa, with her nose in the air, would have him deal with conspiring rivals in the abrupt manner approved by her husband, but once more Manawydan beats a retreat and returns to the land of Dyfed which he loves even as it lies prostrate and helpless under a spell. Resourcefully he takes up farming, sows wheat in crofts and sees a crop heavy with promise. But each time he decides to reap, the following morning he finds nothing but a field of broken stalks and not an ear of corn in sight. He links this with the other disasters and decides to keep an armed watch. At midnight the field is invaded by as many mice as there are corn stalks. Each creature breaks off an ear and carries it away. Manawydan tries to stop them but they escape as easily as gnats, except for one too heavy to move quickly. This one he catches and puts in his glove, tying the glove with a piece of string.

Now the course of events unfolds in a sequence of encounters that are presented for the most part in dialogue. It is a protracted trial scene, but the accused happens to be a pregnant mouse imprisoned in the hero's glove, which would seem superficially to be little more than a whimsical fancy. The author's powers of invention are taking flight and he will be obliged to end his story with a flourish. And yet it must lose nothing of its dialectical significance. To the audience it can still be understood as a philosophical legal argument on the nature of thieving and the problem of making the punishment fit a crime. The story is a comment on *galanas*, the system of compensation based on the value of a person's life according to his status. The story uses the logic of a legal system and quietly calls it into question. How, in fact, can it be related to the unique value of individual life? And beyond this, it suggests the use of legal principles for the settlement of long-standing disputes between rival powers. It is not only on the field of battle that a hero can be called upon to demonstrate courage and endurance. The true leader needs these qualities in negotiation, for the sake of the survival and well-being of his people. In every crisis he will be called upon to demonstrate patience as well as courage, wisdom with endurance, and the moral worth of his own character, and he must learn to prosecute a case with the ingenuity of the most practised lawyer. The qualities of leadership remain constant, however developed a society may become. Somewhat like Azdec in Brecht's *Caucasian Chalk Circle*, Manawydan conducts his own case (as indeed he has conducted his life since his return from the Irish expedition) and in so doing, puts an entire social system to the test.

Cigfa is the first to attempt to persuade him to let his prisoner go free. She is appalled to think of so exalted a personage, and her relative by marriage, stooping so low as to supervise the hanging of a mouse. Any self-respecting court poet would have been deeply insulted to be asked to compose a formal ode in celebration of such a dubious exploit. It was a subject only for scorn and derision. For such a conspicuous member of the hero class as Manawydan it could only mean disgrace and a permanent blot on the most precious asset of all – his reputation. In spite of all this Manawydan is not deterred. With some deliberation he sets out for that magic mound where all the trouble began and fixes up a little gallows. While he is thus engaged he sees a scholar approaching. This undramatic event is in itself something of a wonder. Dyfed has been under a spell and this is the first human creature to pass that way in seven years. In a mediaeval context it was perfectly appropriate that a wandering scholar should penetrate, with absent-minded curiosity, what to anyone else would obviously be a prohibited area. But this wandering scholar knows his Welsh law. Hanging was the standard punishment for theft, but more often than not the sentence could be commuted to a specific fine. The scholar offers to buy the mouse's freedom for the one pound he had managed to collect by begging. Manawydan declines the offer. The scholar goes on his way but no sooner is he gone than a priest on horseback approaches. After polite exchanges a fresh offer is made. This time, three pounds. The life-price of the mouse is going up. The old arguments are advanced based on the unseemliness of a great man soiling his hands with such a menial and unsavoury task. Again Manawydan refuses the offer. The priest goes on his way. The hangman's string-noose is slipped over the mouse's neck. Now a bishop with his retinue appears to plead for the pregnant mouse. With due respect for the cloth, Manawydan suspends operations.

'Lord bishop,' he said. 'Thy blessing.'

'May God give thee a blessing,' the bishop said. 'What work are you engaged at, may I ask?'

'Hanging a thief that I caught in the act.'

'But is it not a mouse I see in your hand?'

'Yes,' Manawydan said. 'And she it is that has robbed me.'

'Ah well,' the bishop said,' since I have arrived at the stroke of doom for the poor creature, let me buy it from you. I will give you seven pounds for it and rather than the world witness so exalted a man destroying so unprofitable a creature, release it, I beg you, and accept my offer.'

'Between me and God, I shall not release it.'

'Well if that doesn't persuade you, let me offer you four and twenty pounds in ready money if you let it go.'

'I shall not let it go, I confess before God, for twice that much.'

'Well if that doesn't persuade you, let me offer all the horses you see on this plain and the seven loads of baggage and the seven horses you see carry them.'

'Between me and God, I shall not release it.'

'If you will not, state your price.'

'I will. Set Rhiannon and Pryderi free.'

'You shall have that.'

'Between me and God, that is not all.'

'What more do you want?'

'Break the spell and enchantment that holds the seven cantrefs of Dyfed.'

'That shall also be done. Now release the mouse.'

'Between me and God, I shall not,' he said. 'I insist on knowing who the mouse is.'

'She is my wife and were that not so I would not ransom her.'

'Why did she come to me?'

'To plunder,' he said. 'I am Llwyd fab Cilcoed and I cast the spell over the seven cantrefs of Dyfed to avenge the insult to my friend Gwawl, son of Clud.'

Rhiannon and Pryderi reappear. The mouse is released and de-enchanted into the most beautiful young woman. Manawydan asks what punishment his wife and step-son have suffered during their two years absence and the answer is a piece of compressed subtlety that characteristically infers yet another *Mabinogi* (*Mabinogi Mynwair a Mynordd*) and also demonstrates how aptly their chastisement fitted the insult suffered by Gwawl, son of Clud, Rhiannon's unsuccessful suitor in the First Branch. Gwawl had been tied in a sack and kicked by all and sundry: his rival's son, Pryderi, was turned into a doorpost to be knocked by the door-hammer and the lady Gwawl lost made to wear the hay collar of an ass – a fitting punishment for a former goddess of the horse.

4   The Military Muse

The most conspicuous legacy of the English crown's effort to subdue Wales is the network of castles that were built at such enormous expense. Architecture tells its own story. Mediaeval Wales was as rich in castles as mediaeval England was in cathedrals. Costly as they were, from the point of view of the crown it was money well spent. For three or four generations after the death of Llywelyn, the Welsh were always liable to break out into fierce rebellion. For the occupying power the pattern of insurrection was very difficult to understand. More often than not, it had the confusing characteristic of a Celtic quarrel dressed up in the poetic hyperbole of Arthurian adventure. There was also a foreshadowing of the most intense forms of European nationalism. In the end, central government was reduced to adopting a purely racialist basis to the daunting exercise of imposing its latest concepts of law and order on this new dominion. The rule of thumb was the notion that all natives were by definition second-rate citizens or outside the law altogether. The derogatory term 'Welsh'* acquired a fresh varnish of opprobrium. A castle and the town it sheltered were off limits. They were required by law to be oases of non-Welshness. In no other way could the territory be kept in even a pretence of control.

The choices, therefore, available to the offspring of the privileged class in Welsh society were limited. But they were all military and this suited the taste of a warrior aristocracy. The first and most attractive choice was to lead or at least to take part in a rebellion. Rebellion was a heady experience, but it had two distinct disadvantages, apart from an insufficient chance of success. The first was being hanged, drawn, and quartered according to English law. This was notably unpleasant, but a worse aspect of the penalty was the forfeiture of ancient land title and permanent disinheritance. It should come as no surprise, therefore, to discover that the most glamorous rebel before the uprising of the great Glyndŵr himself should be a character who may never actually have set foot in Wales.

Owain Lawgoch, a great-nephew of the last Llywelwyn, was brought

* The word 'Welsh' derives from an Anglo-Saxon word for a foreigner.

33

up in Surrey. Nonetheless he was nurtured on the pure milk of the poetic tradition. When Edward III repeated the tactic of Edward I and called his eldest son the Prince of Wales, Owain reacted by attaching himself to the king of France and claiming the Principality of Wales as his inheritance. Successive kings of France expressed their warm support for his cause and Charles V went so far as to provide him with a fleet at Harfleur and three hundred thousand gold francs to furnish an expeditionary force. Owain took Guernsey from the English and his name lived on there as a subject of legend and song, as it seems to have done wherever he went in pursuit of his career as a *condottiere*. A folk song in Switzerland celebrates 'Duke Yvain de Galles with his hat made of gold.' Froissart relates in his celebrated *Chronicle* how Owain was assassinated by an English agent during the long siege of the impregnable castle of Mortagne-sur-Mer. He was stabbed in the back while combing his hair.

His memory quickly became a legend in Wales. He joined Arthur, Cadwallon, and Cadwaladr on the short-list of possible heroes who could return and deliver the Isle of Britain back into the hands of her rightful owners. The remarkable persistence of his legend is demonstrated by an article published in a Welsh magazine significantly entitled *Y Brython* as late as the year 1858. The author, a clergyman and respected antiquary, described a ballad he had heard sung at a fair. The song represented Owain Lawgoch as a hero still expected to return and reign over the whole of Britain. In the meanwhile he was supposed by some to be biding his time in distant lands, and by others to be slumbering in a treasure-cave in the mountainside.

For those to whom rebellion or exile were not available, there remained a possibility of turning outlaw and bandit. (The 'Red Hand' of Owain's surname probably referred to the fourteenth-century term used to denote an outlaw.) To live outside an alien English law imposed on a Brythonic society was in one sense a recession into the anarchic aspect of the Celtic social order and in another a response to an idea of nationhood that depended on a network of kindred relationships and obligations.

The professional poets had no difficulty in adapting the principles of praise poetry to every aspect of the new situation. Through their art they made themselves essential to a new way of life. Viewed from the centre of government, for the two centuries between the fall of the house of Gwynedd and the triumph of the house of Tudor, Wales was a twilight zone where ancient custom and practice were in open conflict with the uncertain attempts of an alien authority to establish systems of law and order that were themselves little more than tentative experiments in uniformity. The life reflected in the magnificent body of Welsh poetry of the period, however, is zestful and joyous and surprisingly civilised. The heroic intensity of the struggle for independence has given way to a freedom from constraint and a delight in the possibilities of a more balanced existence. Now the poets can absorb the influence of the troubadours, enjoy artistic experiment for its own sake, travel freely from one patron to another, and sing the praises of the ancient virtues of hospitality in new modes to match the advent of European standards of luxurious living. Poetry was accepted by the network of aristocratic native families as a high art and the result was the flowering of artistic accomplishment worthy to rank with the very best that the fourteenth and fifteenth centuries could produce. From Dafydd ap Gwilym to Tudur Aled a succession of great poets created a cathedral of praise, a blaze of celebration for a way of life that was the more exhilarating from being frequently threatened by one form or another of danger.

The third channel for the exercise of martial arts, and in practice by far the most popular, was to become a mercenary soldier in the pay, for the most part, of the king of England. The three choices were never mutually exclusive. They frequently overlapped. But the conspicuous growth industry of the period was expeditionary warfare. The Hundred Years War in France created the conditions for a successful export drive. The Black Prince issued his Welshmen with uniforms and thereby established a European precedent. Captains like Hywel ap Gruffydd from the North and Rhys ap Gruffydd from the South organised the shock troops that made the Black Prince's reputation. Their longbows inflicted terrible casualties at Crécy. At Poitiers, when Owain Lawgoch was on the other side, Hywel ap Gruffydd became Sir Hywel of the Axe: the axe that the Black Prince ordered should be displayed in a place of honour in the royal hall and have food served it daily and then distributed in alms. The great poet Iolo Goch was moved to celebrate Sir Hywel's exploits in a mode reminiscent of Taliesin and Aneirin.

> To place, the kind of present a proud man would never want, a halter on the head of the King of France. To be a barber in the style of Erbin's son with lance and sword, the heavy tools of battle: to shave with his hand and strength, heads and beards as they come and swiftly set flowing their blood over their feet. A sad business for some.

Iolo Goch also sang in praise of Owain Glyndŵr, although he did not live to see this patron become the last native Prince of Wales. Iolo sang in the calm before the storm, and his subject was Owain's home at Sycharth as a centre of courtly perfection in a dangerous world. Owain began his military career in the service of the king of England. When he distinguished himself in Richard II's Scottish campaign, the well-born poet Gruffydd Llwyd was instantly ready to apply the familiar prophetic allusions to the rising star of Glyndŵr. This hero would be another

Arthur and inherit the ultimate honour due to a great champion: 'Five score kings, it cannot be denied, of our renowned homeland, ruled in the Court of London, crowned, antlered lords of the island.'

After the death of Owain Lawgoch in 1378, Glyndŵr was the man with the best hereditary claim to the shadowy inheritance of all the royal princes of Wales, North and South. He must have brooded long over this as he listened to the bards singing in the splendid hall at Sycharth. But whether he knew it or not, he was also the heir to the revolutionary pressure of a period of intense economic dislocation. Thus the support he gained from one end of the Welsh-speaking world to the other came from the grass roots. His status as a national figure was established by the way in which he combined ancient aspirations and the creative ideas essential to survival in a changing world. The vision which he held before his followers was a Welsh nation fully equipped with all the institutions necessary for its well-being and preservation. The political cornerstone of his policies was the Tripartite Indenture he made with Mortimer and Percy of Northumberland in 1405. This would have created a solid Welsh state, including the border counties and submerging the ancient frontier of the Dyke in a *Walia Irredenta*. It was for this model that Welsh forces lived and died for almost fifteen years. Glyndŵr had the solid support of all classes, the church and the poets, for at least as long as there was a reasonable chance of success. His legend is without the usual Arthurian betrayal in the last act. He quietly took his place in the cave, which is the Cymric equivalent of a pantheon, and has been sleeping there alongside Arthur, Cadwallon, Cadwaladr, Owain Lawgoch, and all the other heroes, ever since.

Glyndŵr was defeated by Shakespeare's Harry of Monmouth. The founding father of Welsh nationalism was defeated by the founding father of English nationalism, who was also on occasion capable of calling himself Welsh – 'I wear it for a memorable honour; for I am Welsh, you know, good countryman.'

Fluellen's response was also typical, setting a precedent which has been followed down the centuries and is still in use at the present time: 'All the water in Wye cannot wash your majesty's Welsh plood out of your pody, I can tell you that: Got pless it and preserve it.' It was enough to make it easy for so many of the men who fought for Glyndŵr to switch their allegiance. Henry V went to France in order to distract his English subjects from their domestic discontents and to put in practice the military skills he had acquired in Wales. Welsh captains followed him even while Glyndŵr was still alive because he offered them an opportunity to play the great game on neutral ground. When the Abbot of the Cistercian monastery at Llantarnam addressed Glyndŵr's troops before battle, his theme was always a combination of a call to personal repentance and patriotic self-sacrifice. That kind of

Owain Glyndŵr's seal bears comparison with those of greater potentates for elegance of design. It survives in Paris from his treaty with Charles VI. (Archives Nationales, Paris)

religious intensity was completely absent from the joyous excitement of the French adventure.

Guto'r Glyn, one of the greatest poets of the period and a soldier himself, wrote a notable ode in praise of Mathau Goch, known as 'Matago' to the French chroniclers and thought by some scholars to be a possible model for the figure of Fluellen. Guto describes Mathau Goch's campaign as a 'dance through Maine and Anjou'. He and his men in pursuit of La Hire and Poton de Xantrailles are carried away by the excitement of the hunt through the forest and along the roads of France. This is a larger game than the wearisome condition of a lost cause or the stern rôle of defending the integrity of one's own nation. Guto's own career illustrates the pleasures of the chase. He attaches himself to the family of Sir William ap Thomas, the son-in-law of that Sir Davy Gam who died at Agincourt. This family changes its name to Herbert and commits itself firmly to the fortunes of the House of York: so that at the peak of his career, Guto wears 'the king of England's collar', and all his hopes of personal advancement and patronage lie with the powerful family of the new Earls of Pembroke. It was in this fashion that Welsh poetic art, which was the core of assertive

Welshness, became hopelessly embroiled in the struggle for the English crown. Welsh noblemen who were suitable subjects for eulogy became great lords closely related to claimants for the English throne.

The Tudors were related to Owain Glyndŵr. They had been among the first of the gentry to rally to his cause. One of their number, Owain Tudur (the Christian name was significant to the bards), secretly married Henry V's widow. His marriage was the foundation of a Lancastrian party in Wales and ensured that the leading Welsh families would tear themselves apart in 'the fury between the rose flowers'. A category of fifteenth-century verse concerned itself with increasingly obscure vaticination. Prophecy became a minor industry and it was usually couched in vague emblematic terms intended to be reminiscent of the earlier prophetic poetry attributed to Merlin and Taliesin. However boring it may be to read now, at the time it was written this type of verse had much more political importance than all the more aesthetically satisfying output of a great poetic tradition. It was engaging itself in the propaganda of the power struggle and thereby loosening its connection with philosophical concepts of social order reflecting on earth and in human affairs something of the excellence of a divine creation.

Henry Tudor was well aware of the value of bardic propaganda. His appeal to the Welsh was comprehensively nationalist. He named his eldest son Arthur, he flew the flag of Cadwaladr and after his victory hung it in St. Paul's. He gave the Welsh to understand that all the ancient prophecies had been fulfilled and that once more one of their number wore the 'most excellent crown of London'. To the Welsh soldiers in the Tudor army, London was a delectable combination of Troy and Rome and Jerusalem. Military historians have described Bosworth Field as a lacklustre battle compared with the other great encounters of the Wars of the Roses. England had had its fill of civil war. Propelled by a final spurt of myth and the Messianic expectations of his Welsh supporters, Henry Tudor managed to grab the crown when all other claimants had become too weak or too weary or wounded to hold him off.

Guto'r Glyn lived long enough to see it all happen: to see Harri Tudur, *Mab Darogan* (the Son of Prophecy), wear the crown of London. He spent his last years, a blind old man, in care of the abbot of Valle Crucis. His last poems are dedicated to the abbot. With that alarming lucidity that can come with old age, he was able to perceive that the victory of the Tudors would bring no blessings to the poetic order and the high culture which he had cherished all his life. Guto knew that sweet as his poetry had been and pleasurable the pursuit of glory, the age of the military muse had come to an end. The grim truth was even worse than that. The victory of the Tudors would, in the end, make his Wales less Welsh. His praise, and the lifetime's practice of his art, had been for what would now become no more than an unimportant fringe area.

> *Moli bum ymylau byd*
> *Malu sôn, melys ennyd*
>
> (I praised the world's edges, milling sounds for a brief sweet moment . . .)

He knew that the Welsh ruling caste, that had once been dedicated to the maintenance of a native social order, had exhausted itself in the bloody process of carving out the foundations of an English nation state.

5   The Tudor Baggage Train

In the struggle for independence led by the house of Gwynedd, it is possible to discern a protracted wrangle over the copyright on Arthur. Because the Welsh had come to believe that he would return and lead them to victory even at this late hour, two powerful kings of England, Henry II and Edward I, took the trouble to pronounce him dead and buried. In 1165, Henry let it be known that a Cymric soothsayer with impeccable Merlinesque credentials had whispered in his royal ear the exact whereabouts of Arthur's grave. This was shrewd both as propaganda and public relations. Arthur was not sleeping in a cave on a Welsh mountainside, and this information came from the most respectable Welsh source. He was buried in the holy and famous abbey of Glastonbury, still revered by the Welsh for its close connection with Dewi Sant and yet another lost kingdom. In the spring of 1278, a few months before the marriage of Eleanor de Montfort to Llywelyn II in Worcester Cathedral, Edward I arranged a stranger ceremony in Glastonbury. He ordered the opening of the tomb of some West Saxon ruler and his wife and declared the bones officially to be those of Arthur and Guinevere. He had the Archbishop of Canterbury conduct a solemn rite of re-interment during which Edward himself carried what he had declared to be Arthur's relics and his queen, Eleanor, carried what was left of Guinevere. Arthur was dead, and who was better fitted to hold sway on his imperial British throne, Edward Plantagenet who ruled from the Pyrenees to the Tweed, or his client, Llywelyn II with his precarious hold on his mountainous principality, marrying the daughter of Simon de Montfort by Edward's grace and favour?

It was the Arthurian dimension that made the death of Llywelyn such a catastrophe for the Welsh; and by exactly the same token, two hundred and three years later, made the battle of Bosworth in their eyes such a triumph. Throughout the twenty-four years that followed his triumphal entry into London, Harri Tudur – Henry VII – maintained a nice balance between Welsh mediaeval pieties and expectations, and the new spirit of the age. Throughout the middle ages, Arthur was more than an effigy. He represented an enlightened vision of the feudal ideal.

Dante saw him as the successful feudal emperor, balancing Might and Right in either hand with inspired dexterity, an equal weight of virtue and courage. This was the British contribution to the philosophic exposition of the feudal ideal. The homage due to the power of the emperor at the top of the feudal heap was related as much to his legitimacy and his heroic character as to his political and military power. Henry VII carved his way to the throne with his sword, but took care to insure the future of his dynasty by christening his first-born Arthur. The Welsh took this as a graceful gesture, a recognition of the aspirations which had sustained their spirit through two centuries of turbulence. It was certainly a tribute to the massive authority of Geoffrey of Monmouth's *Historia*. By the end of the fifteenth century the English were just as intoxicated on the Arthurian brew as the remnant of the original British. An idealised view of the past is often an indispensable prelude to any radical departure in the socio-political pattern, and it is symptomatic that a people should be obsessed with the ramifications of a notion at the very moment in time when it was being quietly removed from the plane of reality into the world of harmless romance.

It was precisely feudalism that the Tudors brought to an end in England and Wales. When Arthur Tudor died in 1501, his brother Henry became heir to the throne, and this young man was far more interested in Machiavelli than in Geoffrey of Monmouth. Henry VII had already shown a distinct partiality for cultivated Italians. The city states were the laboratories in which the new statecraft was being tested. They had the wealth and the leisure to try out styles in every sphere of human endeavour with what we would recognise as Californian exuberance.

In retrospect it seems wholly appropriate that the scholarly attack on the substance and credibility of Geoffrey's work should have been made by Polydore Vergil from Urbino, already a scholar of European reputation before arriving in Henry VII's London in 1503. Polydore was a cautious man and he knew how much Geoffrey's book had come to mean to the English. It took him almost half a century before he allowed his completed *History of England* to appear, after he had returned to the safety of Urbino. There was little place for scholarly detachment during the prolonged and bloody birth pangs of a nation state in which the monarch was head of both church and state, a secular pope holding in both hands the reins of unparalleled power. The English accepted the dictatorship of the crown because it was patriotic and good for trade. It offered the best prospect of stability for the progress of mercantile capitalism. The Welsh, always more gullible, accepted the new order because it was created by what they imagined to be a Welsh royal house, the descendants of Arthur. They were of course the last people to stop believing in the historicity of Geoffrey's book.

(As late as the eighteenth century, Theophilus Evans was to write a Welsh classic that accepted the main tenets of Geoffrey's historiography without serious questioning.)

Among the English, Geoffrey was not totally abandoned, merely elevated to a strictly literary category. The smoothness of the transition demonstrates the vitality of the new relationship between the Elizabethan power structure and the creative energy of the late Renaissance in England. When Edmund Spenser began his epic *The Faerie Queene* the whole Matter of Britain was transported into the raw material of a new kind of celebratory poetry. Geoffrey's Arthurian vision was transported from a pseudo-historical past into a timeless world of the imagination. Through the golden mist of archaic language the Elizabethan reader was encouraged to catch a glimpse of an exciting possibility: a Protestant world empire ruled over by a virgin queen, herself an improved, enlightened, and generally elevated version of Arthur. It is Spenser's friend, the influential Sir Philip Sidney whose father was for so long Lord President of the Council for Wales and the Marches, who makes explicit the new aesthetic whereby the poet is elevated above the historian and the truth of epic grandeur above mere historic fact. It is at this delicate point that Merlin makes his reappearance.

Sidney and Spenser were both pupils of Dr. John Dee, an intriguing figure who stands at the heart of the English Renaissance. More importantly, so was the Earl of Leicester. In characteristic Welsh fashion, John Dee boasted an ancestry which reached back to Rhodri Mawr (d. 877). This would allow him to claim remote relationship with the great queen herself, and while he was in favour, she raised no objection. Indeed she is on record as having chided him for not coming often enough to court. From the days when he astounded a Cambridge audience with some extraordinary stage devices in a production of Aristophanes, he both enjoyed and suffered the reputation of being a magician. He was a Renaissance version of the 'Dreamer Merlin'. Without his mathematics and navigational scholarship it is unlikely that the exploits of his friends, Frobisher, Gilbert and Raleigh, would have been possible. Spenser, Sidney and Shakespeare came deeply under his influence. He was the most intense exponent of a 'British Empire' with a manifest destiny and a divine mission. He was often referred to as Merlin and it is clear that he did nothing to discourage an obvious correspondence: at every opportunity he would be to Gloriana what Merlin had been to King Arthur and he would summon up every available power, from science to mythology, to serve her. No matter what difficulties presented themselves, like Prospero on his island, he would surmount them with a wave of his intellectual wand.

As early as 1577 John Dee was hard at work in court circles arguing the case for a royal navy supported by taxation and at the same time

John Dee (1527—1608), mathematician, astronomer and magus. A key figure in the adaptation of Welsh myth to English imperial vision, he saw himself as a Merlin at the court of a female King Arthur. (National Portrait Gallery)

setting out the queen's claims to rule the waves of the North Atlantic because King Arthur had colonised all the lands of the Arctic seas from his base in northern Scotland in the sixth century. At the same time he encouraged Welsh historians to present evidence that a direct ancestor of the queen's majesty had in fact discovered America in the twelfth century, long before Columbus claimed the territory for the king of Spain.

Madoc another of Owen Gwyneth his sonnes left the land in contention betwixt his brethren, and prepared certaine ships with men and munition, and sought adventures by seas, sailing west, and leaving the coast of Ireland so far north that he came to a land unknowen, where he saw manie strange things . . . Whereupon it is manifest, that this countrie was long before by Brytaines discovered.

It was not difficult to use Prince Madoc ab Owain Gwynedd as a more factual overseas extension of the Arthurian myth. This section of Humphrey Lluyd's *The Historie of Cambria*, 'corrected, augmented and continued . . . by David Powell', provided the Elizabethan merchant adventurers with just the kind of embroidered cloak of legitimacy that they needed. There was no limit to how far the mythological apparatus of the Welsh could be developed in the service of the Tudor monarchy and the English nation state. The contrast in attitude among the Welsh ruling classes and intelligentsia before and after the Tudor settlement is amazing. The very people who had displayed the deepest and most intense hatred of England and the English became their most devoted and resourceful servants. With surprisingly little heart-searching, they also took on the task of dismantling their own traditional defences of language, religion, culture, laws and customs, so that what was left of Wales could be incorporated 'for ever and henceforth . . . united and annexed to and with this his Realm of England'.

There was a special task of mythological adjustment to be made in the sphere of religion. Once more the Welsh scholars, all sons of leading families or their lesser dependants, demonstrated that they were equal to the task. In Shakespeare's last historical play, *The Famous History of the Life of King Henry VIII*, it is Henry's infatuation with Anne Bullen, who had her own Welsh connections, that is the instrument by which Cardinal Wolsey's pride and power are broken. The twist of the historical plot is based on Polydore Vergil, whom Wolsey had so ungraciously imprisoned in the Tower. And yet its significance derives from the deeper mythological themes of the return of the ancient British kings to the throne, making possible the creation of a purified national church. The play reaches its climax when Cranmer, the first Protestant archbishop of Canterbury, christens the baby Elizabeth, the fruit of Henry's precipitate union with Anne Bullen, and at that moment feels moved to confront the audience with a prophetic utterance in the Merlin tradition, setting out a nice precedent for the doctrine of the divine right of kings.

Anne Bullen, as the audience must have known, did not last very long. A bright young man called Matthew Parker had been appointed her chaplain and accompanied her to the block: it must have seemed singularly appropriate, when Anne's daughter finally became queen, that he should be consecrated the second Protestant archbishop of Canterbury. He was thus in charge of the operation that would make the credentials of the Anglican church beyond question. He was a scholar and an enthusiastic antiquarian, and he knew that there was nothing more relevant to his case than 'the relics of the noble Britons'. The steps of the argument were clear and simple. Once upon a time there had been a Celtic church that flourished independently of Rome. This British Church had been derived from an apostolic source in the person of Joseph of Arimathea. Its nature had been essentially evangelical. It had expanded through preaching and it was maintained by a thorough knowledge of the scriptures which it possessed written down in the native Cambro-British tongue. This was the church that had refused to bow down to the bishop of Rome from the fourth to the seventh centuries. The Welsh scholars transformed Taliesin into a 'noble Clerke Ambrosius Telesinus . . . writing in the year 540, when the right Christian faith (which Joseph of Arimathea taught at the Isle of Avalon) reigned in this land, before the proud and bloodthirsty moonke Augustin infected it with his Romish doctrine'.

If anyone asked where these precious scriptures had gone, the quick answer was given that they were destroyed by the Saxons and the Vikings and the last vestiges of them had been lost during the wars of Glyndŵr. At the palace of the bishop of St. David's at Abergwili outside Carmarthen a bevy of the best Welsh scholars available were hard at work providing Matthew Parker with ammunition in the endless propaganda battle against the Pope and the powers of darkness. In *The Faerie Queene* Edmund Spenser describes a curiously parallel operation in progress on exactly the same territory.

> In Deheubarth, that now South-Wales is hight . . .
> The great magician Merlin had devis'd
> By his deep science and hell-dreaded might
> A looking glass . . .

Magic was in fact performed. The place of the missing scriptures was taken by the work of a small group of Welsh Protestant scholars who as a by-product of all these activities, produced a new and brilliant translation of the Bible into Welsh. They had their material rewards. The relationship between church and state was extraordinarily close throughout this period of radical adjustment, and we have only to consult the genealogical trees, which remained vital documents of Welsh social life, to observe how very efficiently the material benefits of the new order were distributed among the loyal servants of the crown and the church. No doubt this was very much the way in which matters were arranged in the process of consolidating privilege. While it must be recorded that the cautious self-advancement displayed by the Protestant humanists contrasts sharply with the sacrifices of both the Welsh Catholic exiles and of the Puritan extremists of the next generation, they had their own unobtrusive way of showing devotion to the well-being of the mass of their fellow countrymen.

During the Renaissance, to be worthy of preservation, any vernacular however exalted was obliged to prove that it possessed the inherent ability to imitate classical models and modes, in much the same way as Renaissance architecture was expected to base itself on idealised models of the greatest creations of Greece and Rome. Welsh could claim to be a learned language capable of the highest civility on grounds not dissimilar to the exalted lineage of the mythology which had helped to put the house of Tudor in power. In Elizabethan England, aspects of this mythology were still being exploited for the benefit of settlement and active expansion in church and state. If the mythology was valid, so was the language in which it had originally been conceived. Wales had no university, no royal court, none of the attributes of Italianate high culture which would normally be considered essential to allow humanist scholars to work freely and without restriction in the native language. What it did have was a body of literature created in the previous two centuries in a brilliant poetic mode and now jealously guarded by the bardic order. Welsh was saved from premature extinction by an unique collaboration between humanist scholars and a conservative poetic tradition, grimly determined to preserve all the treasures of the past. However much tidy-minded civil servants might object to its presence, the Welsh language was tucked into a corner of the Tudor baggage train, like a cooking pot, along with the crumbling effigies of Arthur, Merlin, Taliesin and Madoc. They could be cast aside when they had outlived their usefulness; the language was not so easily disposed of. A well-made cooking-pot, if preserved for a sufficient length of time, could become a cauldron of rebirth.

6   The Cooking-Pot

Two hundred years before the birth of Christ, Cato had observed of the Celts, 'two things they delight in above all others, to fight well and to speak well.' In the case of the Welsh, Giraldus Cambrensis made oddly similar observations in the twelfth century AD. This fighting flourish, as we may call it, the Tudors sublimated into the tortuous conduct of politics, committee work, intrigue and legal battles. By remaining a virgin, Queen Elizabeth saw to it that dramatic shape was given to the impulse by making perpetual courtship the mainspring of the plot. In this atmosphere the kindred network of the Welsh warrior aristocracy flourished like weeds lovingly transplanted into a hot-house. The rewards of survival were great, and favoured the advancement of talented young members of even the most obscure branches of family networks. A good example of this would be the career of William Aubery of Brecon whose benefactor was his distant relative, Henry Herbert, the second Earl of Pembroke.

Aubery could have served as a cut-out pattern of the ideal Elizabethan. He was a distinguished civil lawyer, head of an Oxford college, a member of Parliament, Vicar General of the province of Canterbury, a former judge advocate with the Earl of Pembroke's forces in France and, inevitably, a member of the Council for Wales and the Marches. He amassed great estates in Breconshire because he was the kind of man who knew which way the wind was blowing even before getting up in the morning. He served Mary and Elizabeth with equal zeal and profit: and when the Leicester-Sidney Protestant interest began to fail, he applied himself with fresh energy to the persecution of Puritans. He took part in the condemnation of his distant cousin John Penry, the supposed author of the Marprelate tracts, who was hanged in 1592. He was also related to John Dee, but when that latter-day Merlin fell from favour and his need became great, William Aubery became 'suddenly unavailable'. The traditional help from a relative was no longer operative under the new system, totally permeated now with the spirit of Machiavelli. In true Renaissance fashion political life in England had become a plot among plots.

For a genial fellow like Aubery it was a pleasure to come down to Wales and refresh himself with outdoor pursuits in his native haunts. It gave an edge to his appetite for the food of his childhood. He also had recourse to the cooking-pot of the old language. For him this could still be a cauldron of inspiration. He still felt an instinct to replenish his genius at the vital source of his being. Or at least it pleased him to come down to his Breconshire estate to 'make merye with his frendes', among whom he numbered the grammarian, Sion Dafydd Rhys. It is this eccentric scholar, who had had the courage to publish a book on the pronunciation of Italian in Padua and a Latin grammar in Venice, who tells us how he managed to copy the words of a song about Taliesin and Prince Elphin from the very lips of William Aubery as they sat before the fire drinking, reciting and singing verses.

As a member of the Council of Wales and the Marches, William Aubery may well have been responsible for commissioning a report on the state of religion among the people of North Wales. Among the collection of manuscripts relating to Wales in the British Museum there is the report written by a spy of the Council which gives us a brief but bright glimpse of the common people enjoying themselves on the western slopes of Snowdonia, once the last stronghold of independent princes and now an 'edge of the world'.

> Upon Sundays and holidays the multitude of all sorts . . . meet in sundry places either on some hill or on the side of some mountain where their harpers and fiddlers sing them songs of the doings of their ancestors, namely, of their wars against the kings of this realm and the English nation, and then do they recite their pedigrees at length how each of them is descended from those of their old princes. Here also do they spend their time in hearing some part of the lives of Taliesin, or Merlin, Beuno, Cybi, Garmon (Germanus) and such other intended prophets and saints of that country.

Through the gift of shape-shifting, Taliesin, above all other historical figures promoted to mythological status, makes himself available to all sorts and conditions of men. It could also be argued that he is able to do this because he was the spirit left in charge of the vital cooking-pot. The original Taliesin was the founding father of the tradition of praise poetry. By the ninth century his charismatic name had become attached to a folk hero and a central figure of myth and romance. This second Taliesin quickly overshadowed the original figure because he was a popular representation in the Welsh world of a characteristic hero figure of Celtic myth, the poet-prophet who enjoys a complex relationship with a sequence of levels of existence of which the physical world that surrounds and sustains us is only one numinous manifestation. Because he lives in folk memory, Taliesin carries with him something of the powers of the gods and spirits of the shape-shifting Celtic pantheon.

'Some part of the lives of Taliesin' and something of the story-telling the people were enjoying on the mountainside, we can gather from a brief outline of the uncanonical book of *The Mabinogion* published by Charlotte Guest under the title *The History of Taliesin*.

Gwion Bach was a boy of humble origin from Llanfair Caereinion. Even now it is possible to imagine the audience on the hillside identifying with a hero who is one of their kind. His story, like theirs, is an epic of survival against overwhelming odds. This local boy chanced to be engaged by a powerful but misshapen witch by the name of Cyridwen. His job was to keep an eye on the blind man who fuelled the fire underneath her cauldron of inspiration. Cyridwen had a severe personal problem. Her only son and the apple of her eye was the ugliest male in the world and, until she could do something about this, there was absolutely no hope that he would ever be received in polite society. Her plan was to transform her repulsive offspring into the world's outstanding intellectual. To this end she proposed to boil every known type of virtuous herb in her cooking-pot cauldron and produce within a year and a day a magic essence – three shining drops which, when swallowed by her ugly son, would give him full knowledge of the past, the present and the future.

All this was extremely hard work and by the end of the year the witch Cyridwen was overcome by the desire to put her feet up and take a nap. Before doing so, she took the precaution of placing her hairy boy in position so that the three precious drops, when they came, should land in his open mouth. This was an opportunity which Gwion Bach could not allow to pass. While the witch was snoring and the blind man was stoking, he contrived to change places with Cyridwen's son at the crucial moment. Humble as he was, he had understood that in history everything was a matter of timing. When the three hot drops hopped out they landed on his index finger which he promptly popped in his mouth to cool. Thus by accident or design, but not by education, he became the wisest man on earth, sensed his immediate danger and fled for his life. There follows a chase that sounds like a folk symphony of shape-shifting. He became a hare to improve his speed, and the angry witch became a greyhound. He jumped into a river and transformed himself into a fish. She became an otter. He surfaced and became a bird. She followed him like a hawk. When she was on the point of catching him, he landed on a heap of winnowed wheat and hid there in the shape of one of the grains. Cyridwen turned into a black hen and scattered the grain with angry feet until she found him and gobbled him up.

This was the end of an historic first act. It was followed by a nine month interval during which the seed of promise grew inside her. The ordinary mortal who had contrived to become the wisest man was reconstituted in the womb of a witch and born again as a baby of such beauty that, in spite of her wrath, Cyridwen could not bring herself to destroy him. Instead she had him sewn up in a skin bag and tossed into the sea. On the night of 1st May in an undated year, a bankrupt young 'prince' named Elphin was watching the catching on the weir, and hoping for enough fish to pay his debts. He was in the throes of disappointment when he noticed the skin bag caught against one of the poles. It was shaped like a baby's cradle. Elphin took out his knife and, cutting the stitches, uncovered the forehead of a baby some three days old. *'Tal-iesin'* said the prince, by which he meant 'What a beautiful shining white brow!' which was the first of the three meanings the people could give to the word 'Taliesin': these were, a forehead, a value, and a payment. Much to the prince's astonishment the baby responded. *'Taliesin bid,'* the baby said, which in the succinct Welsh of mediaeval storytellers meant 'Very well, Taliesin let it be.' He was graciously accepting his name and all the responsibilities that went with it. This was a point in the story when the storyteller could expect a murmur of approval and even applause from his audience, whether of high or low degree.

This was the prince with the infant genius in his saddle-bag that was the subject of William Aubery's song.

Elffin deg, taw a'th wylo

(Fair Elffin, cease thy weeping)

But it was a song that Aubery's social class was less inclined to listen to as it grew wealthier and more successful; and for whom therefore it was less and less intended. A valid song has a life of its own, and only those who show it respect are entitled to enjoy it. A growing preoccupation with the social root of this aesthetic problem can be clearly traced in the output of the major representatives of the Welsh poetic tradition throughout the sixteenth century.

Tudur Aled was a great poet whose zest for life is brilliantly reflected in the exuberant skill he displays in his verse. He was by choice a man of the Renaissance with great hopes of preferment. But even as he writes his polished verses to celebrate the success and ease and wealth that had come with the Tudor settlement, Tudur Aled was uneasily conscious of the adverse effect of the new prosperity on the most salient virtues of the old Welsh way of life. He focuses on the new danger: 'This will become an age of office-seeking, the kind of competition to give us cause to hate each other . . . Wales will be the worse for this exposure, and only England will thrive on our corruption.'

In the absence of any form of political independence, a chain of relationships, carefully defined by the art of genealogy, and the celebration of the loyalties and obligations and qualities of character that went with it, were an essential framework to sustain the sense of nationhood. Throughout the middle ages wherever the poets sang, an effective Welsh polity came into existence from one end of the country to the other. Their song was capable of giving the most modest household regal dimensions: the very strength of their technique was sufficient to sustain an edifice of pride and celebration. Under the conditions which prevailed, loyalty, co-operation, courage, generosity, and independence of spirit were Welsh political imperatives. When Wales was swallowed whole by the Tudor nation state of Henry VIII, there was no longer any place for these ancient virtues. A nation state in the Italian style designed by Machiavelli was held together by the grim combination of fear and self-interest, a nice balance between juicy rewards and fearsome punishments.

Tudur Aled's favourite pupil, Gruffudd Hiraethog, collaborated wholeheartedly with William Salesbury, the translator and learned humanist. They were both well aware that they were engaged in an emergency rescue operation. On a journey they make together from the banks of the Conwy to the banks of the Thames, Salesbury copies out with his own hand one of his friend's manuscripts and insists on publishing it because, as he says, there was so little time to waste. There was certainly no time for bickering between the guardians of the old bardic law and the advocates of the new learning. In 1552 Salesbury dedicated a book on rhetoric to Gruffudd and makes a gentle pun on his bardic name.

> You are so *hiraethog* [the word is the name of a mountain near Gruffydd's home and it also means 'full of longing' or 'anxious'] about the state of the language . . . that you take too great a load on your individual shoulders, namely that you search high and low for every dog-eared manuscript and mouldy mottled book to study and examine in order to discover any help to support this language which is beginning to stumble.

Gruffudd prepared in manuscript the prospectus of a great book in which he would set out the professional secrets of the bardic schools. It would include 'the best things of Taliesin' and 'Taliesin's wisdom'. Inevitably he died before the project could be set in hand. His elegy was composed by his most cherished disciple William Llŷn who lived in Oswestry, a town much loved by a remarkable sequence of skilled poets. The elegy was cast in the form of a dialogue between himself and his dead master. The poem displays many of the characteristic beauties of the *cywydd* form, but it also contains a note of sadness and melancholy that is new to a tradition hitherto aggressively zestful and joyous. The poet makes us feel that we are at the graveside of the last great master of an art in decline. William Llŷn was the author of many passionate appeals to the aristocracy and land-owning class to attend to their traditional responsibilities. It is significant however that he preferred to stay at home in Oswestry, and was less inclined to go on poetic intineraries. His recriminations grew more bitter as he grew older. Only one more generation and the 'good ould squier' of Beaupre could think it something of a humorous gesture to toss Meurig Dafydd's 'cowydh' 'into the fier'.

7 An Endangered Species

The unmentionable snag in the otherwise fruitful concept of a Virgin Queen was that she could not, at least by natural means, produce any offspring: and not even her most sycophantic Welsh courtier would have dared to express a desire for an Anglican Virgin Birth. She had to die 'like any man or any owl' and with her passing the mythological life-support system, which had been the unique Welsh contribution to Tudor well-being and the expansion of her empire and her glory, were tossed out of the back doors of the palace like discarded dressings into a hospital incinerator. When James VI of Scotland became James I of England, the value of Welsh shares on the stock exchange of royal favour took a distinct downward turn. James had little interest in Welsh mythologies which had outlived their usefulness.

The smarter families were well advised to become English as quickly as possible. A chasm was opening across which even the most fluently bilingual aristocrat could not easily stride. William Herbert, the first Earl of Pembroke, brother-in-law of Catherine Parr, executor of Henry VIII's will, governor of Edward VI, Master of Horse and Knight of the Garter, friend of both Catholic Mary and Protestant Elizabeth, was more at home in Welsh than in English to such an extent that in London it was whispered that he was illiterate. His son, the second earl, was still praised by the poets and described as *'llygaid holl Gymru'* (the eye of all Wales). The third earl, the patron of Shakespeare, who dabbled in verse himself, was still eligible for his modicum of Welsh praise. In his case it came from the author of more humble verses, the Vicar Pritchard, who would never have dared attempt a full-blown eulogy in the strict metres. He called his William Herbert *'colofn y deyrnas'* (the pillar of the realm). The fourth earl, Philip, also had literary tastes and proved himself a faithful servant of the Stuarts. In his youth he was teased about his Welsh accent. Although he had Welsh and English poets among his tutors, including a herald bard and genealogist and the great poet George Herbert, his links with Wales grew tenuous as he grew older, and well before the end of the century the family was thoroughly anglicised.

In 1604 Dr. John Dee made a desperate appeal to King James I that he should be cleared of the slander that he had been 'a conjurer or invocator of spirits'. There was no question that Dee had in fact attempted to commune with spirits and interpret their messages. There is some suggestion that it was this Merlinesque habit of his that gave Shakespeare the idea of Glendower summoning spirits from the vasty deep and of the ageing Prospero deciding to abandon his rough magic, break his staff, drown his book. Unfortunately for Dee, the king considered himself a world expert on demons and witchcraft. The old man's petition was refused. He died in poverty and disgrace. In any case the age of mythological syntheses was over. The polarisation of religious ideologies characteristic of the seventeenth century had begun. After the economic misery that dragged the German people into the gruesome Thirty Years War, England became the storm centre of ideological conflict.

No corner of the British Isles escaped the bitter winnowing process. It would not have been too surprising if under such conditions the Welsh identity and language disappeared altogether. The country had been totally integrated into the English political and ecclesiastical system. It remained overwhelmingly royalist and like a rudderless dinghy bobbed up and down in the waves created by the larger vessel. The Welsh were hanging on grimly to what they were now able to convince themselves was their venerable loyalty to the crown. Cromwell may have been a Williams with Welsh ancestry, but the pedigree of a Putney brewer would never be long enough to satisfy a people still besotted with the mirage of their Trojan ancestry. Cromwell's network of relatives fitted snugly inside the House of Commons, at one point all twenty-one of them. None of them had what the Welsh would consider blue blood. However, trial by battle proved which family backing was the more effective. It seems somehow appropriate that the Welsh-speaking Welsh should have been so attached to the losing side: ancient pride and an undeveloped economy provide the perfect breeding-ground for a lost cause.

In a time of trouble, when the foundations are shaking, any literature calls out for the help of a writer of genius. His pen must be the seismographic needle that will enable his people, both his own generation and their posterity, to increase their understanding and strengthen their capacity to endure the upheavals with which their little world is afflicted. In Wales, the lordly poetic tradition could no longer fulfil the vital rôle of sustaining the morale of a whole people. The high bardic tradition had exhausted its power to develop. It was a system that had begun to inhibit rather than stimulate the native imagination. It was only an eleventh-hour collaboration between the humanists and the last masters of the bardic schools which provided the language with a new strength and gave the writer of genius the medium that he needed to complete his work.

Morgan Llwyd was born in 1619 in a magical corner of Wales called Ardudwy. In the *Mabinogi* this is the home of Blodeuwedd, the wife made of flowers, and it seems appropriate as the birthplace of the man who was to become the greatest imaginative prose writer in the language after that anonymous genius who composed the *Pedair Cainc y Mabinogi*. This territory was sufficiently isolated to preserve many of the features of the more ancient Welsh way of life. It was also an area that enjoyed a degree of economic self-sufficiency and freedom from excessive external interference. Therefore it was able to produce men notable for self-reliance, independence, enterprise and courage. In this period these qualities were conspicuous in the characters of four men representing four quite different points of view. First there was Huw Llwyd, Morgan's grandfather, who in his younger days had been a soldier of fortune with Sir Roger Williams in the Low Countries. He returned home to enjoy the traditional pleasures of the Welsh country gentleman. But in addition to being a celebrated hunter, he practised as a physician, experimenting with the old and new sciences, so that he gained the reputation of a magus and a soothsayer. He was also a capable poet in the old style. Not far from Cynfal, their ancestral home, John Roberts was born. He reverted to the old faith at Oxford and left for Valladolid to join the Benedictine order. He pioneered the revival of the order in Britain and became its first martyr, executed in 1610 in London at the age of thirty-four. Just over the hill still stands Maesgarnedd, the birthplace of the formidable John Jones. Of all the Welsh John Joneses not one was more powerful in his day than he. 'The most universally hated man in North Wales', John Williams, Archbishop of York, said of him in 1647. As a native of Conwy and a former Lord Keeper of the Great Seal, we can assume he had some experience in making such judgements. But since he was a royalist out of royal favour, it is also possible that his view was jaundiced. Jones went on to be a member of the Council of Six, a Governor of Ireland, brother-in-law to Oliver Cromwell and 'Regicide' before he himself was hanged, drawn, and quartered after a celebrated show trial in the autumn of 1660.

Thus, remote as it may have seemed, Ardudwy was as acutely conscious as any part of the British Isles of the dangerous nature of an age of transition. Native curiosity drew the sons of every family of any substance towards the universities that were the gateway to the new learning, to the new professions, and to the more exciting forms of advancement. But ambition was never in itself enough: it had to be reconciled with old loyalties and cultural tradition that continued to flourish. And the conflict of loyalties had to be resolved at a time when religious faith dominated the thinking of educated men. Of all the sons of Ardudwy, it was Morgan Llwyd who was destined to wield the most lasting influence over the future of Wales. He was involved in Puritan politics and served as a chaplain in Cromwell's army; but his permanent influence flowed from the imaginative intensity of his writing. His style marks the passing of the Taliesinic spirit from its imprisonment in the strict metres into the freer range of prose. It remains essentially poetic with a degree of intensity and fervour which is all his own.

Llwyd was deeply involved in the effort of the Commonwealth to transform Royalist Wales into a Puritan province. This revolutionary project conditioned his brief literary career. Unlike Charles Edwards, the other great prose-writer of the period, he never had time to spend on revising his work. It took Edwards three editions to achieve his mature masterpiece *Y Ffydd Ddiffuant* (A History of the True Faith). We last hear of him in London in 1691 trying to publish *An Afflicted Man's Testimony Concerning His Troubles*, and clearly suffering from some form of persecution mania. The difficulties of Edwards' personal life had been too close a reflection of the misfortunes that overtook the Puritan cause after the Restoration. Llwyd, however, did not live to see the failure of the experiment. He died in 1659 at the age of forty.

He knew well enough that Wales was not ready for change. The Commissioners appointed were given wide-ranging powers to reorganise the life of the country. They set about their work with righteous enthusiasm. Three hundred clergy were ejected from their livings, not only for supporting the late king but also for being drunken and ignorant and unable to preach in the Welsh language. The prominent Welsh Puritans were extremists who compelled themselves to attempt the Herculean task of activating a country listless with sullen inertia. Both Morgan Llwyd and Vavasor Powell were Fifth Monarchy men. For them Christ's empire on earth was at hand; and for that a mere Oliver Cromwell was no substitute. They made no distinction between religion and politics and Morgan Llwyd drove himself to attempt to make his own mystical experiences available to his fellow countrymen.

The poetic imagination that governed his prose style could only appeal at best to a minority of readers and as political propaganda it was even more limited. Colonel John Jones, the Regicide, was a great admirer of Morgan Llwyd: but as a man of action he could become impatient with his friend's unworldly stance. Like his brother-in-law, Cromwell, he was something of an eagle. Writing from Dublin Castle in September 1653 he thanks Llwyd for a copy of one of his pamphlets and then adds:

> I confess the discourse is exceedingly good and spirituall according to my understanding, yet my selfe and many other sober wise Christians heere conceive that if it had beene penned in a language or still less parabolicall, and in more plane Scripture expressions, it would be more usefull. Babes must be fed with milk.

Circumstances thrust the visionary Morgan Llwyd into the classic dilemma of the artist caught up in a revolutionary movement. Had there been time, he had the capacity to construct on a Miltonic scale the kind of intellectual system every culture needs to confront an age of revolutionary change. But there was no time. Both the culture and the identity of the species he belonged to were threatened with extinction. Only in another world could their continued existence be guaranteed and the ancient promises fulfilled. His output became conditioned by a conscientious attempt to provide babes with milk, in simple verses as well as in prose. Both the note of desperation and the idiosyncratic sensibility are fuelled by the crisis of his time and the depth of his concern for his people.

O People of Wales! It is towards you, O inhabitants of Gwynedd and Deheubarth, that my voice is raised. The dawn has broken and the sun rises for you. The birds sing: awake, O Welshman, awaken. And if thou art unconvinced by words, be persuaded by events. Look about thee, and see, for behold, the world and its pillars give way. The earth is in tumult. Thunder and lightning strike through the minds of peoples. Behold, many hearts tremble (though they do not admit it) as they contemplate the things that will come to pass. The great day of the Lord searches out and proves every secret thought: and many seek to hide among their own leaves and under the aprons of the old Adam: the wise are bewildered and the strong made to bend. The eloquent swallow their words and the cunning chew their tongues. Dear friends accuse each other and almost every man is divided in himself and the great houses are split and the small houses have cracks . . . The life and time of everyone runs like the weaver's shuttle and the great world of eternity closes in on us all and to you who read or listen.

8   Poet and Peasant

It is at this juncture in the history of the Welsh that the forms of *canu gwerin* (folk poetry) emerge from the shadow of the majestic but crumbling architecture of the bardic tradition and the elaborate structures of the strict metres in time to make themselves readily available both for the age-old preoccupations of the common people and for the more urgent propaganda needs of a period of transition. The first to make use of simple folk verse quatrains in order to get his message across was the Catholic martyr from Llanidloes, Richard Gwyn, who was executed in Wrexham in 1584. He composed five long poems which he called carols in which he made fierce attacks against Protestantism and a passionate appeal to his fellow countrymen not to leave the Catholic Church: 'The branch that is broken from the tree will not be long in withering; the member that breaks away from the body will deprive itself of the food it needs.'

The most popular verses in this style were as one might expect composed by the 'Old Vicar', Rhys Pritchard of Llandovery, a stalwart member of the established Church. He was a career cleric and did well in the church but the hundreds of moralising verses he churned out did not take hold of the popular imagination until they were collected in a popular edition towards the end of the seventeenth century by the Puritan, Stephen Hughes, who realised their value as 'wall newspapers' that would help to impress the truths of religion on the impressionable minds of ordinary folk. The collection was known as *Canwyll y Cymry* (The Welshman's Candle) and it came to occupy a position on the bookshelf of a respectable home alongside one of the translations of the *Pilgrim's Progress*.

The Old Vicar subjected his muse to the yoke of the pastoral duties of a parish priest. The result is sometimes plodding and repetitious, but never without a charm which owes something, too, to the patina that lies on the surface of a way of life no longer with us.

The countryman is an early riser.

The first act of the skylark at daybreak is to praise his maker: and that

should be the first act that men should be obliged to do, praise God from
the depth of the heart.

And the housewife occupies a noble place in the Old Vicar's scheme of
things.

Pillar of gold in silver mortice, tower against death for a feeble man,
crown of beauty, most excellent part, a grace upon grace is a gracious
woman.

The husbandman has his own prayer in verse.

Designer of this earth, helper of man, author of the seeds of the fruitful
soil, giver of rain, augmenter of labour, hearken to the prayer of the busy
husbandman.

The goal of his simple verses is to set all the activities of a rural society
inside the framework of the articles of faith of the established church.
The extent of their appeal is therefore the true measure of his success.
The Old Vicar made a substantial contribution to a social order that
contrived to remain monoglot Welsh and yet a law-abiding well ordered
and loyal corner of the realm. To please God in the Old Vicar's
world-view was to work hard, honour the Anglican church and obey the
King and all those set in authority under him. But he had his more
imaginative moments. It is when he contemplates the fragile nature of
man's existence on earth that he comes closest to the authentic music,
the still sad music, of true folk poetry in the Celtic tradition.

As the sun runs towards the night, as the wax candle wears, as the white
rose petal falls, as the mist on the lake fades,

So they wear, they run, they fail, believers fall, and man's life fades, and
so we finish one by one.

Nothing of our trace remains more than the track of a snake across a
meadow, or the wake of a ship at sea, or the thin flight of an arrow through
the air.

What then is a man but a vapour, a smoke, a mist, a straw, a brief
disgrace: a shrivelled glass, a frost, a rose, an earthen vessel, a breeze, a
speck of foam?

Like a shepherd's hut we shall be shifted
Like an earthen pitcher we shall be shattered
Like a garment we shall be cast aside
And like hoar frost we shall disappear.

Morgan Llwyd struggled to use the same simple forms for unliterary purposes. But his restless spirit was more at home in prose. In his work it is possible to see how a mysterious reversal has taken place: the use of the imagination to penetrate the stubborn surface of material reality, which was at all times an important if unspoken function of the Taliesinic tradition, is transferred to prose and the simplicities of the new verse in his hands is left with humbler didactic functions. There remains something awe-inspiring in the effort Llwyd makes to get his message across to ordinary mortals in the bald statements of a folk verse style.

> It takes but a short time to break a kingdom, a moment only to raze a city, men are only shadows, and this world only the shadow of death.

> This world is only a small thing and Wales is smaller, the least part. The whole earth is like a garment that can be changed within the year.

He is desperate in his desire to create a new society, a new Wales. He has no time for the finer points of social criticism. He attacks Welsh weakness and strikes out where it hurts most. He wants to transform a people who still insist on sustaining their self-esteem by parading their pedigrees and extending their estates.

> All our gentry, vaunting and boastful, are no more than greedy malicious little worms, crawling the face of the earth along the track of pride to the house of mourning.

> I saw less and more than my fathers, my sons will see more than I saw. The great spinning wheel turns in this earth, but woe to the blind, to the dumb, to the deaf.

The crude rhythm of his verse drives relentlessly forward and the dynamic is his burning desire to make his message available to the simplest listener. The recurring thrust of the accent is like the jabbing of a preacher's finger, and can hardly be reproduced in translation.

Duw a'm carodd, Duw a'm cofiodd,
Ceisiodd, cafodd, cadwodd, cododd . . .

> God did love me, God remembered
> He sought, he found, he saved, he raised me up
> The sun of my life by means of death,
> The fountain of my spirit, the sum-total of my longing (*hiraeth*) . . .

Folk poetry was not the only escape route from the cracking walls of the labyrinth of the old tradition. The great Edmund Prys, Archdeacon of Meirionydd, in a brief epistle to the reader that introduces his metrical translation of the Psalms, sets out precisely why he decided against translating into any of the twenty-four strict metres. In the first place, he did not feel it was his business to truss up Holy Scripture in such sophisticated forms. Giving pleasure to aesthetes could give offence to God. Secondly, the Psalms were intended for congregational singing among the Godly: a *cywydd* or an *awdl* would be too complex and difficult to set for popular choral singing. Lastly a simplified versification would be easier for uneducated people to learn by heart. The stanza he invented for this purpose had a sophistication of its own, with internal rhyme, variable accent and felicitous touches of *cynghanedd* that give it an enduring charm. Prys had a mastery of the old and the new forms and an understanding of European styles which enabled him to lay a discreet foundation for many later developments in Welsh poetry. His powers of invention made possible the adaptation of the styles of Petrarch and Poliziano: but the potential for change was severely inhibited by his ecclesiastical function and by the weakness of a debilitated literary tradition that lacked the support of secular institutions, of courtly culture, and of urbanised centres of learning.

The sober reality of the situation is demonstrated clearly by the long career of a royalist poet like Huw Morus (1622–1709). He had great natural gifts and that technical mastery which is the *sine qua non* of the ambitious poet. But his vision was limited and his social function a limping imitation of the old praise tradition: so much elegance and craftsmanship dedicated to an outmoded convention. In Huw Morus's poetry there is often a noticeable contrast between the sophisticated manipulation of language and the relative simplicity of what he has to say. This feature of his work is often pleasing: but it is never capable of touching the heart-strings with that artless simplicity that is the authentic hallmark of the anonymous *penillion telyn* (verses for the harp). This flourishing art form was totally rooted in the everyday tribulations and joys of common folk and in the soil of given localities. It was independent of the turbulent events in the spheres of politics and of learning and intellectual concern. The defection of the upper class to the attractions of anglicised culture may have undermined the supremacy of the bardic tradition, but it also removed restrictions that held back the development of new forms capable of sustaining a fresh upsurge of national vitality. Folk poetry is important not only because of its own intrinsic value; it is an indication of the emergence of an entire class of people over the threshold of history. It gives them a voice of their own. It presents them with those necessary tools of articulation and self-expression that have to be mastered before they can organise themselves to demand a larger say in the management of their own destiny. In the Welsh experience folk poetry is the first evidence for the existence of *y werin*, an evocative word which means more than 'the peasantry'; '*y werin gyffredin ffraeth*' (the wise witty common people), the only true repository of common sense, political wisdom and no-nonsense understanding of the true nature of human existence. The popular songs of the ordinary folk crystallise the human condition in a manner that no other poetry can equal, even when it chooses to make the attempt.

> As I was doing the washing in the shadow of Cardigan bridge I had a golden drubbing stick in my hand and under it the shirt of my lover. I was approached by a horseman mounted on a broad-shouldered, speedy, proud stallion and he asked me if I would sell the shirt of the lad I loved most.

> And I said I would not sell even for a hundred pounds or a hundred loads, even for two hillsides of wethers and white sheep, even for two hedged fields full of oxen under yoke, even for the whole of Llanddewi filled with crushed herbs. And that was the way I intended to keep the shirt of the lad I loved the most.

In the *canu gwerin* experience of life becomes part of the process of nature itself, apparently impervious to historical movements and responding only to the cycle of birth and death and the comforting certainties of the progress of the seasons. We can see now that this was something of an illusion; but we can also see that the illusion was sufficiently agreeable for the Welsh people to cherish it and even continue to develop it throughout two centuries of unprecedented social change. There would seem to be a certain incongruity in contemplating, say, an unemployed miner singing the following words in the streets of Cardiff or London during the Depression:

Diofal yw'r aderyn . . .

> The bird is without responsibility, it does not sow, it does not reap even one grain. Without any care in the world except to sing year long. It perches on its branch examining its wing without a penny in its purse, wheeling about and full of joy. He will eat his supper tonight without the least idea of where his next meal is coming from, but that's the way he likes to live and leaves God to arrange his feasts.

Because of its timeless quality, folk poetry may seem an unpromising area for sociological speculation. But it has occupied so prominent a position in Welsh consciousness over the last three or four centuries that some study of the phenomenon cannot be avoided. It may well be that a people who consider themselves put upon, oppressed, overly restrained and unfulfilled, inevitably conjure up an image of the past that has to be charged with the romantic energy that belongs to a version of Arcadia or even the Garden of Eden.

> I served for one season near a farm called Ty'n-y-Coed and that was the

most agreeable place in which I ever worked my time. The little birds were always singing and the woods were alive with whispers. But in spite of all this, that was where I broke my heart.

When I die will you bury me in the woods under the leaves of the oak tree; you will see a golden haired youth stand on my grave to play the harp.

If I fail during my lifetime to get the smallholding I so much wanted, when I come to the graveyard in Aberdare I shall be given my share of the soil.

There is no end to the ways in which the songs reflect, often with piercing accuracy, the lot of the common people. They did not need to be reminded that life was sweet and fleeting, that work was hard or that death was never far from the door.

There was a night when I lay in bed. Throughout the night unable to sleep since my mind without any doubt was filled with concern for my earthly journey.
I called for a basin of water that I might wash in the hope that washing would cheer me up. But before a water drop reached my cheeks, on the edge of the basin I saw Death perch.

It is in the folk poetry that we first discern the lineaments of a new composite hero emerging to take the place of the warrior aristocrat or the princely defender of a nation under siege. In his raw form the new hero figure is a simple countryman: the patient ploughman and honest husbandman replace the fearless fighter. But a hero must be a hero and the original figure is embellished with sterling qualities that will themselves be capable of sustaining a cherished way of life. He is loyal, wise, pious, hard-working, and sufficiently sensitive both to enhance a traditional way of life and to celebrate it. His character becomes a substantial addition to the genius of the place. Like any pagan deity he is deeply rooted in his locality. His nature is not only in tune with Nature; it is capable of infinite expansion and thereby actively assists in the subtle social process of pinning down posterity and binding generations yet unborn to the landscape which will become the place of their birth.

The words and music of these songs are still in circulation and are very much part of the mainstream of Welsh popular culture to this day. It is no mere coincidence that the music publishing house at Llangollen which holds the copyright for many of the versions and their arrangements was also chiefly instrumental in founding the International Folk Eisteddfod in that town. Consider this verse:

Mi a glywais fod yr 'hedydd . . .

I heard that the skylark lay dead on the mountain. If I could be sure the words were true, I would take out a party of armed men to bear the body of the skylark home.

It has been suggested that the skylark would be a pseudonym for a fifteenth-century outlaw and that the folk verse is making use of the convention of the time whereby heroes are referred to as animals or birds (Henry Tudor was often 'the seagull', and Rhys ap Thomas 'the raven'). Thus the metamorphosis which has taken place is also a continuity between the aristocratic and the popular traditions. And perhaps even more remarkable, the tradition is still being added to. In our lifetime, the poet Cynan (Rev. A.E. Jones), a veteran of the Macedonian campaign in the first world war and probably the best known archdruid of the national eisteddfod in this century, composed two additional verses with such skill that they blend in perfectly with the original and could still be interpreted as a valid comment on a political situation as well as an innocuous evocation of a romanticised episode of moorland life.

I heard that the hawk is still seen above the moor and that his wings, as they pass over the skylark's corpse, know the cowardly tremble of a murderer's heart.

I heard that the lapwing tries to scare off the guilty one from the marsh, but he will still have even as he escapes and lurks under the thorns, the bittern to bother him.

I heard from the swallow that the Fair Kinfolk would provide the skylark with a crystal coffin and with a shroud from the apple tree without removing too many petals.

But in spite of mustering an army with weapons, and in spite of putting fear into the hawk, and in spite of crystal and of petals and the Fair Kinfolk and all their gifts, the song of the skylark will never come home.

The *penillion* present a lively and accurate picture of the everyday life and preoccupations of the common people. In a collection published in 1940 the editor, the late Sir Thomas Parry-Williams, assembled his selection of 741 pieces under several headings. Over two hundred are cheerful verses designed to amuse and display unsophisticated wit. The section on the ever interesting topic of love, courtship and marriage is of the same length, and there is in fact a considerable overlap, as one would expect. The smallest section is concerned with history and verses that contain direct historical references. This would seem to confirm the general impression that, before the advent of democracy, great historical events made little impact on the consciousness of a hard-working peasantry. The remaining headings are 'wisdom', verses of 'advice' and 'proverbial distillation', 'daily life', 'carousal', 'festive songs' chiefly concerned with drinking and smoking; 'direct celebration of music'; 'primitive nature poetry'; and quatrains summing up particular experiences, some happy, but more sad. Favoured topics in this section are death and that peculiarly Celtic form of nostalgia known as *hiraeth*.

> You, men great with knowledge, tell me what is *hiraeth* made of: and what material woven in it that fails to wear out with the wearing.
> Gold wears away and so does silver, velvet wears and so does silk:
> The most ample dress wears out: and yet *hiraeth* never wears.
> *Hiraeth, hiraeth*, walk away, don't weigh so heavily on me: the thing has taken tenancy for one full year of a smallholding located in my breast.
> A great and cruel *hiraeth* is breaking my heart: even when I lie in deepest sleep at night, *hiraeth* comes to touch and wake me.
> The sun will rise, the moon will set, the sea will move in waves of green and the wind will lift as high as it wishes: but *hiraeth* will never lift from my heart.

A remembrance of things past is of course an important literary category. Among the Welsh *gwerin* it has been developed over the centuries into a minor art form, and always in the minor key. Grief or sadness after the departed is a basic right for every individual and a necessary attribute of civilised man. But in the Welsh context this condition can quickly expand itself into a longing for a lost world, and when this happens *hiraeth* can take on something of the morphology of an endemic disease. It is in clear parallel with the long-held historic notion of a chosen people being turned out of the earthly paradise and being left with a gnawing yearning to return. At its strongest this emotion can give poetic expression an added depth because it is such an accurate reflection of the nature of the human condition. In the Welsh poetic tradition an heroic exaltation combines with a sharp sense of loss in the very earliest poetry of Taliesin and Aneirin. It is later that the note of doom and despair and a sense of tragic failure make themselves felt in the Llywarch Hen sequence. Both these strands of feeling develop side by side in mediaeval praise poetry. But it is fair to say that, until the rise of the Tudors, it is the note of joy and triumph which most frequently prevails. By the time the *hiraeth* motif re-emerges in popular poetry it is wistfulness that predominates. *Hiraeth* has become the innocent opium of a people obliged to remain helpless and inert without the capacity or the desire to take control of their own destiny.

> My heart it is as heavy
> As the horse that climbs the hill.
> I long to be light-hearted

But fail, try as I will.
My little shoe is pinching
In a place you cannot see
And my heart is breaking
With unspoken misery.

9   Sailing Westward

Before the Restoration, England had been to the handful of Welsh Puritans what Italy and Spain were to the Catholics, a refuge and an inspiration. In the rhyming quatrains that he called *Hanes Ryw Gymro* (The Story of a Certain Welshman), Morgan Llwyd recites his ports of call during his English pilgrimage. 'And apart from these towns I stayed at Bath, I travelled through Chichester, I lodged in Leicester and at Winchester I saw a town in fear, a heavy plague in Guildford. Derby welcomed me but Shrewsbury thought I was of no account.'

The writings of the Puritan in either language were printed and published for the most part in London, and their most successful cells were established in the Border country within reasonable travelling distance to the kind of English cities where the exiled Manawydan would have gone to practise the unfamiliar skills of a golden shoemaker. It was from Wrexham that Morgan Llwyd sent two of his close associates to seek out George Fox in the north of England and learn direct from that prophet himself the exact nature of his revolutionary teachings which appeared to be so close to Llwyd's. He was already talking Quaker language before he made contact with the new movement.

> Be on watch every minute lest the power of the flesh (like a hurricane in the world) snatches up thy thoughts . . . be at home always ready to welcome [the] Christ on the hearth of thine own heart . . . We have the true Evangelist standing in the pulpit of our minds . . . and in place of every voice calling outside, let us follow and let us obey the Voice inside us and the Light that shines within.

One of Llwyd's men, John ap John, attached himself to Fox and became the apostle of the Quaker faith among the Welsh. It seems strange to find the people of peace and silence among the first to raise what was virtually a standard of Welsh independence after the suspension of specific nationality and the prolonged euphoria induced by the Tudor Settlement. Unlike the majority of their fellow-countrymen, the

Welsh Quakers showed no reluctance to take control of their own destiny. It must be one of the paradoxes of the nature of European man that the more his beliefs tell him to incline his ear to the will of God or to hearken to the whispered threads of the meaning of history, the more he is encouraged to act in his own behalf, to shape the future and even to sacrifice his own life in order to hasten processes that his beliefs teach would be bound to occur in any case.

In the early days disputes between the Quakers and the Baptists were particularly acrimonious; they were competing for the same limited clientele. But the persecutions which followed the Restoration made both sects turn their eyes westward. The North America they looked to was an extension of the thrustful English Puritan world that could still maintain its way of life in spite of the change of government in London. To Welsh eyes, the new continent had additional attractions. The lingering spell of Celtic mythologies about the islands of the blessed, the region of eternal youth, was rekindled in a totally different religious context. Ancient imaginings offered additional substance to holy experiments. To the imprisoned faithful redemption became linked in the imagination with emigration. 'Speak O Lord, for now thy poor servants hear. Redeem us from the vanities of this world to be a peculiar people unto Thee.' Pitar Price of Pales in Radnorshire, where the oldest Quaker Meeting House in Wales still stands, writes from prison in Presteigne, at the age of seventy-eight, that he has lost count of the number of his imprisonments and the litigation and sequestration of his property, but still has sufficient strength remaining to rejoice daily in his faith. In Radnorshire and the Border counties John ap John translated the burning sermons of George Fox to the monoglot Welsh.

Their mission was most effective among two distinct social classes: in the Border country among skilled artisans and owner-occupying smallholders, and in the remote valleys among ancient families with long pedigrees and independent minds, 'Morgan Llwyd's people', as they were sometimes called among the Welsh. The story of the Welsh Quakers is yet another example of the Welsh survival syndrome at work: that unexpected combination of ancient and modern, of the oldest and newest beliefs that appears to make a renewal of identity possible, as it were, at the very moment of extinction. It is this characteristic that presents us with a spectacle of a tattered standard of independence being raised by the partisans of peace. The very last patrons of the pedigree poets and the ultimate heirs of the strict metre bardic tradition embrace the literal interpretation of Jesus Christ's most revolutionary teachings in their own version of the vision of William Penn:

> Let us learn war no more, so that wolf may lie down with the lamb and the
> lion with the calf and nothing that destroys be entertained in the hearts of

the people . . . Freely forgive, yea, help and relieve those that have been cruel to thee and do not take revenge, but endeavour through patience to overcome injustice and oppression . . . Love thine enemies. Bless them that persecute thee. Do good to them that hate thee. Pray for them that despitefully use thee and persecute thee.

In their remote country houses or their small farms and cottages, the Welsh Quakers remained intensely mindful of their lineage. The customs of many centuries were impossible to cast aside. Like the majority of the educated Welsh, they clung with increasing fervour to the version of history that owed most of its impetus to the mythologies plundered by Geoffrey of Monmouth and refined and propagated by the Welsh Protestant humanists of the sixteenth century. Every prose writer of importance with the slightest interest in history up to and beyond the second edition of Theophilus Evans's *Drych y Prifoesoedd* (The Mirror of the First Ages) in 1740, held on grimly to the same old articles of faith. 'This is the island that first received the true gospel in the time of Llês fab Coel . . . the Welsh who first discovered America . . . our ancestors the ancient Britons were faithful unto death in their stand for the True Faith.'

To the Welsh mind, Pales in Radnorshire was only three miles from the abbey of Cwm Hir, the last resting place of the headless body of Prince Llywelyn. There was no distance at all between Dolobran, the home of the Lloyd family of Quakers, and Mathrafal, the ancient court of the princes of Powys. For such people, as they embraced the dangerous new faith, it was not difficult to believe that this was an act of pious solidarity with the ancient British tradition of which history had appointed them to be the heirs: their remote ancestors had been the first to receive the pure gospel and it was now their bounden duty to set it all out afresh in New Testament order.

Notable families surnamed Lloyd and Vaughan abound in the history of Wales after the Act of Union, but none were more remarkable than the Lloyds of Dolobran. They were prototypical in their descent from a mythical king, in their support of Owen Glyndŵr, of the bardic tradition and of the Tudors all in turn. But their individuality comes into full focus with the generation of three brothers, Charles, John and Thomas, after the Restoration. Charles became a Quaker in 1661 and spent ten years in Welshpool prison. John remained a cautious Anglican, which was just as well for the family estate. Thomas became a Quaker exhorter and emigrated with his family to Pennsylvania.

In the shelter of the expansion of two English-speaking empires on either side of the Atlantic, the Lloyd family was poised to expand its influence, wealth and power. In banking, in the growth of the iron industry in the English Midlands, and in public administration in the United States and the British Empire, the family, which still owns the ancestral home and preserves the records of its lineage in the traditional style, made a lasting and distinctive contribution. The Welsh Quakers had been the first to respond to Penn's appeal for clients to buy tracts of land in the New World. These people in the main were driven less by poverty and persecution than by the desire to recover the substance of two dreams which not so long ago had appeared within their grasp in their own country.

Thomas Lloyd was appointed a president of the Provincial Council in 1684 and served as William Penn's Deputy Governor until 1693, when Pennsylvania became a colony of the Crown. His wife was the first person to be buried in the cemetry at Arch Street in Philadelphia. His cousin David became Chief Justice of Pennsylvania and a legislator of considerable importance in the early history of the commonwealth. David Lloyd's translation of Roland Ellis's *Anerch i'r Cymry* was published in Philadelphia in 1717 under the title *A Salutation to the Britaines*.

Penn had a special attraction for the Welsh Friends. Some of them believed he was of Welsh origin, and associated his surname with Penmynydd in Anglesey, the ancestral home of the Tudor family. This was clearly a wish-fulfilling extension of the type of ancient myth that claimed that the British were descended from the Trojans; even among the most enlightened people it is evident that old myths die hard. And it is possible that William Penn himself was ready to take advantage of Welsh gullibility. They believed that he had chosen 'New Wales' as the name for his colony and it was an unfeeling monarch who insisted on calling the place Pennsylvania in memory of William's father and the debt he owed him! But it is certain that Penn verbally promised the Welsh Friends that they would be allowed autonomy in their new country if they would purchase 40,000 acres in 5000 acre lots. He promised them that they would be allowed to establish a 'barony' (an extraordinary resurrection of a mediaeval Marcher term) where they would make and administer their own laws, speak their own language and worship in their own way. Penn commissioned Gabriel Thomas, a Quaker from Newport, Monmouthshire, to write a flattering account of the material attractions of the New Jerusalem across the ocean.

> Already fine houses and gentlemen's estates are to be seen in the country . . . As for the fruit trees, when planted they reach perfection in half the time they would take in England and bear great fruit.

> I saw no old maids in this country: most women be married before twenty and rarely is a young wife without a child in the womb or on her lap.

For some time the Welsh Friends continued to hold William Penn in high esteem. They noted his special concern for the native Indians.

There is a celebrated painting that demonstrates the version of the godly merchant, a comfortable image of the wealthy sober Quaker, standing among the naked savages and insisting on paying for the land that he was taking from them, even though they were still unaware of the idea of property and the intrinsic merits of buying and selling. The picture is a memorable portrayal of the confrontation of the Puritan ethic with the noble savages who happen also, somewhat inconveniently, to be the aboriginal possessors of the stage on which the New Jerusalem is scheduled to be built. From the moment the Proprietor sets his dainty shoe on the mud of Dock Creek in the City of Brotherly Love, the great American dilemma comes into existence. It is this dilemma that has constantly to be reconciled with the sentiments of the Declaration of Independence of the thirteen United States of America. (For the Welsh reader it is no small irony that the author of this Declaration, Thomas Jefferson, claimed to be of Welsh descent. In his autobiography he states that his forefathers were born 'in the shadow of Snowdon'.)

There can certainly be no question about the Welshness of the Welsh Quakers or of their desire for independence; or about the extraordinarily permanent and pervasive nature of their Welsh dilemma. They were double-crossed by Penn's agents, probably with the Proprietor's approval, and their so-called 'barony' was split up by the selling of parcels of land to speculators and settlers of other ethnic groups. For a while the Welsh Friends protested vigorously:

> We the inhabitants of the Welsh tract . . . are the descendants of the ancient Britons . . . always in the land of our Nativity, under the Crown of England, have enjoyed the liberty and privilege as to have our bounds and limits to ourselves, within the which all causes, Quarrels, Crimes, and Titles were tried and wholly determined by officers, magistrates, juries of our own Language, which were our Equals . . . because it was promised unto us before we came that these ancient privileges would still be ours in the New World.

The story of the Welsh 'barony' in Pennsylvania is worth contemplating because it demonstrates in microcosm the exact nature of the difficulty inherent in every attempt to perpetuate the condition of Welshness. Even in the first secular state in the history of the world that claimed to be founded on brotherly love, no allowance could be made for Welsh autonomy, not even the mildest form of devolution. The Welsh reaction also was characteristic. After much protesting, they withdrew to lick their wounds and then re-emerged to occupy crucial roles in the opposition to the Penn establishment.

Thomas Lloyd stood up to Penn and also became a key figure in the renewed interest in the existence of Welsh Red Indians. In mythopoeic

terms there can be no avoiding the links between these two minorities
and their aboriginal status. But it was Lloyd's cousin David who
became the most bitter opponent of the Penn family and one of the
founders of popular democracy in Pennsylvania. Here again we
encounter a recurring motif of the Welsh condition. There is a curious
similarity between the career of this David Lloyd and another Welsh
lawyer called David Lloyd George who, at the end of the nineteenth
century, turned from an abortive struggle for greater Welsh independence to exploiting his manipulative and oratorical talents in the
parliamentary assembly of the ruling power.

To give full support to the validity of a theory apparently as fanciful
as this, it is necessary to go backwards as well as forward in time and to
test it among a group of people who remain Welsh, but otherwise have
totally different religious and political affiliation. For the Welsh
Catholic exiles during the reign of Queen Elizabeth the Welsh language
became a potent badge of nationhood and in some sense a guarantee of
the ultimate loyalty of everyone who spoke it to the old faith. Doctor
Owen Lewis, a native of Anglesey and later Bishop of Cassano,
established the so-called English College in Rome in 1578. A Catholic
Bishop of Bangor, Morys Clynnog, was appointed Rector and was soon
embroiled in a power struggle with the Jesuits. The Welsh exiles lost
the struggle for control of the seminaries chiefly because they were
outnumbered by the English exiles, who had the ear of the Pope, who
was in this instance very much the Proprietor. There are historians who
see this as the moment when the Catholic party lost their chance of
winning Wales back. But in the context of the present argument the
crucial factor, and the recurring factor, was that the Welsh were too
few. It is this situation after all that has a permanent bearing on the
Welsh character.

It is in the isolated examples of experiments such as these that we can
most clearly discern the effect of permanent minority status on the
psyche of the individual Welshman. As in the case of David Lloyd and
the Welsh tract, when the talented leader is frustrated by the crippled
and ineffective nature of the society to which he acknowledged his first
allegiance, he is liable to emerge on a larger stage as a natural centre of
turbulence. He has been relieved of the restraints of tribal loyalty and
the moderating decencies that are part of the force that a well-adjusted
social order exerts over the behaviour of its members. He seems
responsible only to his own talent and ambition and, when the
opportunity arises, he is capable of conducting himself with an
autocratic arrogance which must in some measure be a compensation
for the failures of the society that gave him birth.

10 Pax Anglicana

Whatever the fate of Welshness abroad, any form of national consciousness in Wales itself remained in a largely comatose state from 1588, the year of the Spanish Armada and the publication of William Morgan's magisterial translation of the Bible, to 1789, the year of the fall of the Bastille: or even to that precise moment when the stonemason Edward Williams, released from Cardiff gaol, decided to become Iolo Morganwg full-time. The political and religious upheavals of the powerful English state purged the small dominion of Wales of its extremists: dissenters were forced underground or to North America, and the active Catholics into permanent exile in Europe. The established church had the field of Wales to itself. It was the only institution with any pretensions to intellectual activity: and after a period of civil strife and revolution it seemed in the best interests of the state to keep intellectual activity to a bare minimum. The highest virtue was loyalty, and its natural expression was obedience. These virtues were the basis of good behaviour and good behaviour was the message to be spread abroad through the entire network of the lethargic parishes. This was the essence of the Pax Anglicana and as prosperity slowly returned after the wars it continued as a background noise, like the hum of bees and insects in the quiet glades of the Welsh Arcadia.

In the secular Welsh world, a supine squirearchy became increasingly anglicised and a tired peasantry found relaxation in the comforts of their monoglot condition. It was in the security of this monoglot world that the ancient language lodged itself to be content for the most part with its local pursuits. This was not altogether a loss. Every language should be able to return to the shrines of local deities to renew its creative power with the spirit of the place. In such Virgilian tranquillity, undisturbed by the harsh voice of authority, by bureaucratic usages or even the rod of the pedagogue, that power of dialect which is also the source of poetic power was able to reassert itself at its own leisurely pace. The reward of quiescence and obedience was a cultural drip-feed operated largely by the lower echelons of the Anglican church.

It was wholly fitting that the first substantial work to appear under this order should be Elis Wyn's translation of Jeremy Taylor's *Holy Living*. Elis Wyn was educated at Oxford and began life as a lawyer: but it is clear from his prose masterpiece, *Gweledigaeth y Bardd Cwsg* (The Vision of the Sleeping Bard) that the grotesque cupidity of the class to which he belonged was repugnant to his fastidious nature. The spectacle of human greed at too close quarters was too much for him and, as in the case of Dean Swift (who might have written a similar book had he been a Welshman), he sought refuge in the church. He was in every sense well-connected. In the first place he was a native of that seed-bed of literary talent to which we have referred earlier, Ardudwy. His father was the grandson of the eldest brother of Colonel John Jones the Regicide; but the family had long since made their peace with the new dispensation. Their credentials were above reproach. They were connected by marriage with the descendants of Edmund Prys, the poet archdeacon of Meirioneth, and it was his cousin Humphrey Humphreys (probably the last Bishop of Bangor for a long while to take an active part in patronising Welsh culture) who ordained him and presented him with the quiet living of the parish of Llandanwg near Harlech. But it is possible that the bishop hoped that here the talented writer could continue, like Dante, to follow up his 'Vision of the Way of the World and of the Courts of Death and Hell', with his 'Vision of Paradise'. This did not happen: but there is ample evidence of the energies the new rector gave to his parochial duties during the thirty years he spent in the ministry. His remains were granted the unusual privilege of being buried under the altar of his church.

In 'The Court of Death' of his 'Vision' he had a brief encounter with both Myrddin and Taliesin. This gives him an opportunity to reflect on the decay of the bardic tradition.

'What are you called?' he said.

'You can call me what you like in this place, but in my own country I am known as Bardd Cwsg.'

On the word I saw a lump of hunchbacked old man, with his two ends like a ram pointing earthwards, straighten himself and glare at me more hostile than the little red devil, and before uttering a word, he hurled past my head a great skull and I have to thank the gravestone that gave me shelter.

'Leave in peace, sir, I beseech you,' I said 'a stranger who was never here before and will never return, if only I could find the start to the way home.'

'I'll remind you you were here,' he said.

And he launched himself on a second devilish attack against me, this time with a thigh-bone, and me doing my best to avoid him.

'What,' I said, 'this is a country most discourteous to strangers. Don't you have one Justice of the Peace?'

'Peace,' he said, 'what peace do you deserve? Who insist on disturbing people in their graves.'

'Good sir, I implore you,' I said, 'let me know your name for I am not aware that I ever did disturb anyone from this land before.'

'Sir,' said he, 'know that I, and not you, am Bardd Cwsg and that I have enjoyed the stillness here for nine hundred years and have been left alone by everyone except you.'

And he started to challenge me again.

'Stop that, brother,' said Merlin who was standing near. 'Don't get too heated. Be grateful rather to him for the reverence with which he preserved your memory on earth.'

'Great respect indeed,' says he, 'from such a blockhead as this one; and can you, sir, manage the four and twenty measures, can you trace the lineage of Gog and Magog and the pedigree of Brutus ab Silvius as far back as one hundred years before the fall of Troy? Are you able to prophesy just when and what will be the end of the wars between the lion and the eagle and between the dragon and the red stag? Ha!'

'Hey there, let me ask him a question,' said another one who stood by a great cauldron that was boiling with a *soc, soc, dy-gloc dy-gloc*.

This new interlocutor is no less a person than Taliesin, chief poet of the West. The satire grows more savage and when the poet appears before King Death he watches the trial of a Youth and a Maiden.

He was once known as the Good Companion and she a Gentle Maiden, or easy with her body: but in this place they were given the naked names of Drunkard and Whore.

'I trust,' said the drunkard, 'that you will look on me with favour, since I sent many plump victims floating towards you on a flood of good beer; and when I failed to kill any more I willingly brought myself as a sacrifice to feed you.'

'With the Court's permission,' said the Whore, 'it was more than half I sent to King Death as burnt offerings, and indeed roast meat ready for his table.'

'Hey, hey,' said Death, 'all this was done to satisfy your cursed lusts and not for the sake of feeding me. Bind them both together, face to face, since they are old friends, and cast them into the Land of Darkness and let him vomit into her mouth and let her piss fire into his guts until the Day of Judgement.'

In Elis Wyn's 'Visions' life is always on the edge of nightmare. He is compelled to deploy his sense of humour in order to preserve his sanity: the penalty of being a realist in a world that has worn out a sequence of visions and lies panting on the shore of eternity uncomfortably aware of the bestial origins of the human species. The old Welsh traditions are gone, Taliesin is only the occasion for a prolonged joke and, but for the strength inherent in the structure of the established Church of

England, the Cambro-British world would collapse into a state of disgusting anarchy.

Theophilus Evans was another loyal servant of the Church of England and his attitude to his labour of love, *Drych y Prifoesoedd* (The Mirror of the First Ages), is cautious and mournful.

> It is an onerous, sad, and vexing task to relate the misfortunes of the Cymry; their difficulties and their worldly troubles in every age and every land that they inhabited from that time when the language was compounded in the Tower of Babel. For is it not a sad and sorrowful thing to relate how ungrateful they were to God, how ready to fall into the temptations of the world, the flesh and the devil, how inclined to rebel against him, all of which being responsible for their afflictions and lack of success.

It was only in the second edition of a work first published in 1716, that Theophilus Evans, vicar of Llangamarch in Breconshire, took his courage in both hands and embellished his history with the powerful extended similes, largely modelled on the classical epic tradition, that made the book a national epic. As a historiographer who also wore the mantle of a people's remembrancer, he was obliged to make the attempt to reconcile plain fact with cherished myth. The similes are important, not only because of their own intrinsic liveliness, but also as a measure of the intensity of the poetic imagination that was necessary to fuse these two conflicting aims and create a synthesis which would make the work acceptable and useful to succeeding generations in their flagging efforts to maintain and even recreate a sufficient thrust of patriotic sentiment. It is some measure of the success of his enterprise that no other Welsh book, except of course for the Bible, had so many editions on either side of the Atlantic.

On the title page of the second edition the author explains that he has divided his account into two parts.

> Part I which treats of the ancient lineage of the Welsh and from whence they came: the wars that occurred between them and the Romans, the Picts and the Saxons. Their former manners, before becoming Christians.

> Part II which treats of the Preaching and the Progress of the Gospel in Britain: the Doctrine of the original church. The manners of the original Christians.

In the first part he is obliged to attempt a reasonable summary of all the cherished notions about the origins of the nation, from its source in Troy to the high point of its achievement under King Arthur. Evans is not unaware of all the attacks of scientific scholarship from Polydore Vergil onwards. There were stories he was prepared to abandon: even figures of such mythological importance as Merlin. The sticking point was the historicity of the person of Arthur. 'And it is as undoubtedly true that there was such a king as Arthur as that Alexander existed even though the life-history of one and the other has been clouded with ancient tales.'

The dramatic sweep of Theophilus Evans's version of history needed Arthur just as much as the British vision of Geoffrey of Monmouth. Evans's aim was to preserve the king as the national hero of the Welsh and, by implication, make his return a remote but tantalising possibility. He could not extol the antiquity and gentility of the Welsh without also giving them some hope for the future: and it is this element which made the work of an Anglican Tory such an important document to generations of Welsh reformers and radicals for the next two hundred years.

The second part of his epic was concerned with the myth of the primitive purity of British, that is Welsh, Christianity. He identifies so closely with Gildas that he is able to adopt his stance and treat his readers as a modified version of the wayward British of the sixth century. This is in itself an astonishing demonstration of the continuity of the Welsh tradition. But the theory of original Protestantism Theophilus Evans has inherited from William Salesbury and the sixteenth-century humanists, and along with it a lively, not to say virulent, anti-Papist attitude. His version of history was vital to the credibility of his position as a responsible priest in the Church of England. The Church of Rome was the anti-Christ and the enemies of England were the enemies of the Church of England. The church he served was the legitimate heir of the ancient British church and therefore there could be no inconsistency in the two parts of his work or in the two loyalties that governed his life. To be a good parson and to be a good Welshman were merely two sides of exactly the same coin.

Evans was engaged in reviving Gildas's concept of an erring chosen people and adapting it to his own understanding of the position of the Welsh of his own day in relation to what he regarded as the mother church. His appeals to the *Brut*, to folklore and to the poetic tradition are constantly reinforced by biblical reference. He wishes his readers to become convinced and active Protestants, aware of a telling parallel between their own history and the history of the Jews. No matter how small the Remnant, as long as it remained united in obedience to the will of God it would never disappear. In this sense Arthur could come again: both parts of the myth, the people and their Church, could be fused, in spite of the contradictions implicit in their origins, and the Welsh provided with an optimistic epic holding out the possibility, against all the odds, of a more brilliant future.

As so often happens the parson-historian achieved more than he intended. The robust dramatic style of his work was a lusty sermon that provided the emerging Welsh consciousness with the good news it wanted to hear. In the spirit of an age that was still dominated by religious concern, the Welsh were very willing to swallow all the dire warnings about dissension and neglect of their duty: it was a very small price to pay for a more cheering view of the national destiny. In any case a people long used to one form or another of failure have little difficulty in accommodating an increasing load of guilt. A collective sense of sin must add spice to the prospect of salvation.

The progress of Theophilus Evans's work through the next two centuries of Welsh life is in itself a revelation of the development of the educated Welshman's psyche. He added authority to his dramatic style by adopting, as it were between the scenes, a profoundly scholarly manner. And his scholarship was substantial. He wrote well in Latin and in English and his knowledge of Welsh manuscripts and ancient poetry was impressive by the standards of his time. But the most infectious element was his patriotic zeal and his readers accepted this gratefully, in the old world and the new, until the revival of Welsh scholarship that began at the end of the nineteenth century.

11 Perpetual Curates

Our understanding of history is always relative and partial. Had we ourselves lived in the eighteenth century and been in a position to indulge in leisurely speculation about the spectacle of human endeavour unfolding around us, it is unlikely that we would have been in any way aware of the seeds of the future being sown like explosive charges right under our feet. Even when it is at its most scientific, a view of history is driven to express itself in approximate metaphor. In this instance, our thoughts might resemble those of the fortunate young men who enjoyed the Grand Tour and were entirely taken up with the cultivation of their sensibilities among the ruins and the grandeur of the classical past. These young men were not unaware that it was ruthless land enclosures, the wealth of the new world and the growing profits of the slave trade that were paying for their expensive trip: they just preferred not to think about it. The hard facts of economic life were not the most attractive parts of history: they had little excitement to offer compared with painting ivy-covered castles in Arcadian landscapes or contemplating mortality on a full stomach in a melancholy churchyard.

At such a time a revived interest in the land of Wales and in the Welsh language was part of the cult of the picturesque. The language was a particularly interesting ruin. It was a remarkable fact that in this comparatively accessible corner of a burgeoning greater British Empire there continued to exist a peasant people largely ignorant of English and using an ancient tongue that some insisted was as venerable as Hebrew and as old as the druid circles. The attitude of authority continued to be as ambivalent as ever to this quaint phenomenon. To those directly responsible for civil and ecclesiastical government it was an inconvenience and even a potential threat: like the dialect of Corsican bandits it could always become an instrument of disaffection. John Wesley was more sympathetic than most; to him a soul was a soul whether it belonged to a countess or a Cornish tin-miner. But even he felt that preaching to the Welsh was more frustrating than attempting to exhort the Cree or Cherokee Indians. Earnest Welsh clergymen seeking support for publications of uplifting material in the Welsh language were driven to argue that this was the most efficient way of teaching a ploughman his duty. The native language was cheaper and more efficient as an agent of good government. Writing early in the eighteenth century, John Morgan, the scholarly vicar of Matching in Essex, was opposing the use of English in Welsh charity schools on the following grounds:

> It is a grand mistake to teach poor children their duty in a foreign tongue, which takes up a good deal of time to little purpose; for when they are employed for some time at the plough, or cart, the language is lost, and they are as wise after five or six years schooling as they were before; whereas were they taught in their mother tongue, it would take but little time and charges.
>
> This method is as ridiculous and preposterous, as if English charity boys should be instructed in Latin and Greek, in order to know their duty, and the consequence at last will be barbarism, which necessarily introduces ignorance and irreligion.

Like the mantle of Arthur, the language barrier had the mysterious and sometimes irritating quality of suggesting another world that was not visible to the naked eye. The manufacture and proliferation of myth is one of the few creative activities left to a people with unreasonably high expectations reduced by historic forces into a marginal condition. Influences are as intangible as myths. Notions of romantic Arcadia were early linked with the ancestor worship and genealogical refinements that the Welsh aristocracy had brought with them when they infiltrated the more pragmatic English networks of influence and power. Welsh pedigrees went up in value when druids became fashionable. An English milord, when he returned from the Grand Tour, could be agreeably surprised to discover that there would be no reason at all for him to be ashamed of a Welsh maternal grandparent. The druids were very well connected and as fine a subject for the poet or the painter as anything in classical antiquity, and also more mysterious and therefore more romantic. There is no better example of this development in a Welsh context than the relationship between the young Sir Watkin Williams Wynn II and the unhappy curate Evan Evans.

The founder of the Williams Wynn dynasty had been an Anglesey cleric with an interest in the law. His son had risen to be Speaker of the House of Commons and had married into the network of old families in North Wales. Sir Watkin Williams Wynn I had been a Jacobite and his home the centre of the secret Circle of the White Rose. But his son, Sir Watkin II, showed more interest in the arts than in politics, and delighted in his friendship with Sir Joshua Reynolds, George Frederick Handel, and David Garrick. He wished to be known as a generous patron of the arts and to prove his interest in the native tradition he became the second President of that influential London-Welsh organisation the Honourable Society of Cymmrodorion.

Evan Evans was a farmer's son from Cardiganshire. It is not unlikely that his pedigree, as pedigrees went, would have been every bit as good as Sir Watkin's. He was educated at Ystrad Meurig school, a distinguished institution in eighteenth century Wales, and Merton College, Oxford. Before going to Oxford he came under the influence of the redoubtable Lewis Morris, (the greatest of the Morris brothers, who inspired his brother Richard in London to found the Cymmrodorion). Evan Evans found the confidence to take up the practice of traditional poetic art, to devote his life to scholarship. He entered holy orders in 1754 and was licensed to his first curacy at Manafon in Montgomeryshire. In less than a year he moved to a curacy in Kent and the peripatetic nature of his life-style began its unsteady progress. He served as a curate in at least eighteen different parishes and spent brief intervals in both the army* and the navy. His obsession was the discovery and the copying of any ancient manuscripts that might have something to do with the history and the literature of the Welsh. His weakness was for strong drink; not uncharacteristic of his profession or his time. Dr. Johnson described him as a 'drunken Welsh curate' and it would be easy enough to declare that like so many Celtic poets of his kind he was obliged to take to the bottle as a supplementary invocation of the *Awen*, the Muse in charge of inspiration. The record is sufficiently daunting to suggest that a universal inclination of poets can be exacerbated by a condition of cultural disinheritance.

Drink made the curate aggressive. His bardic name was Ieuan Brydydd Hir, (Ieuan the Tall Poet) as well as Ieuan Fardd. A fellow poet and member of the Cymmrodorion describes meeting him in a tavern in Caernarfon where they had a row.

> He was very ragged . . . He called a volley of opprobrious names and epithets upon me, that would have been a valuable acquisition to Billingsgate College . . . I noted three remarkable features about Ieuan – his pride, his bad manners, and the big scar under his chin.

It seems that in a moment of desperation Ieuan had tried to cut his own throat. The symbolism of the action was not altogether lost on his contemporaries. The throat was the point of entry for the drink and the proper exit for the *Awen*. Even before he went to Oxford he had been lauded as a boy genius by such shrewd and authoritative critics as Edward Richard and Lewis Morris. To be a good poet and a great

* He was in the army for four days: 'To whom it may concern. This is to certify that Evan Evans was enlisted in the 34th Regiment of Foot, but being disordered in his mind and finding him to be the Rev. Mr. Evans, is hereby discharged. Ogle, Capt. 34th Regiment of Foot. London April 6th, 1768.'

scholar would appear to be a worthy enough ambition, but he soon realised that there was nothing in the structure of the society to which he belonged that could help a young man to sustain such an ambition. He needed the security of patronage, a secure niche in some venerable college, a properly ordered outlet of publication. But none of these facilities existed in any consistent form in Wales. In his life, as we see it reflected in his letters, the force that drove him throughout his wanderings was a profound belief in the resources of the Welsh language and the existence of hidden riches, sleeping, like Arthur and his warriors in their cave, in the library cupboards of those old families who had begun to neglect their native inheritance. The gentry for their part were inclined to treat him as a joke or an irritation.

> Dear friend . . . of the library at Gloddaith I can give you little account because the knight was set upon shooting woodcock with his friends that morning . . . but I made the best of my brief moment when I got inside, and he was good enough to lend me five of the best volumes . . . This was all I found curious upon so short an examination.

The great pursuit had its moments of glory. One such is captured by Lewis Morris in a letter to Edward Richard sent on August 5th, 1758. It was meant to read like a despatch from the front.

> Who do you think I have at my elbow . . . as happy as ever Alexander thought himself after a conquest? No less a man than Ieuan Fardd, who hath discovered some old mss lately that no body of this age or the last ever as much as dreamed of. And this discovery is to him and me as great as that of America by Columbus. We have found an epic Poem in the British called *Gododdin*, equal at least to the *Iliad*, *Aeneid* or *Paradise Lost*. Tudfwlch and Marchelw are heroes fiercer than Achilles and Satan!

It was one thing to discover manuscripts: quite another to edit them and see to their publication. Ieuan proved himself a remarkable scholar but there never seemed to be a convenient printing press within his reach, and the tedious method of publishing by subscription took up too much of his time. He had none of the skills of an entrepreneur and many of the local poets and dilettanti with whom he sought to collaborate let him down. From 1771 to 1778, when the parishes where he served were all in North Wales, he was able to rely on the patronage of Sir Watkin Williams Wynn II. He was given reasonable access to the excellent library at Wynnstay and was able also to visit Hengwrt and Peniarth; and Sir Watkin provided him with regular sums of money. He knew that Ieuan was highly thought of by the famous poet, Thomas Gray, and the influential antiquarian, Bishop Percy. To look after a scholar who held so many secrets of the nature of ancient poetry was a feather in the cap of a man who wished to be recognised as an outstanding patron of the arts. For his part Ieuan was now able to publish a volume of sermons in Welsh which he considered to be urgently needed; an English poem dedicated to Sir Watkin on 'The Love of our Country', by which he meant Wales; he could prepare important manuscript material for publication, and sharpen his attacks on his *bêtes noires*, the *Esgyb-Eingl*, the Anglo-Welsh bishops.

> I cannot without the utmost indignation observe the unnatural behaviour of the modern Welsh clergy and gentlemen of the principality of Wales. They have neither zeal for religion nor the interest of their country at heart. They glory in wearing the badge of their vassalage, by adopting the language of their conquerors, which is a mark of the most despicable meanness of spirit and of a mind lost to all that is noble and generous; and our clergy contrary to their oaths, perform divine services in a language, that one half of the congregation doth not understand; and thus they rob those of the means of grace that pay them their tythes. This is no better than mere popery.

Ieuan had a strong case. For a century and a half no bishop who understood the Welsh language was appointed to any of the Welsh sees; and the tendency of such career clerics was to license their English dependents to livings that were inhabited by monoglot Welsh people. Even by the standards of the *Pax Anglicana* this exploitation of benefices would do nothing to teach the common people 'their duty', and thus the established church could be accused of failing in its duty to the state, quite apart from any consideration of the welfare of the language or the spiritual wellbeing of the people.

> But as they take upon them the care of souls, whose language they do not understand, I think it is only for filthy lucre's sake and they seem to me to be only tools of a government that sets religion aside; at least makes it subservient to its destructive and ungodly policy. Such I reckon the depriving of any people or nation of the candlestick of God's word and of pastors who understand to preach it in their own language.

His words are a curious echo of the protests of the Puritan John Penry published by his secret printing press at the end of the sixteenth century. Penry was hanged for his pains and Ieuan's fierce attacks against the bishops and their malpractices did him very little good. In spite of the obvious quality of his mind, his excellent intentions and the justice of the cause he was so determined to champion, Ieuan's devotion to drink and to the Welsh language were insuperable obstacles to preferment.

His career offers a shadowed contrast to those of the two English literary figures with whom he was in correspondence. Shy and retiring as he was, Thomas Gray was driven to hide from the brilliant light of his own reputation. Thomas Percy was a grocer's son who became a bishop more on the strength of his literary reputation than the rather tenuous claim that he made to be the last of the great line of the Percys. The tone of his letters to Ieuan is a good deal more genial than Shakespeare's Percy's abrupt way of addressing Owen Glendower: but the balance of power across the vanished frontier remained steadily unaltered. Ieuan's striking lack of success in contrast with the other two is not to be attributed merely to his individual weakness; it also reflects the comparative state of two cultures at that moment in time. Ieuan was trudging around Wales in an attempt to salvage the mouldering fragments of an ancient tradition for the sake of the dwindling posterity of that tradition. Gray and Percy were showing a cool and cultivated interest in antiquities in order to be able to adapt them to the needs of a culture conscious of the massive political and economic power behind it. When Thomas Gray wrote 'The Bard' he could easily have used the gaunt figure of Ieuan Fardd as his model.

> On a rock, whose haughty brow
> Frowns o'er old Conway's foaming flood
> Robed in the sable garb of woe,
> With haggard eyes the Poet stood,

Ieuan's enemy was not the ruthless King Edward but his spiritual successors, the *Esgyb-Eingl*, who were in his view doing just as much damage. In Ieuan's experience the great struggle was still in progress, and even the climax of Gray's Pindaric Ode where the Bard, having completed his prophecy, hurls himself over the edge of a cliff, was in some sense a reflection of the anguished curate's attempted suicide.

Gray's poem was a great success. The Bard in his decorous English garb was able to use a mixture of Pindaric enthusiasm and the mythic prophetic gift of Taliesin. His metrical version of British history renewed the political scenario whereby the Tudors and their successors were still to be acclaimed as the appropriate heirs of the British tradition. Gray was fulfilling the appointed task of a national poet in translating the historic hymn of triumph into contemporary idiom and making a source of aesthetic and spiritual strength available to yet another generation of empire-builders. There is a glittering invocation of the figure of the Virgin Queen that is followed by the celebrated line: 'Hear from the grave, great Taliessin, hear!' But it is doubtful whether even that shape-shifting genius would have understood the transformation which had taken place; and even if he understood, would have in any way approved. Arthur had been spruced up and sent to Eton and he, Taliesin, offered the post of Poet Laureate which Gray himself had shyly declined. Nevertheless for the English world of the eighteenth century and much later this remained a serviceable transformation.

Some kind of literary rough justice had been seen to be done and honour was sufficiently satisfied all round to keep the natives happy. As late as the 1860s, Matthew Arnold could hike around Llandudno with his brother Tom waving his arms and roaring out at intervals, 'Hear from the grave, great Taliessin, hear!' as he enjoyed the first intimations of yet another serviceable theory called 'Celtic Magic'.

Gray and Bishop Percy encouraged Ieuan to publish in 1764 *Some Specimens of the Poetry of the Antient Welsh Bards*. The book was designed to satisfy the growing curiosity among English antiquarians and men of letters about Welsh literature. The impression it made was limited because a shrewd Scottish forger, James Macpherson, was already in the field. As usual Ieuan's publication had been delayed for several years by his peripatetic habits and printing difficulties. Macpherson's *Fragments of Ancient Poetry* had set the poet Ossian off on his astonishing journey into the mysterious hinterland of the European creative imagination. The influence of Ossian the poet became second only to that of Arthur the king. His origin was a similar potent compound of original Celtic fact and judicious fabrication. In entrepreneurial terms Macpherson, like Geoffrey of Monmouth, was smart enough to see that a great market existed for romantic fantasy of Celtic origin and he set out deliberately to supply it.

The Welsh were never taken in and, reassured by Ieuan's solid scholarship, they refused to accept Macpherson's work as genuine translation. Macpherson counter-attacked with the instinct of a skilled publicist. He went straight for the cultural jugular vein and poured contempt on the Welsh poetic tradition. It was not worthy of notice. Meanwhile Ossian continued to ride the crest of a wave. In a few years the young Goethe made his tormented hero in *Die Leiden des Jungen Werthers* recite the translation he had made of Ossian's *Songs of Selma*. It is true that Goethe's admiration for Ossian wore off and that he was to observe in later life, 'I made my hero quote Ossian when he was mad, but Homer when he was in his right mind.' But it was his interest and Herder's that vastly extended that influence of Ossian in European culture and which brought the young Mendelssohn as far as the Hebrides in the 1840s.

The modesty and restraint of Gray's muse was in strong contrast to the flamboyant excesses of Ossianic poetry and it was this Augustan English tradition that appealed to the conservative spirit of the Welsh, and particularly the men of scholarship and talent who belonged to the Morris circle. Ieuan's best known poem, his *englynion* to the ruins of Ifor's court, would probably not have been written but for his admiration for Gray. But the power of the poem derives from his understanding of the brooding passion of the great Welsh elegies of the ninth and thirteenth centuries. The fact of a defeat, with the pain unassuaged by the passage of time, gives a cutting edge beyond romantic melancholy. Brambles cover the ruins of splendour, the halls of song are the haunts of the owl, and the qualities of generous noblemen and a whole way of life are less than stones in the sand.

When Ieuan visited the ruin of the court of Ifor Hael (which is now probably under the M4 outside Newport, Gwent) he was accompanied by one of the strangest figures in the history of modern Wales. His young guide was a stone-mason called Edward Williams, the Bard of Glamorgan who became famous in Wales under his bardic name, Iolo Morganwg. Although the date is uncertain, it was an occasion of some significance. Iolo himself was deeply moved by the sight of the ruin. For him it had an added significance. This was the court where the great poet of the fourteenth century, Dafydd ap Gwilym, had been made welcome, and in his more inspired moments Iolo had already begun to believe that he himself was the eighteenth-century equivalent of the great Dafydd and that it was therefore his duty to supplement the known works of that genius with effusions of his own. Inside Wales, Iolo's forgeries had an even more profound influence than the outpourings of Macpherson-Ossian in romantic Europe.

They were an oddly assorted couple, Ieuan and Iolo. The force that drew them together was Taliesinic; a devotion to the faltering Welsh poetic tradition bordering on the demonic in the case of Ieuan, and in the case of Iolo well beyond it. They were both initiates, the more conscious of some mysterious and even prophetic form of poetic consecration because they were the two living men most deeply versed in the ancient language and the myths and legends and history of what was rapidly becoming a lost world. It was a great burden to bear and, if we are to believe Iolo, the learned curate was very ready to share it with him. In a letter to Owen Myfyr, a well-to-do London Welshman, then assistant secretary to the Honourable Society of Cymmrodorion and later to become its guiding force, Iolo wrote:

> Ieuan the priest and the poet is now minister at Maesaleg, but he will not find there a single Ifor Hael. The poet has become a very sober and religious man, but his worldly state is very low. I believe he must be the poorest man in his profession in the whole island. It would be no great expense for the Cymmrodorion to present him with eight or ten pounds, which kindness would be of great benefit and a service to him at this point in time.

In tracing their dealings with each other, the reader has the impression that Iolo is handling Ieuan with a pair of tongs. He needs the authority of the older man to reinforce his own position. They are both South Walians and Iolo is well aware that a lifetime of disappointments has given Ieuan a deep-seated suspicion of the North Wales literary establishment, of the Cymmrodorion, and an irrational hatred of

English bishops. These are weaknesses that he would be very ready to exploit for his own purposes, but he is equally well aware that Ieuan Fardd is not a man to be manipulated, and that these transient passions would pale into nothing alongside his scholarly devotion to the truth. The drunken curate who had stubbornly refused to accept the Ossianic forgeries would never have allowed a similar activity to flourish inside the field of Welsh antiquities that he had spent a lifetime cultivating. Iolo had good reason to keep a sharp and respectful eye on the movements and welfare of the older man. As long as the Rev. Mr. Evan Evans was alive, he was obliged to keep a tight rein on his own impetuous imagination.

Another 'eternal curate' discovered, promoted and sporadically supported by the Morris brothers and the Cymmrodorion was the celebrated Goronwy Ddu o Fôn, Goronwy Owen of Anglesey, who was to become a Welsh culture hero in the nineteenth century. Eight years older than Ieuan, he was considered by his contemporaries an even greater genius. The Morris brothers backed him to scale the heights of Parnassus and vindicate their claims for the 'copiousness' of their ancient language. Goronwy's ambition was no less than to compose a Welsh epic poem worthy to stand comparison with Homer and Virgil and above all with the great John Milton whose massive shadow seems to have dominated the literary imagination of the eighteenth century, leaving the Welsh even more mesmerised than the English. The young Goronwy appeared to have all the necessary qualifications: he could 'compose in the four and twenty metres'; he was of humble origin, which suited the expectations of indulgent patrons and discoverers of flowers 'born to blush unseen'; he was well schooled and spent three years at Oxford and his letters indicated that he had an acute understanding of the nature of the problem which confronted him. All along, again in the spirit of the cultivated opinion of his day, the central question was the problem of form.

However, Goronwy's career, like Ieuan's, was too early launched on the sea of liquor and he was soon running before the storm from one curacy to another, after 1748 all of them outside Wales. Unlike Ieuan, he entered the bonds of matrimony so that his financial difficulties were soon compounded. As things transpired the only epic he ever wrote was the odyssey of his own life. He served as a curate in Shropshire, Liverpool and Northolt near London. His mood and opinions are vividly reflected in his letters which are worth comparing with the letters of Dylan Thomas. There is a striking resemblance between the two men, between their aims and ambitions and their weaknesses; and it could be argued that they are both at their best as poets of exile and the evocation of a lost paradise. In London the impoverished curate despaired of ever obtaining a good living. He was constantly short of money and the father of three small children. When his vicar obtained

for him an appointment as headmaster of the grammar school attached
to the William and Mary College, Williamsburg, Virginia, it seemed a
last chance to avoid bankruptcy and a debtors' prison. He appealed to
the Cymmrodorion and they made a collection to pay his passage. It
proved a fearful voyage. Elin his wife and Owen his youngest son both
died and were buried at sea. He arrived in Williamsburg in April 1758,
four months after leaving London, a widower with two sons to care for,
almost four thousand miles from the island of his birth. In spite of the
bitter disputes poisoning the life of William and Mary College at that
time, he managed to hang on to his job and within six months he
remarried a widow who was the Principal's sister and matron of the
college. He was made Professor of Latin and Greek and began to earn
four times as much as he had ever earned before. Fortune seemed to be
smiling on him at last. But the new comforts were short-lived. In less
than a year his second wife died. As in the old days, Goronwy found
refuge in the tavern. He quickly developed a dislike for the people of
Williamsburg.

> Savage Babilonish sots
> Usurpers worse than Hottentots
> Rank heretics alive with pox and plots . . .

His drinking companion was a young English academic even more
contemptuous of the local citizenry than Goronwy. In their cups they
were a fiery and impetuous pair. They caused a great scandal when,
armed with pistols and swords, they led the college students in a brawl
with the town apprentices. His colleague was dismissed on the spot and
Goronwy asked to resign. By August 1760 he seemed a broken man,
without a job and without a home.

His muse was no longer capable of an epic but he managed lines that
brought some shred of dignity to his disgrace and defeat.

> A man's life . . . as short as the life of a leaf.

It was a simile which he copied from Homer and Llywarch Hen; but in
Goronwy's case, it was literally a leaf which came to his rescue. He was
given a living one hundred miles south-east of Williamsburg. He
married for the third time, and he was able to buy land. In Virginia the
politics of church and state depended on the tobacco crop. He became a
planter himself. Quarrels in the vestry were settled in bundles of golden
leaf. Goronwy was able to bring up a new family on a stipend of tobacco
before he died at the age of forty-six. According to his will, his most
valuable piece of property was a negro wench named young Peg who
was worth £40. He had also managed to preserve 'a parcel of old
authors, in number 150, Greek, Latin, Hebrew, Welsh and a French

grammar' and these were valued at £3. 0s. 4d.

Perhaps his most lasting legacy was his life story, because it offered the legend of a thwarted genius driven into exile by unkind fate and the hostile authorities of his native land. He composed memorable stanzas about the beauties of Anglesey and the Welsh language, and these became part of the equipment used for the celebration of those ever-increasing festivals of Welsh diaspora that were the inevitable side-effect of the spread of two vast English-speaking empires. In Wales itself the literary canons he set out in his letters became a form of holy writ to the nineteenth-century eisteddfod poets. But the real problems of form, which he identified so early in his career, he never solved. He was incapable of reconciling his devotion to the ancient forms of the Welsh literary tradition with the rigid standards of his classical education and his unquestioning subservience to current English literary fashion. He became so absorbed in the cultivation of his own poetic gifts that he took only a limited interest in the social and moral problems of the world around him. As a natural conservative he does not seem to have felt the need to defend or celebrate the *status quo*, only to take it for granted. All he ever asked for was some small preferment that would give him the time he felt he needed to solve the aesthetic problems posed by his private, cloistered, ambition. In spite of all his travels, he was unaware that he was living in an age of rapid transition. He never understood that there were forces in the world outside himself capable of snatching up his cherished problems and solving them overnight.

12 The Wind of Heaven

Under any conditions a religious revival is a mysterious and unaccountable event. With the wisdom of hindsight that belongs to historical analysis, we can sometimes point to economic and social conditions that would foster the outbreak of such a phenomenon and even condition its course and long-term effects. European and American experience shows, time and again, how religion offers among the oppressed and the deprived a solace for material deprivation and physical infirmity – 'balm from Gilead'; and the definite promise of improved conditions in an undefined future, the Promised Land, either in this world or the next. When a religious revival occurs it is powerful enough to forge a link between personal salvation and the survival of a whole society. By some means beyond the pedestrian processes of analysis, the spark of personal mystical experience is endowed with the power to ignite a whole population. The need, the appetite, the longing can be traced: the social organism, like nature itself, abhors a vacuum. The difficulty is, to isolate that point in time when the personal convictions of a handful of men take possession of an entire people so that transcendental belief is suddenly transformed into a social necessity.

Like so many comfortably placed eighteenth-century parsons, Theophilus Evans was not without bees in his bonnet. With all the authority of the respected author of *Drych y Prifoesoedd*, in 1752 he published a book in English with the title *A History of Modern Enthusiasm*. Bolstered up by his ancient British pride, Theophilus shared the distaste of the cultivated Englishman for the unseemly excesses of religious revivalism. John Locke had provided the philosophical basis for natural religion which was much to be preferred to the dubious claims of the supernatural. The government and the established church were engaged in genial co-operation: teaching the common man his duty, and organising a spirit of thanksgiving for the manifold blessings a benevolent providence had seen fit to bestow on the English nation and its lesser dependencies. All this was conventional enough. Where the bees begin to buzz is when he suggests that the Quakers were nothing more than a fifth column insinuated into the ranks of Protestantism by the wily Jesuits in order to undermine the will to fight of the Protestant powers. To those who remember Senator McCarthy accusing General George Marshall of being a Communist sympathiser, this kind of fantasy, born of irrational suspicions, must have a familiar ring. Theophilus also wanted to prove that all nonconformist sects were in some way crypto-Papists, and particularly those infected with the emotional disorder of 'Enthusiasm'.

He had good reason to be worried. As an experienced historian of the unsteady progress of a chastened chosen people through the wilderness of this world, he knew that providence was not always to be relied on. Some mischievous sprite in the service of the Spirit of the Years had arranged for a certain Mr. William Williams, of Pantycelyn, to be appointed one of his curates in 1740. This earnest young man, born of a nonconformist family, had intended to become a doctor until the day he was to celebrate for the rest of his long life: 'The morning I shall remember for ever when, through the awe-inspiring sound that he made, I heard the voice of heaven, and I was held for ever by the summons from above!'

Williams was referring to an occasion two or three years earlier when he heard Hywel Harris preaching in the churchyard at Talgarth; an occasion which was soon to become part of the mythology of the Welsh Methodist revival. *Y Diwygiad* (the Revival) began with the conversion of three would-be curates, two of whom were ordained, Daniel Rowland and William Williams. Harris was refused ordination because of his 'irregular preaching' and, in all probability, the unstoppable force of his personality. Theophilus Evans soon discovered that the milder-mannered Williams could also be as disturbingly 'irregular' as the imperious and impetuous Harris. He visited people's houses to discuss with them in private the condition of their souls. He held private prayer meetings and had even invented an institution called '*seiat brofiad*' (the society for the sharing of spiritual experiences) in which the members laid bare their most intimate thoughts and openly confessed their sins. This was more than Theophilus could stomach. The business of confessing confirmed his rumbling suspicion that the new movement was nothing more than Popery in disguise. He refused to recommend his curate to the bishop for final ordination as a priest in the Church of England and thus, unwittingly, played a tiny but significant role in the transformation of the history of a country which he himself had celebrated in epic style. Williams was released and the southern counties of Wales were soon to experience a sustained missionary effort from what amounted in its first phase to a club of revolutionary curates. The leader, Hywel Harris, first among equals, was in fact a part-time schoolmaster with the Rev. Griffith Jones's circulating schools, which had already begun the task of transforming the peasantry of Wales into a literate community and was soon to form the basis of a new market for Welsh books and periodicals. Howell Davies, the Apostle of Pembrokeshire, John Powell of Monmouthshire, Peter Williams of Carmarthen, Daniel Rowland of Cardigan: these Methodist clerics were possessed with volcanic energy, and the very fact that they were kept down by the established church created a pressure that added force to their eruption. They were able to collaborate with sympathisers among the old dissenters, but they themselves took the full brunt of the opposition. Their progress was astonishing in the face of increasingly fierce persecution. The first qualification for an early Welsh Methodist was physical courage. Hywel Harris was a particular target. In many places thugs were employed to attack him and more than once in front of stone-throwing mobs he seemed to be courting martyrdom. But the brand of religious enthusiasm that Harris pioneered throve on persecution and Harris himself possessed the eloquence, the dictatorial temper, the organising powers and drive to awaken an entire population from the state of inertia.

Harris, also, was the link with English Methodism. In fact in England his complex character seems to undergo something of a transformation. The storm centre becomes the peace-maker. He was intimate with both Wesley and Whitfield and he did what he could to keep the two sides together in the conflict over Calvinism. English Calvinistic Methodists, through the Countess of Huntingdon, had Tory connections and their hope was that one day Bolingbroke would become prime minister and make George Whitfield a bishop. When this happened he could set about ordaining Methodist preachers and exhorters, even Hywel Harris himself. It says much for the power of Harris's personality that when Whitfield was in America (1744–8) he became the leader of Calvinistic Methodism in both England and Wales. Leadership came easily to him. He was of an autocratic disposition; but these self-same qualities brought about splits and controversies. His affection for royalty (he paid the expensive entrance fee to the Chapel Royal in order to be able to boast that he had prayed alongside his king) did nothing to prevent English Methodism from being infiltrated with the spirit of nonconformity. And in Wales an attachment to a married convert, in particular his close ties with the prophetess, 'Madam Griffith', who had been driven out of her home by her drunken husband, and the over-dramatisation of doctrine in his preaching split the new movement into two. It was from this time forward that William Williams became the central creative force of the movement. His patience and forbearance were the chief factors in the preservation of unity and the eventual reconciliation between Harris and Daniel Rowland who was generally accepted as the pillar of orthodoxy and Methodist rectitude. Rowland was a magnificent preacher and mass orator, and thousands of people came by land and sea to hear him and take Communion from his hands. But he had little

*Hywel Harris (1714—73). The young Williams Pantycelyn heard him preach 'like a summons from heaven'.
(National Library of Wales)*

gift of organisation. It was Williams who continued the Harris tradition of establishing a network of cells all over the country and linking them up with an efficient denominational organisation. Like the Celtic saints, the Methodists stamped their impression on the calendar. The *seiat* and the weekday meetings were woven into 'churches' and these in turn linked to territorial monthly presbyteries which were associated with assemblies whose meetings became 'high festivals' in the spiritual calendar.

Williams possessed the creative power to invest this solid framework with the pulse of life. He knew from his own experience both as a convert, and as an exhorter and spiritual counsellor, that emotional appeal, however profound the upheaval, was never enough. The new way of life was something that had to be worked at, and the duty of the leadership was to provide every flock with sufficient spiritual food that would last, not only for their lifetime, but for generations to come. The prejudices of Theophilus Evans may seem to us to be comical enough, but in the context of the continuity of Welsh social life Harris, Williams, Rowland and their co-workers, did in fact restore to the people an indigenous structure that was in many respects a revised and updated version of a community life that had maintained the Welsh identity throughout the middle ages. The revival placed great emphasis on love and loving-kindness, so that it is not altogether incongruous to imagine these early young Methodist heroes awakening a sleeping country with a spiritual kiss. Love was their central concern, and it sprang from the concept of a Creator being so in love with his creation that he sent his son as his own representative to die on the Cross for the sake of mankind. In Harris's imagination God himself died in the course of this cosmic rescue operation, and this is why he was accused of the heresy of Patripassianism. Harris was in close touch with the Moravian Brethren and it was from them that he acquired his preoccupation with the mystical nature of the Saviour's blood. This became the symbol of God's life-giving love and through the hymns of Williams Pantycelyn and his successors, blood became a symbol of the reviving power of the movement.

> It is the blood of thy cross that raises up the weakling and transforms him into a great conqueror.
> It is the blood of thy Cross that will subdue and bring down a host of strong giants.
> Let me feel the wind that breathes from Calvary Hill . . .
>
> It was blood that wrote on the wooden cross, powerful, divine, unstinting love;
> And it is only with blood that thy words will be properly inscribed on my heart.
> And this is the writing that will outlast the world.

Harris and Williams had both enjoyed a thorough English education and in theory there would have been nothing to prevent them pursuing extensive and successful evangelical careers outside Wales. Harris in particular was often drawn in this direction. When they wrote to each other as they frequently did, since they were always on the move, and the needs of their organisation demanded close contact and a continuing understanding, the language of their letters was English more often than not. In politics they were both Whigs and perhaps because of their Tory connections, in times of crisis, such as the Jacobite Rebellion, they went out of their way to demonstrate their militant loyalty to the Hanoverian succession. But once they were committed to the conversion of Wales, Wales took possession of them. In spite of their profuse, almost daily protestations of unworthiness and of humility, they were men of Napoleonic ambition. They intended to save the souls of all their countrymen and they planned their campaigns with military precision.

Religious reformers as men with an urgent mission are usually the first to realise that the native language is more often than not the soul of a nation. For the conversion of Wales, the Welsh language had to be the chosen weapon. But once the process was set in motion, repercussions were far-reaching.

The Methodists were to Protestantism in several important respects what the preaching friars had been to mediaeval Catholicism. But for poverty they substituted that industrious frugality which contributed substantially to the growth of capitalism. Their religious societies were inclusive rather than exclusive, so that in the case of a small country like Wales it is not too great an exaggeration to visualise an entire population being shepherded gradually into chapels and conventicles that were the extra-mural equivalent of the religious houses of the mediaeval church.

These young men had no desire to do more than save the souls of all the Welsh that they could persuade to listen to them. This was ambition enough. It was never any part of their intention to create a new nation. But since the language of their activities was Welsh, all sorts of ancient seeds were re-activated. To revert for a moment to one of the mediaeval metaphors, they lit a fire, and in no time the cauldron of rebirth was on the boil. It is chiefly as a result of their mission that the language, either by its absence or by its presence, continues to be the central fact of Welsh existence.

It is unlikely that Williams ever preached as powerfully as Harris or Rowland. He does not seem to have shared their unaccountable power to sway large assemblies of the faithful. People travelled by sea and by land to remote Llangeitho in Cardiganshire or to 'the family' established by Harris at Trevecca, to submit themselves to the authority of Rowland's or Harris's ministry. Pantycelyn never gained the shrinelike status of Llangeitho or Trevecca. Williams did not share the tempestuous temperaments of his two friends, and it was often his rôle to make peace between them. But his was the most far-reaching influence in the growth of the movement and in shaping so much of the emotional life of his country and even producing new psychological features that would soon be accepted as integral parts of the Welsh personality.

Practical necessity forced him into the rôle of poet of the movement. As soon as he began to exercise this function the power of his inspiration was so great that he was able to achieve, as it were by accident, what more fastidious poets like Goronwy Owen had decided was an impossible dream. Williams ignored the restrictions of the Welsh bardic tradition, and inspired by English works as different as *Paradise Lost* and *Pilgrim's Progress* he hammered out two book-long poems which were in fact epics. *Golwg ar Deyrnas Crist* (A View of Christ's Kingdom) is an extraordinary exercise in theological song. It celebrates the order of the material universe and the wonders of creation and attempts a synthesis of contemporary scientific knowledge with his own understanding of the needs of his own nature.

> It was my own wild nature that brought me so close to the Fire and nothing in my own endowment of gifts or talents or virtues would have been able to save me; it was Thy wisdom and care when Thou didst take me by the hand when my foot was on the edge of the fiery torrent that made it possible for me to step back.

Bywyd a Marwolaeth Theomemphus (The Life and Death of Theomemphus) follows more closely the spiritual experiences of a representative Christian, Theomemphus, through the crucial stages of religious conversion. It is a portrait of the progress of the soul through a Methodist revival that Williams wishes his readers to understand as a turning point in history. Because the turning point is so important he feels obliged to trace all the essential experiences and temptations of his representative hero from the cradle to the grave. Since the eighteenth--century revival also proved to be the rebirth of a nation, or even the creation of a new one, Theomemphus must stand as a substitute for the second part of a national epic. Theophilus Evans had taken his cue from Gildas and the sixteenth-century Welsh humanists: his curate Williams was endowed with a more prophetic power to place himself in touch with the very source of Christian feeling. Conversion was the one method left to create the new man and by so doing make a new Welsh nation an historical possibility.

The force of his inspiration impelled Williams to achieve the impossible. He became a great artist by accident. He reached that level of creation which is reserved for men of unique vision, and it is these achievements, all by-products of a burning, unartistic and unselfish ambition to bring salvation within reach of the greatest number of his compatriots, which make modern Welsh literary critics acknowledge him as Wales's greatest poet.

They do so with some reluctance. He shows so little respect for the inherited beauties of the language, the sheer music of utterance cultivated over the centuries by professional poets infatuated with its resources and determined to take every opportunity to display their own technical brilliance. At every stage in his development, Williams is preoccupied with the practical problem of channelling the great power of his own experience into the spiritual reservoirs of his *seiadau* (societies), and making it easily available to every individual member. He composed over a thousand hymns as a means of communicating his experience for their benefit and the fact that so many of them are great poetry is only an incidental bonus. There are so many apparent contradictions involved in any sustained appreciation of the nature of his work. He was, after all, engaged in expressing the inexpressible: in translating the language of his understanding of the Godhead into a language that could be understood by the simplest member of a congregation. The first lines of so many of his hymns have that warm memorability and breathlessness of immediate experience that an English reader finds in the first line of, say, a Shakespeare sonnet.

Jesu, the delight of my soul that cost so much to buy, is to gaze on thy countenance . . .

I never cease to stare at the distant hills in search of Thee; Come my beloved, it grows late and my sun will soon have set . . .

I see the black cloud is now being put to flight and the wind from the north by small degrees begins to turn . . .

Guide me Lord, sick pilgrim that I am through the barren land . . .

Unseen, Invisible, I love thee, so strange is the power of thy grace: drawing my soul with such gentle sweetness away from its greatest pleasures; Thou didst achieve more in one short minute than the world with all its time. Winning for thyself a session of sweet silence in the stony hardness of my heart.

Williams's strange combination of transcendental obsession and idiosyncratic eloquence makes him a solitary figure in the Welsh scene. It is a paradox that the very nation which he helped to bring into being has never really come to grips with the full significance of what he had to say. A towering figure can be isolated by its very size. Even before his death lesser men were engaged in transforming him into a totem-pole. Succeeding generations cultivated the habit of bathing in the medicinal waters of his verses. Hard won perceptions were transformed into popular incantations. To this day, a Welsh rugby football crowd can roar out a verse of Pantycelyn with impressive fervour, even though most of them have long ceased to be chapel-goers. English supporters have yet to be heard making the Twickenham girders re-echo to 'Jerusalem'. It may be that the Welsh have managed to siphon off something of the emotional power of Williams's muse to put to their own devious uses. The fact remains that this man was able to express the most rarefied experience with a penetrating simplicity that made a sustained lyric output available to everyone who spoke the language.

In almost all his writing Williams was obliged to be a pioneer. He was a man of strong scientific bent and he had been well trained in the new learning in the tradition of the South Wales nonconformist academies. Over fifteen years his energies were engaged in the publication of a remarkable encyclopaedia of comparative religion called *The Pantheologia*. The purpose of science was to reveal to the Christian the wonders of God's creation and help him discern aspects of the divine order in the exploration of nature. He felt concern for the unenquiring mind of the monoglot Welshman, and his desire was to awaken in him a spirit of inquiry that could be directed into constructive religious and social channels. It is a reflection of the organic nature of his activities that once again he was able to adapt the rich spoken language of his native Carmarthenshire and combine it with the discipline of science and humanistic literary learning to reach the widest possible readership, aided by the increase of literacy brought about by Griffith Jones's circulating schools.

Williams possessed an all embracing vision of the nature of the Christian life on earth. In his view, the triumph of Christianity would be to discover a proper balance between the passions. The theological explanation for the condition of mankind was relatively simple. As a result of the Fall of Man human desires were dangerously out of hand. The energy inherent in human affections, like any other uncultivated elemental power, contained the seeds of its own destruction. The practical task of a Christian church was to guide these essential energies into a new harmonious relationship so that a mass of conflicting desires could be transformed into a network of creative love. The evangelical message declared that the only effective means of securing this miraculous transformation was to tap the divine love of the Creator on the cross so that the church would be sustained by what was in fact a spiritual blood-transfusion. Williams's command of the Welsh language and his extraordinary literary gifts made it possible for him to impose his vision on the small world of Wales. His raw material was a nation aware in its collective unconscious that it owed its survival down the centuries to one form or another of religion. Its very condition of slumberous inertia made it more susceptible to the impact of Methodist eloquence and the new visions given the power of permanence in everything that Williams wrote. His hymns were the most obvious and audible part of the awakening and they remain what has come to be regarded as a national characteristic. The power of his song inspired others to sing. In his native Carmarthenshire alone, within a twenty mile radius of Pantycelyn, three poets were inspired in sustained outbursts of composition to celebrate in popular hymns the mysterious nature of divine love and the greatness of the suffering Lord; Morgan Rhys of Llanfynydd, Dafydd William of Llandeilo Fach, and Dafydd Jones the drover from Caio. Before Williams died the singing of hymns was well established in Wales and in the next century it acquired the status of a national pastime.

Williams was well aware of the dangers of facile emotionalism. His *Templum Experientiae Apertum*, cast in the form of seven dialogues between two religious friends, discusses practical problems of religious counselling with the dramatic liveliness of Platonic dialogues. Williams was as wise as he was inspired. He travelled thousands of miles to nurture the *seiadau* which became, as it were, the revolutionary cells of the movement: the nuclei around which a church would gather and the human source of spiritual power that would have the authority to revise behaviour and impose new standards on what was yet another refined version of the chosen people. The book demonstrates Williams's powerful psychological insight and understanding of human nature, and like a true classic it reads as freshly today as the day it was written.

It is no fault of Williams Pantycelyn if the Methodist *seiat* in the nineteenth century acquired habits of arid and unbending rigidity. If the founding fathers have done their work well, the seeds of renewal will always be present in their writings. And this seems increasingly true in the case of Williams the more closely his great output is examined. Had his spirit been sufficiently considered, it is doubtful whether the conflict between the people of the *seiat* and the 'people of the world' would have become such an unprofitable undercurrent of Welsh life. He was no prude. He understood better than most the power of the temptations of the flesh. This understanding, combined with his intense scientific interest in human behaviour, allowed him to anticipate many of the insights of twentieth-century psychoanalysis. His *Ductor Nuptiarum* is a classic statement of the Christian attitude to the problems of physical infatuation, sex, and enduring marriage. The nature of the dialogue demonstrates with vivid frankness that sexual freedom is no escape route from the human predicament. It is itself, however romantically expressed or however perversely unrestricted, a form of slavery which ultimately drags the individual down to a dungeon of misery and a sub-human level of existence.

The balance between the untamable strength of personal desire and the stability of any social contract remained a central concern. The books he wrote were intended, as he said, 'to make Godliness attractive'. They were written to guide and encourage the new societies and to help them understand the challenge of reconciling every new freedom with a new responsibility. As a man of the eighteenth century, somewhat in the manner of the founding fathers of the American Republic, he was inclined to look upon the independent farmer as the best raw material for leadership in both religious and secular life. But this individualist had to bend his way of life in accordance with genuine religious experience. It was important that his worldly dealings should be free from any discreditable activities. It was his duty to avoid the extremes of extravagance and avarice. In Williams's view of the world, moderation was a great social virtue. He was perfectly aware that his movement was soon to be confronted with the advent of large scale industrialism. The subtle but accelerating rate of change around him made him uneasy. He understood the power of the profit motive in the rise of capitalism, and he feared that unrestricted development would sweep aside any sense of social responsibility and authentic religious duty. The ruthless practices of the slave trade would be extended to the new centres of industry by the same appetite for profit. Once again his answer to so vast a problem has a modern relevance. The resources of the earth are not inexhaustible: a fundamental part of the discipline of their exploitation would only come from a profound inner conviction of the need for restraint, and a moderation that would be a practical expression of absolute justice.

There remains an extraordinary sense in which the vision of Harris and Williams was a continuation of the ideal society canvassed by the strict-metre poets of the fifteenth century in conscious imitation of what they conceived as the Taliesinic role in the Cymric world. Both Harris and Williams shared the eighteenth-century interest in Welsh antiquities and there are accounts of them discussing the contents of the ancient manuscripts. In the event, strictness of metre was replaced by strictness of behaviour, and the code of honour of the Round Table replaced by the stern standards of the *seiat*. The leaders of the Methodist revolution were providing for peasants and workers a more effective and organic social organisation than the skilled *cywyddwyr* of the fifteenth century ever succeeded in persuading their more wilful and anarchic patrons to adopt. They wove a social fabric that was to last the best part of two hundred years.

13 The Fruits of Heresy

To understand a nineteenth-century Welshman, and indeed for a twentieth-century Welshman to understand himself, it is essential to know to which denomination or religious sect his immediate ancestors belonged. This does not mean that denominations operated a mechanical mould that turned out the typical Baptist or Unitarian or Anglican. However the process worked, it must always have been complex and organic. But there are underlying rhythms which can be identified. The sect had to occupy its position in a changing social structure brought about by the rapid expansion of a capitalist economy and imperial political structure. Similarly the family in communion with the sect had to adjust its position in the chapel pew with its changing fortunes in the world outside. It becomes obvious that an attempt to understand the characters of such notable Welshmen as Robert Owen, Thomas Gee, Henry Richard, Sir Hugh Owen, David Davies, O.M.Edwards, Mabon, Tom Ellis, or David Lloyd George, must involve an examination of their denominational background; and the same is true of their Cambro-American counterparts, men like Jefferson Davis, Jenkin Lloyd Jones, D.W.Griffith, Frank Lloyd Wright, Charles Evans Hughes and John L.Lewis.

The dissenter by definition has a conspicuous inclination towards doctrinal disputation. The young William Williams of Pantycelyn left the Congregationalist (Independent) church of which his grandfather had been a minister because he was surfeited with bitter wrangles over points of doctrine. It is true that after the first flush of conversion the Methodist leadership sailed into even rougher waters, but at least the quarrel between Harris and Rowland was a matter of living concern to a substantial part of the population and part of the growing pains of a great historical movement and not just a grinding argument droning on behind the closed doors of a separatist conventicle. It was however the Methodist movement that brought the old arguments back into the open. It brought the fire of revivalism into the ranks of the 'old dissenters'. From the year of the temporary split between Harris and Rowland in 1749 to the final registration of the Welsh Calvinistic

Methodists as a new nonconformist body in 1811 the irregular progress of this transformation creates what is in effect a secret history of Wales. The agricultural and industrial revolutions, the population explosion, the wars against France and in North America and against Napoleon governed the common history of Great Britain and Western Europe. What is unique to Wales, and what governed the development both of the concept of Welsh nationality and the Welsh personality in so many of its characteristic facets, is the progress of doctrinal differences among the forces of organised dissent. The Welsh situation offers as it were a transparent receptacle in which it is possible to see how a disinherited and unenfranchised people struggled out of their hard won religious defensive positions to reach out for democratic power in a secular world.

Present-day nonconformists in Wales would be hard put to it if asked to tick off the five headings that summed up the reaffirmation of Calvinist doctrine at the Synod of Dort in 1619. It is possible that active socialists would find it equally difficult to recite the resolutions of the Third International. But in nineteenth-century Wales *Y Pum Pwnc* (The Five Canonical Points) were part of the familiar conversation of every chapel-going person. To make the pattern even more complex, the response to these five Calvinist commandments penetrated every sect, so that it was possible to be, say, a Calvinist Baptist, or an Arminian Baptist; and even among the Calvinistic Methodists there was an important distinction to be made between the High Calvinist and the Fullerite with the less exclusive version of Calvinism. The Wesleyans who came late to the Welsh feast were of course all Arminian, but even among these latecomers there were disputes about methods of church government. Loyalties were deep and fierce. We have to bear in mind that among the Welsh there was an almost total absence of the steadying influence of native secular institutions on a local or a national level. A resurgence of a sense of identity and particularity also entailed what might be described as a rekindling of the contentious inclinations of a mountain people, coupled with the innate cellular structure of ancient Celtic tradition. The response to *Y Pum Pwnc* could condition the allegiance of a family to their particular sect and, in so doing, condition the lives of succeeding generations far more than any intervention, short of war or imprisonment, by government or judiciary.

The Five Canonical Points were referred to by number. One, the nature of divine predestination that granted unconditional salvation to the elect; two, the view that Christ's death was an atonement limited to the elect; three, man's total incapacity, due to his corrupt nature; four, the irresistible power of divine grace; five, the promised perseverance of the saints in a state of grace. This was the norm and the dynamic of Calvinist orthodoxy. Initially dissenting churches were cells of believers who put applicants for membership to strict test before allowing them to join. This sense of importance attached to membership remained central to the nonconformist outlook until the period after the first world war when the power of the chapel at last began to wane. But the intellectual reaction against the uncompromising rigidity of Calvinism had begun in the seventeenth century. It is again the figure five that helps to indicate the stages down what the strict Calvinist would call the slippery slope, that could only end in what he would regard as the dark pit of free thought and atheism.

The first position became known as High Calvinism. This was orthodoxy and total adherence to the small print of the Canons of the Synod of Dort. The next step down was Low Calvinism, of which there were several versions. It was 'Low' because of a certain easing in the conditions of grace. It did not require, for example, the belief that God had pre-ordained the Fall of Man. A far greater step led to differing degrees of Arminianism, of which the most extreme implied that salvation was available to all because Christ had died for all mankind. John Wesley was a moderate Arminian. However the Welsh Methodist leadership remained Calvinist so that their denomination eventually became known as Calvinistic Methodist. A swift slide from the Arminian position landed the venturesome in an ancient heresy, first propounded by Arius in the fourth century. Arius taught that Christ was not of the same essence as God the Father. He was the first and the greatest and the highest of any being ever created, but since he was not of the same essence as the Father, the Trinity could not be said to exist. Beyond this came Socinianism and the differing shades of Unitarian belief. These points of view took much encouragement from the development of philosophical and scientific ideas in the eighteenth century. However by the middle of the nineteenth century Welsh Calvinists could hotly argue that Unitarianism had held the door open to an aggressive liberal humanism that was bent on reducing Christianity into a mere exhibit in an anthropological museum.

In 1726 a young man by the name of Jenkin Jones, member of a Congregational church in south Cardiganshire, began to preach Arminianism. This divided the congregation: but the young man had sufficient means to build the first Arminian chapel in Wales at Llwynrhydowen. He wrote books with titles like *Y Cyfrif Cywir o'r Pechod Gwreiddiol* (A Correct Account of the Original Sin) and by the time he died in his early forties several ministers and churches in that area had adopted his new ideas. His ministry at Llwynrhydowen was continued by his sister's son David Lloyd. (In itself this is an interesting echo of a special relationship in early Celtic society, and it was a relationship to be continued generation after generation in the history of this family.) David Lloyd ventured further into the hazards of heresy. He became an Arian. Like all advanced thinkers of the eighteenth century, David Lloyd was a man of independent means. Indeed, in the traditional Welsh manner, he could boast a pedigree. His father was directly descended from the Lord of Castell Hywel, who in turn was of the line of the Lord Rhys. He was, moreover, an excellent scholar in Latin, Greek and Hebrew. He spoke French and Italian fluently and he was one of the few accomplished poets in the strict metres outside the charmed circle of the Morris brothers and the London-based Cymmrodorion. As a poet he was known as Dafydd Llwyd, Brynllefrith. Both uncle and nephew were products of those dissenting academies in South Wales which offered the most advanced education at that time. (Oxford and Cambridge were of course still closed to dissenters and Catholics.) The career and accomplishments of David Lloyd, secure in his south Cardiganshire *bro*, offer an interesting parallel with an exact contemporary who was also a product of the nonconformist academies of South Wales, Dr. Richard Price. Their contrasting careers offer one more illustration of the apparent choice the bilingual condition presents the talented young Welshman. We have seen the process in operation among the aristocracy in Tudor times and it is not difficult to trace it on its way down what used to be called the social scale. The eighteenth century presents the illusion of a moment of equilibrium and of paradox. It is the literary minded Welsh Anglicans who zealously promote the old language and their enthusiastic curates who place it in a position to dominate Welsh life from about 1760 onwards in a way that it had not been able to do since the fifteenth century. In their early phase the Welsh nonconformist academies concentrated on an English scientific education and the perfect product of their austere regime was a man like Richard Price from Llangeinor in Glamorganshire.

Price was also able to boast of a pedigree. His father was a dissenting minister who kept an academy. He became part of legend in his role as the stern guardian of the Maid of Cefn Ydfa whose sad love story gave rise to the celebrated folk-song '*Bugeilio'r Gwenith Gwyn*'. The influence of his uncle Samuel, the friend and collaborator of Isaac Watts, removed Richard to London where he became a dissenting minister himself, a Presbyterian with Arian views. At the age of thirty-five he published his *Review of the Principal Questions in Morals*. His work as a statistician and economist made him virtually the founder of life-insurance and as a leading intellectual among the dissenters, in spite of his amiable and retiring nature, he was in the forefront of the struggle for political freedom. Price was an eloquent advocate of the American revolution. From the beginning there was a special relationship between the emergence of the United States of America and the disadvantaged minority status of dissent in Britain. It was a logical development of the demand for the removal of all religious disabilities to welcome the revolt of the American colonies. In the fateful year of

1776 his *The Nature of Civil Liberty* passed through fifteen editions. He, more than anyone else, raised the level of the debate from a question of customs and taxes and the jostling for mercantile advantage between ports on either side of the Atlantic to a discussion of the principle of liberty based on the natural rights of man. His arguments made the American War of Independence an extension of the English Civil War in the long memory of history. John Wesley thought Price was mad, replacing the Divine Right of Kings with the dominion of an insubordinate rabble. Price for his part described both the American and the French Revolutions as heralds of the dawn of a better era in the history of mankind.

Price never went to America, except in spirit, in spite of the pressing invitations. David Lloyd devoted his life to his ministry at Llwynrhydowen, and the society which he created in his small corner of the world became a beleaguered outpost of those advanced democratic views which inspired the constitution of the United States. Richard Price only spent his summers in Wales, but his eloquence and his writing made a deep impression on the minds of the extreme dissenters who saw their own battles for religious and political freedom as a significant microcosm of the greater struggle. The Unitarians were the pioneers of libertarian principles and democracy in Wales, but as a religious organisation they were lacking in popular appeal. Llwynrhydowen enjoyed the leadership of a succession of gifted ministers who were also tireless educators, and it remained one of their rare successes within the orbit of the Welsh language. It flourished to such an extent in the district of Llandyssul that in the orthodox Calvinist Wales of the early nineteenth century that area became known as *Smotyn Du* (Black Spot). But it remained only a spot, a blot on a Trinitarian nonconformist landscape.

The only other important centre was Merthyr Tydfil, and there the Unitarians made lively contact with the new force of industrialism. This minority group seems to have been the first to realise that the democracy which they cherished was a force at work capable of creating new nations. Indeed across the Atlantic it had already done so. Their problem was how to infiltrate the consciousness of a Welsh people, apparently entranced by the joys of 'vital religion', with the possibilities of democratic nationhood. Help in the execution of this work of supererogation came from an unexpected quarter, the fertile imagination of one man of genius, Iolo Morganwg.

14 Old Iolo

Iolo, old Iolo, he who knows
The virtues of all herbs of mount or vale . . .

Whatever lore of science or of song
Sages and bards of old have handed down.

This was how the poet Robert Southey saw Edward Williams, or, to be more precise, that was how the Glamorgan stone-mason wished to be seen by the English poet, and by literary and revolutionary circles in London. Iolo was a Jacobin, also a forger and a romantic in the same league as 'Ossian' Macpherson, Chatterton the 'marvellous boy' and Psalmanasar in the south of France. But Iolo's methods and motives were different. Indeed they were so complex that it has taken almost two centuries to unravel them and the work is still unfinished. An outstanding Welsh scholar, Professor G.J.Williams, devoted a good part of his working life to unravelling fact and fantasy in Iolo's vast output and died without completing the task. The first volume of his authoritative *Iolo Morganwg* appeared a quarter of a century ago and it remains the only safe entrance into the labyrinth.

Iolo wished to be seen above all as a bardic figure, the heir of druidic and Taliesinic mysteries that had been miraculously preserved by the bardic tradition of his native Glamorgan. 'I am giving you the Patriarchal religion and theology, the divine revelation given to mankind, and these have been retained in Wales until our own day.' Viewed from a safe distance this seems an absurd fantasy. The unnerving element in everything to do with Iolo is the surprising way in which fresh advances in scholarship are forced to concede the presence of traces of truth even in his most outlandish fantasies. His cottage in the Vale of Glamorgan was his bardic lodge. Like Cyridwen in the story of Taliesin he possessed a magic formula and out of the bubbling cauldron of his mind he would produce the essence of wisdom by discovering the correct balance between the wild herbs of out of the way fact, the authentic remnants of cultivated tradition, and the spices of his own imagination. To begin to understand him we have to accept his self-appointed bardic rôle. Contemporary records describe him as a small man with an electric personality, a spell-binder capable of dominating any company in either language. In some ways a prototype of the Glamorgan character, bustling, self-confident, convivial, vital, endlessly curious, with an unshakeable faith in his own ability.

And yet his zeal and love for his secret labours, about which the world knew nothing, sprang not from a desire for personal glory and reward, but from an irrepressible urge to revive in as elaborate a form as possible what he believed to be Europe's oldest living literary language, and not only restore its ancient glory but embellish it and make it powerful enough to embrace an even more glorious future. In his younger days he travelled on foot calling in great houses all over England and Wales to copy manuscripts and to make himself the best informed among Welsh antiquarians. Once Ieuan Fardd was dead and gone, Iolo knew that there was no one left who could question his authority in the rarefied subject of British antiquities and early Welsh literature. His business from now on was to elaborate the trappings of a revived Welshness. To be truly effective the task had to be conducted in secret. He disciplined his natural gregariousness, and like a wonder-working magician in the Taliesinic tradition, he went underground. All night in his stone-mason's cottage he worked away at his forgeries and the nature of his activity was never revealed even to his closest family. His method was never to be too original; rather gently to extend the corpus of existing work, so that, for example, the brilliant *cywyddau* of Dafydd ap Gwilym should be multiplied by almost equally brilliant effusions of his own, executed in the manner of the master with an almost comparable ascendancy over the strict metres.

His poetic forgeries were only a small part of his herculean labours. He was one of the first men to understand the significance of folk culture and his interests included the idea of a national museum and a national library, as well as his cherished dream of a national eisteddfod. His fierce local patriotism also demanded that the history of Wales should be realigned, and everything of the greatest value in the Welsh tradition, including Taliesin, be demonstrated to have its real roots in Glamorgan. Some real or imagined slight from prominent North Walians in the Cymmrodorion aggravated this obsession and he forged away furiously at additional triads and historical monuments that were all directed to proving the primacy of Glamorgan. This is an extra-ordinary example of an imaginative man anticipating historical development. Long before his death, the valleys of Glamorgan and Monmouth had become the workshop of Wales and the source of a new wealth which was to make the realisation of many of his dreams social realities. It seems oddly appropriate that Iolo should have spent his declining years in Merthyr Tydfil, offering lectures, among other subjects, on engineering. No small feat for a man who claimed never to have enjoyed a formal education. The lectures on engineering certainly bore fruit. His grandson Edward became an ironmaster, with extensive works in Middlesbrough (Bernicia) as well as in South Wales: the kind of historical fact that would have amused the original Taliesin as well as 'Old Iolo'.

We have already seen that the Welsh were being inducted into a vibrant form of nonconformist religion by the genius of the leaders of the Methodist revival. Iolo was not in sympathy with that mass movement. As so often happens with imaginative sceptics, he was deeply suspicious of the emotional content of revealed religion. If there was such a thing as the supernatural, he would take it upon himself to control it and give it instructions. He already had a vision of the direct link between the pure religion of the ancient druids, of whose existence he was absolutely convinced, and the rational religion of the Unitarians and the Deists and Jacobin doctrines of political freedom.

In London on Primrose Hill on June 21st, 1792 he took upon himself the authority to reassemble the druidical court of the 'Bards of the Isle of Britain'. An interest in druids was a conspicuous feature of eighteenth-century romanticism, but it was Iolo who provided the rules and regulations of the mystic rituals whereby the *Gorsedd*, also of his creation, would assemble in druid fashion inside the circles of large standing-stones, to make proclamations and to supervise the chairing and crowning of poets and give the authority of antiquity to the support of the eisteddfod as a central institution in the life of the Welsh nation. 'Old Iolo' was only forty-five at the time but such was his personal authority that he was able to persuade a cultivated assembly that he was the lone survivor of the ancient order of Glamorgan druids who had preserved a knowledge 'sages and bards of old had handed down' of the 'patriarchal religion' of the ancient druids. On the strength of this authority he was able to make proclamations 'in the face of the sun and in the eye of light' and to raise the voice of 'the Truth against the world'.

By 1819 he was able to persuade the benevolent Lord Bishop of St. David's, a learned Englishman called Dr. Burgess, to take part in a *Gorsedd* ceremony at the Carmarthen Eisteddfod and to lend his substantial support to the revival of the regional eisteddfodau. Iolo's sorcery had a dual effect as time went on: it convinced the peasants and the Welsh working class that their homely speech was in fact glowing evidence of untold riches from the past and untold possibilities for the future. It was only a short step from this conviction towards the agreeable discovery that peasants as well as princes could be a chosen people.

Iolo would have been an exception to the romantic rule if he had not also dreamt of a settlement in the New World where the precepts of freedom and equality could be carried out free from the restrictions imposed by the tyrannical regimes of European monarchs. Notions of

Iolo Morganwg (1747—1826), stone-mason, poet, visionary and literary forger; he was architect of all the more colourful embellishments of nineteenth-century Welsh nationalism. (National Museum of Wales, Welsh Folk Museum)

human perfectibility were in the air. Later his friend Southey was to draw up with Coleridge a scheme for a communal farm on the banks of the Susquehanna, and Iolo, of course, was his main source of information (and misinformation), for Southey's immensely long *Madoc*, which must have some claim to be the least read epic in any language. (It may be of interest to note that the poem was dedicated to Charles Watkin Williams Wynn, a successful politician and the son of that Sir Watkin who had for a time been the patron of Iolo's literary guide and companion Ieuan Fardd, Evans the curate. Charles kept up the family tradition of patronage with an annuity of £160, until Southey was appointed Poet Laureate.)

The Madoc legend and the rediscovery of the Welsh Red Indians was a cause very close to Iolo's heart. It was an essential extension of his vision of Welsh greatness which links him directly to the Elizabethan

Dr. John Dee. In contemplating the connection between these two extraordinary men we may almost witness the uncanny spectacle of two magicians nodding at each other across the centuries. Dr. John Dee consciously played the role of a Protestant Merlin at the court of the Virgin Queen who also contrived to be a female version of King Arthur. As an act of deliberate policy, and probably in good faith, he started the paper boat of the legend of Madoc on its journey down the river of time. It was then inevitable that the thing should have been picked up and refurbished by a Taliesin waiting further down the bank exactly for this purpose. If this seems far-fetched, it is nothing to the connections between the two men that are being uncovered by recent scholarship. Iolo's frenetic researches into the druids had brought him into contact with the teachings of occult philosophy and the doctrines of the Jewish Cabala. This was precisely the field of speculation which sent the Elizabethan magus on his journey to the court of the King of Bohemia. At many points we become conscious of Iolo picking up signals rather like a druidic radio-telescope from some region of the summer stars already occupied by a John Dee now released from his terrestrial disappointments to enjoy an infinity of Merlinesque experiments.

There can be no question of the elective affinity that Iolo Morganwg felt towards the figure of Taliesin. He went to great trouble to make the founder of the poetic tradition completely at home in South-East Wales, forging a series of manuscripts giving him deep roots and a pedigree in Gwent. It therefore comes as no surprise that Iolo named his first-born Taliesin. He himself was in the debtor's prison in Cardiff at the time, but when he turns to the business of poetry, his unquenchable spirit revives. He is able to write to his friend and admirer William Owen (later to become the industrious if misguided lexicographer William Owen Pughe), a simple and upright North Walian, who later most appropriately christened his first-born Aneurin and who never had any inkling of what Iolo was really up to: 'I hope my Taliesin will live to be the Editor and Translator of the works of his ancient namesake . . . There will be a dawning of a New Age in Welsh Learning and it will be known to posterity as "The Age of Taliesin".'

1792 which saw the birth of *Gorsedd y Beirdd* was also a peak year for Madoc fever in Wales. William Jones, an antiquarian and country doctor who had cured himself of scrofula, circulated an address at an eisteddfod in Llanrwst declaring that the Welsh-speaking Indians descended from the followers of Prince Madoc who had discovered America in 1170, had been contacted beyond the wide Missouri. They lived there as a free and distinct people who had preserved their language and ancient liberties 'and some trace of their religion to this very day'. This Jones was an individualist and a strange mixture of eighteenth-century characteristics. He modelled himself on Voltaire, disliked Englishmen, Methodists, and Sir Watkin Williams Wynn. At the same time he was a zealous Anglican. If a man like William Jones believed in the Welsh Red Indians they just had to be there.

For a romantic like Iolo, however, there was a Messianic content in the whole notion. The existence of a tribe of Welsh Indians descended from Prince Madoc and his followers would supply the keystone to the soaring arch of his vision of the world. His Welsh Red Indians would be the noblest of all the noble savages, since they retained untainted the secrets of the mother tongue and even that crystal clear gospel that the Elizabethan humanists had insisted was the true inheritance of the aboriginal British. When this lost tribe was discovered, the wheel of history would have come full circle; mysteries long hidden would be made plain; the endurance of the centuries, the endless sufferings and disappointments would at last be justified and rectified, and a new era in the history of oppressed peoples and of all mankind would begin.

> I thither fly with anxious haste,
> Will brave all danger of the waste,
> Range tangled woods about:
> Pierce every corner like the wind
> Till Death forbids, or surely find
> My long-lost brethren out!

The Bard of Glamorgan was moved to indite in English numbers and when he did so, it was in a streamlined version of Thomas Gray's 'The Bard': remembering his friendship with Ieuan Fardd, this was not wholly inappropriate.

> Boast Cambria, boast thy sceptred Lord
> 'Twas He, thy Madoc, first explored
> What bounds the Atlantic tide.
> He from the tumults of a Crown
> Sought shelter in a World 'unknown'
> With Heav'n his only guide . . .

News of the Madocians took different Welshmen in different ways. The desire to prove their existence became a curious rallying point for an upsurge of national feeling that spread right across all barriers of creed and class. When the liberal Baptist Morgan John Rhys, who distributed Protestant Bibles in revolutionary Paris, launched a new magazine, *Cylchgrawn Cymraeg*, he declared that all the proceeds would be devoted towards an expedition to discover the *Madogwys*. Even in those days there must have been an air of unreality about the promise. A magazine that was a mirror of all the advanced ideas in Wales at that time – political freedom, anti-slavery, druids, education, missionary zeal, more and better eisteddfodau – would hardly be likely to make enough profit to finance a day-trip in a paddle-steamer. Nevertheless when the time came Morgan John Rhys himself emigrated to the New World, preached to the armies of the Republic on the banks of the Ohio, defended Indian rights, and thundered against slavery in the streets of Savannah.

Iolo was determined to go. He went into training for the arduous journey and took to sleeping out of doors under the hedgerows of his native Glamorgan. He entered into an arrangement with a young North Wales Methodist called John Evans from Waenfawr in Caernarfon-shire. Each would make his own way to Baltimore where they would meet and enjoy the benevolent hospitality of Welsh Americans before setting out on the great journey. Iolo was forty-six. He suffered from asthma and was in the habit of taking laudanum. John Evans was twenty-two and one of his brothers was already dying of tuberculosis. His family were pioneer Methodists and noted for their piety. His initial motivation was simple enough. As a Methodist exhorter he could not bear to think of his long-lost brethren across the ocean bereft of the privilege of William Morgan's Bible and the knowledge of the great revival encapsulated in such treasures as the hymns of Williams Pantycelyn. The spirit of missionary zeal abroad at that time was channelled in Evans's case into an acute sense of personal destiny. He approached the Rev. Thomas Charles of Bala who had taken over the leadership of the Welsh Calvinistic Methodists after the death of William Williams, and he was given encouragement and financial support. He moved with some speed, and by late October 1792 he was in Baltimore.

Iolo never joined him. It would be unfair to say of him, as has been said about so many of his compatriots, that the word was an adequate substitute for the deed; or to draw on the alternative scenario that the wily South Walian stayed home while the innocent 'Northyn' went plunging on into a wilderness of disaster. Iolo's outdoor training had brought on lumbago to add to all his other ailments. His Jacobin sympathies were getting him into trouble and he had a growing family to support. In any case they would have been an ill-assorted pair. Propelled by his irresistible sense of destiny, the young Evans marched westwards into a series of incredible adventures that landed him in a Spanish prison in St. Louis before he made his epic journey of 2,000 miles to reach the Mandan villages in the headwaters of the Missouri river. This was a difficult and dangerous journey through territory dominated by hostile tribes. The Mandans were reckoned to be the most likely candidates for Welsh descent among the Indian tribes. They lived in earth lodges, practised agriculture, and were reputed to have fairer skin and blue eyes. The would-be missionary from Waenfawr was transformed by his experiences into a professional explorer. He was received by the Mandan as the accredited representa-tive of the king of Spain. From them he learned much more of the course of the rivers and the routes to the great mountains. He understood that the distance across the Rockies was far greater than any European had previously imagined. He spent a terrible winter in the Mandan villages and survived an assassination attempt by French-Canadian fur traders who had come in from the north. His journal is a vivid account of the first contacts of three powers, Spain, the United States, and Great Britain, with the Indian tribes who had hitherto escaped their menacing attentions. His greatest disappointment must have been the realisation that the Mandans had no Welsh connections. At the end of a long letter which he wrote from St. Louis in July 1797 to his friend Dr. Samuel Jones in Philadelphia comes the verdict. 'Thus having explored and charted the Missurie for 1,000 miles and by my Communications with the Indians this side of the Pacific Ocean from 35 to 49 Degrees of Latitude, I am able to inform you that there is no such People as the Welsh Indians.'

Evans was asked by the Spanish governor to lead a new expedition to discover the best land route to the Pacific coast. But time was running out for both the Spanish empire and the young explorer in North America. The legend survived them both. John Evans died of fever and drink in New Orleans at the age of twenty-eight. Louisiana fell into the hands of Napoleon who sold it to Thomas Jefferson. But the ghosts of Merlin, Taliesin, and Madoc were still hovering over the expansion of an empire. Jefferson, whose ancestors like John Evans himself came from the shadow of Snowdon, obtained from Congress a grant of 2,500 dollars for an expedition led by Meriwether Lewis, his private secretary, also of Welsh extraction, and Captain William Clark. The president took a personal interest in providing Lewis with all the information available. In January 1804 before the expedition started he wrote to Lewis:

> In my letter of the 13th inst. I enclosed you a map of a Mr. Evans, a Welshman, employed by the Spanish government for that purpose, but whose original object I believe had been to go in search of the Welsh Indians said to be up the Missouri. On this subject a Mr. Rees of the same nation established in the Western part of Pennsylvania will write to you.

The Mr. Rees in question was none other than Morgan John Rhys who was now busy building his Beulah, his own Welsh City of Brotherly Love, in the Allegheny forest. Whatever Morgan John wrote to Meriwether Lewis has not been preserved. But it was a combination of John Evans's map and the guiding hand of an Indian woman, Sakakawea, that saved the expedition from failure and made the continental empire of the United States, Jefferson's dream – something which at one time, like the wording of the Declaration of Independence, had existed in his head only – an historical reality.

Even at that dawn in which it was bliss to be alive, the executive powers available to a humble stone-mason in the Vale of Glamorgan were microscopic compared to those of the president of the United States. Iolo could shape stones and words but little more. Considering his station in life, his dangerous opinions and nocturnal forgeries, it comes as something of a surprise to learn how much practical influence he did in fact exercise during his lifetime. He was acquainted with the leading Unitarians of his time and he was among the company who founded the *Cymdeithas y Dwyfundodiaid* (lit. Society of the One-Godists) in South Wales in 1802. He was the author of the *Rules and Regulations* published in the following year. It is plain that the Unitarians, who were noted for their rational turn of mind, had every confidence in Iolo's legislative and philosophical powers and intellectual integrity. This small man and this tiny denomination would continue to have an influence in Wales and in the world out of all proportion to their size.

15 Prince of the Pulpit

In 1811 the Welsh Calvinistic Methodists somewhat reluctantly registered themselves as a nonconformist denomination. Their position inside the Church of England had become untenable. They were running out of curates, even in South Wales. In the North there had never been many and by 1811 it was the North that was the stronghold of Calvinistic Methodism. This transformation in itself was a repetition of one of the abiding themes of Welsh history. Calvinistic Methodism was born in the South. Every single one of the leaders of the revival came from the South. But in the second phase of consolidation and entrenchment the leadership moved to the North among men of conspicuously conservative temperament. 1811 was also the date of the second official census in Great Britain. The population 'explosion' was on its way and the Methodist leadership like everyone else felt the tremor of the machine age beginning to disturb the ground under their feet. But this was not their immediate problem. In 1811 Napoleon Bonaparte was at the height of his power. He had placed his relatives on various European thrones and it looked to the world as though he had succeeded in establishing a permanent dynasty. A greater British patriotism flourished as it had not done since the days of the Spanish Armada. Once again it was the wooden walls of England that protected all the inhabitants of these islands from the unspeakable horrors and unknown terrors across the sea. Once again it was the English-speaking Protestants versus wicked Catholic foreign powers and once again there were two weak points in the islands' immutable defences: the subversive separatism of the Catholic Irish now made more virulent by dangerous viruses from France; even worse, the enemy within, Republican radicals still mouthing the French and American inspired notions of the Rights of Man.

Iolo Morganwg took refuge in his own eccentricities. In spite of his fiery words and deeply held republican convictions, he was never the man to mount the barricades. As the war progressed, like Southey, Coleridge, Wordsworth and the rest who executed the great somersault from unquestioning idealism to iron-clad conservatism, Iolo was able to oblige with a patriotic poem or two when the need arose. As long as the sea route was open the more extreme radicals like Morgan John Rhys could escape to America. But that route was closed by the sea war; and by 1812 the United States was at war with England.

Much to their horror, the Calvinistic Methodists found themselves a suspect organisation. On the local level those paragons of loyalty, the parson and the squire, were able to point at the *seiat* as a secret meeting. Nobody could know outside the membership what went on, and this meant that they were essentially subversive. The Methodist leadership was pushed further along the road to nonconformity by such accusations. They had to register their conventicles in order to gain what protection the law could afford. In addition to such practical measures they had to convince the authorities that their apparent lack of interest in politics and preoccupation with the condition of their own souls did not mean that they were anything less than devotedly loyal subjects to the English crown. The business of West Wales in particular would continue to be turning out the ideal infantry man for the British army, five-foot-four tall, stoical, able to put up with anything and live on nothing, devoted to his comrades and a conveniently small target. It is arguable that the descendants of the megalith builders would have been more at home building chapels than empires. Economic necessity recruited them to the larger task and once they were about it, habits of obedience and endurance inculcated by Calvinist theology served their masters well.

It was not altogether a loyalty reflex that made the Calvinistic Methodist leadership move closer to High Calvinism. The new century saw the incursion of Arminian Wesleyan poachers into their territory and but for the short-sightedness of the English Methodist Conference and the traditional lack of insight into Welsh conditions, they would have penetrated much further than they did. When the war was won, and the field of conflict was transferred from the playing fields of Eton and Waterloo to the growing centres of industry, the influence of Calvinistic Methodism was on the side of dutiful submission to those set in authority. If the road to heaven lay through an earthly vale of tears, there was still the prospect of consolation in eternity.

The vital relationship between evangelical religion and industrial capitalism has to bear much of the responsibility for the astonishing transformation from an old Wales of sleepy squires and frustrated curates to that of an aggressively nonconformist people. It is almost as if the conversion of souls provided the original pattern for business expansion. A business which fails to find new markets behaves like a denomination which fails to make an adequate impression on a growing population. Denominations behave like rival firms adapting their product to the rigorous processes of free market competition. It can be argued that this process helped to regiment the deracinated work force as it flowed in to the new industrial centres and made the people more open to the exploitation of industrialists. But it also offered them minimal protection even in the early stages and consolation which came from its own source of spiritual capital.

The original spiritual capital of Welsh nonconformity was created by the founding fathers in the pre-industrial stage of the movement's development. It was their first-hand experience of the love of God and the inexpressible sense of relief that came with conversion and the sense of salvation, that provided the pioneers with a reservoir of strength they needed to effect the change in society that was there for everyone to see. Again it is the element of mystery in the process which forces an historian to resort to metaphor in order to account for what went on. The phrase 'Great Awakening' conveniently covers social, economic and religious change; but it is the awakening rooted in the experience of one individual which is most difficult to explain. A late example of this would be the strange story of Ann Griffiths.

This lively girl spent all her short life on a hill farm in Montgomeryshire. She was fond of the old way of life and devoted to dancing and singing until she heard a dry enough sermon by an ageing nonconformist preacher in the local market town. She experienced conversion and took instruction in theology from a Methodist exhorter. She began to compose sacred poems in her head as she went about her daily tasks and recite them to her friend and companion Ruth Evans who memorised them and later married the same Methodist exhorter who wrote them down. Ann herself married a local farmer and died in childbirth at the age of twenty-nine, leaving behind only a few letters to friends, which are themselves regarded as classics of Welsh religious prose.

> I am reverently ashamed and I rejoice in astonishment to think that He who has to lower himself even to look at things in heaven, has yet given Himself as an object of love to so poor a creature as myself . . . It amazes me to think who it was on the cross . . . My mind drowns in too much astonishment to be able to say anything more.

Her hymns are based on a strong intellectual understanding of Calvinist theology and particularly the doctrine of the sovereignty of God and the debt of homage she owes and longs to pay. The language she uses belongs to the Welsh of the Bible and the Book of Common Prayer and the period of intense preoccupation with religious experience. In some ways it is familiar and yet in others it lies far away across the barriers of secular education. It is the strength of her poetic utterance that is capable of transfixing the modern reader with a shaft of light that comes through her voice direct from an altogether different level of existence.

> O my soul behold the place where the King of Kings, the author of peace lay still, creation moving in him, and He dead in the grave . . .

She possessed a remarkable ability to express in poetry her experimental understanding of the depth of truth of a particular doctrine. A translation can only give a suggestion of the paradox inherent in the process.

> My grieving soul, when it remembers the payment, leaps into joy; sees the law honourable and the great transgressors against it set free; putting the Author of life to death and burying the great Resurrection; leading in eternal peace between the heaven of heaven and the humble earth.

The social historian is confined to dealing with events in time and space. He has no means of quantifying spiritual experiences. Nevertheless he is bound to recognise that such things exist and to take them into account and consider their influence on the course of events. The phenomenon of an Ann Griffiths occurring on a remote but beautiful hillside in Montgomeryshire can be accepted as a typical fruit of the first phase of the great religious awakening in Wales. Ann lived and died in a self-sufficient pre-industrial context. She was an exact contemporary of Jane Austen. Authorities on Christian mysticism compare her to St. Teresa of Avila and Julian of Norwich. To succeeding generations of Methodists, experiences like hers were something infinitely precious that somehow had to be preserved through a period of unprecedented economic and social change, and distributed like sacramental wafers among an ever increasing membership. There is an account of Thomas Charles, the man who led the Calvinistic Methodists out of the Church of England in 1811, visiting Ann in her home and coming away speechless with fear and excitement. Charles was a great scholar and administrator and a strong link between two phases of Methodist development. His rôle was to be a Moses among his people. Having somewhat reluctantly led them out of their Egyptian captivity, his *Scriptural Dictionary* became the essential companion volume to the Bible in even the poorest home; and it was his model of the Sunday School that replaced the circulating schools of Griffith Jones and became an integral part of the nonconformist way of life. It was Thomas Charles more than anyone else who composed what amounted to the tablets of the law for the guidance of the growing church and generations to come. He and his collaborators provided the new denomination with a complete apparatus of church life from a Confession of Faith to a Sunday School rule book and a handbook for teaching

(a)

(b)   *The National Museum of Wales*   (c)

The Herbert family, a Tudor success story. *(a)* William Herbert, created Earl of Pembroke by Edward VI in 1551, was grandson of the patron of Guto'r Glyn, and himself patron of Sir John Prys of Brecon, pioneer of Welsh historiography and printing. The 1st Earl was more at home speaking Welsh than English. *(b)* Henry, 2nd Earl, and one of the richest peers in the kingdom, also took pleasure in being acclaimed 'the eye of all Wales' for his patronage of Welsh poets. *(c)* William, the 3rd Earl, was Shakespeare's patron.

The Bard, by John Martin. After his conquest of Wales, Edward I was reputed to have ordered the massacre of all the bards. In the mid-eighteenth-century vogue for Celtic antiquities the legend inspired Gray's ode of the same title, and this in turn fired the romantic imagination of many English artists.

(a)

(b)

(c)

National Museum of American Art

The Welsh Red Indians. *(a)* One of the Mandan villages of the headwaters of the Missouri visited 1796-7 by John Evans in his quest for the lost descendants of Madoc. Evans eventually admitted the Mandans had no Welsh connections, but the myth lived on, supported by the American painter George Catlin, who produced these pictures in 1832. *(b)* Mint, a twelve-year-old girl whose albino-streaked hair Catlin saw as evidence of Madoc's ancestry. *(c)* Four Bears, a Mandan chief who, like Gray's bard, cursed the invader and hurled himself off a cliff when his people were wiped out by the white man's smallpox.

(a)

(b)

(c)

The Methodist Revival. *(a)* William Williams Pantycelyn and *(b)* Daniel Rowland. These portraits gained wide circulation as unofficial icons and Williams Pantycelyn's can still be found in Calvinistic Methodist chapel vestries and homes. *(c)* Trevecca, where Hywel Harris established his religious 'family'.

(a)

(b)

The exploitation of Wales's mineral wealth reawakened a sense of nationhood.
(a) Penrhyn slate quarries in 1852. The ant-like quarrymen are dwarfed by the
towering faces. (b) The iron works of Dowlais in 1840.

The stern statue of Sir Hugh Owen seems to turn away in utilitarian abhorrence from this assembly of the numerous heirs of Old Iolo. Members of the Gorsedd (the Bards of the Isle of Britain) pose for the camera at the Caernarfon eisteddfod of 1893.

(a)   *Keystone Press*

(b)   *The National Library of Wales*   *(c)*   *Photograph: Ron Davies*

Lloyd George, *(a)* found no difficulty in adapting nineteenth-century pulpit oratory to the new medium of broadcasting. *(b)* Mabon, William Abraham (1842-1922), first President of the South Wales Miners' Federation. *(c)* Gwenallt, David Gwenallt Jones (1899-1968). A Marxist in his youth, he became an outstanding Christian poet. He is seated here in the Shanghai Chair which he won at the Swansea eisteddfod in 1926.

(a)

The National Library of Wales

(b)

BBC Hulton Picture Library

(a) Lewis Valentine, Saunders Lewis and D. J. Williams, photographed on their way to the magistrate's court in Pwllheli in 1936 after informing the police they had burnt the RAF installations at Penyberth. *(b)* Aneurin Bevan in 1942, defending the freedom of the press before an audience of 3,000.

Welsh spelling. Charles died in 1814 and the leadership passed to a gaunt individual of imposing presence who is usually referred to as the greatest of Welsh preachers, and a prince of the pulpit, John Elias o Fôn, John Elias of Anglesey.

Ann's chosen means of communication was poetry spoken to her confidante and very often the only other person in the house. A link had to be forged between the miracle of poetry and a much wider means of communication to be pressed into the service of an urgent mission in a rapidly changing society. The obvious answer was the power of preaching, and in the case of John Elias the power of dramatic preaching. The *seiat* continued to exist and remained a vital organ of social discipline in the increasingly complex life that revolved around the chapel. The hymns of Pantycelyn and Ann Griffiths and all the others were sung with increasing fervour and volume. In the industrial areas, the chapel choir developed as an essential expression of communal experience and solidarity. But the centrepiece of chapel life was the sermon. Every denomination boasted of its great preachers and the architectural prominence of the pulpit was a symbol of the accepted rôle of the preacher as the leader of the people.

It is fair to judge any national awakening by the type of personality that it produces. The most easily recognisable type to emerge in nineteenth-century Wales has to be the great popular preacher and we are therefore obliged to accept him as the first fruit of the refurbished if not entirely new Welsh identity. John Elias was the kind of culture hero of whom Staffordshire pottery statuettes were widely sold during his lifetime. Recollections of his amazing prowess continued to be written half a century after his death. Because of the strength of his convictions, the power of his oratory, based on remorseless reasoning steeped in minute knowledge of the scriptures, and an acting ability reputed to put him on a par with Edmund Kean, John Elias exercised a kind of authority over the multitude in some ways more far-reaching than that of a twentieth-century dictator. His eloquence was in direct competition with the increasing roar of machinery, as if the orator from his balcony was attempting to turn back the tide of traffic by the lonely gesture of isolated human speech. Evangelical religion was challenging the super-human might, the gigantic power, of an industrial machine for the right to control the destiny of a people and the shaping of their character. A preacher like Elias was also a social engineer of the kind whose services would still be welcome to any society in the throes of transition.

With his passion for purity and temperance he took the easy-going social habits of the natives of Anglesey, for example, and transformed them from being the Welsh equivalent of the cheerful poteen makers of Connemara into convincing imitations of New England Puritans, neatly ranged in pews rented a year in advance. But no one engaged in social reform could afford to belittle his achievement. In Dr. Owen Thomas's biography of another great preacher, John Jones, Talysarn, published in 1874, there is an extraordinarily vivid account of John Elias's method in dealing with drunkenness at a mass meeting in Holyhead in 1824. The young Owen Thomas was present as a boy of twelve, and fifty years later, he is able to give a detailed account of the occasion. Elias makes his first appeal based on the proposition that the Welsh Calvinistic Methodists have no defence against their enemies except their good name. Then he stretches forth his arm and proceeds to conduct an auction. He will sell the drunken element to absolutely any body or power that will be prepared to take them. But no one wants them. Not the Anglicans, nor the Congregationalists, nor the Baptists; every one of the denominations has excellent doctrinal reasons for not accepting them.

> Then, stretching his hand out as though he were holding them in it, and casting a glance over the crowd, he shouted at the very highest volume of his voice, 'Who will take them? Who will take them? Who will take them?' Then in an instant his whole nature was convulsed; his eyes flashed and he made a most odd movement; he turned his face towards his left, and in a rather low voice and yet distinct enough for the whole congregation to hear, he said, 'I rather thought I heard the Devil at my elbow saying, "Knock them down to me; I will take them." '

By this time the vast crowd was suffering from an unbearable emotional tension. The preacher's awe-inspiring penetrating eyes were burning in his pock-marked face as he searched the congregation with his gaze and held his pause longer than any but the greatest actors can afford to do.

> And then he turned again to his left and pointing with his right forefinger at his left elbow, he moved it up and down, once, twice, thrice, and then shouted with tremendous force until his voice echoed through the town, 'I was going to say, Satan, that you could have them: but . . .' and he raised his eyes towards heaven and with a victorious, yet tender voice, he cried, 'I hear Jesus shouting, "I will take them; I will take them; to wash them of their filth, to sober them in their drunkenness; to purify them of all their uncleanness in my own blood." '

John Elias was an autocrat. When Thomas Jones of Denbigh died in 1820 there was no one with enough authority left to restrain the absolutist temperament of a man who by that time was universally acknowledged as Wales's greatest preacher. After 1820 even the most reactionary government would have no cause to imagine any subversive trend among the Welsh Calvinistic Methodists. Historians have rightly pointed out that it was the influence of John Elias above all others that made his new denomination politically Tory. A man of such conservative temperament could behave on occasion like a nonconformist Bourbon in his efforts to turn back the tide of inevitable change. To the dismay of his admirers he even went so far in accepting the aristocratic embrace as to marry as his second wife the widow of a baronet. But since she herself had been a beauty of humble origin the result was in effect a bourgeois compromise that set the North Wales Calvinistic Methodists on a middle-class course, from which they have not deviated to this day.

This was not a popular move. Many of the membership didn't like it and found the courage to say so. But John Elias's grip was so tight that, like all his other unpopular policies, they were obliged to accept it or suffer excommunication. It was not for nothing that he was dubbed 'the Pope from Anglesey'. He demanded complete ideological obedience and exercised his influence through all the assemblies of the organisation. Many of the other denominations were to benefit from the talents of young preachers who could no longer bear the tyranny of John Elias. He set his face against so many of the forces of change that even he came to realise in his old age that he was fighting a losing battle.

> The spirit and attitude of the old Methodists is slowly disappearing from our Body. There are people coming up in our midst who love the poorest features of other denominations and strive to introduce them among us. There are those who desire to follow 'The Spirit of the Age' and to swim in the stream of popular opinion: and are even prepared to say, as the atheists of this country are already saying, 'that the voice of the people is the Voice of God'. But it is in his revealed word alone that the Voice of God resides.

In spite of his evident shortcomings, there was no denying John Elias's greatness. He set such a pace that all the other denominations were obliged to accept the basic characteristics of his development of Methodism if they had any ambition to stay in the race for popular support. It became obligatory for each one of them to have its own brand of pulpit giant: Christmas Evans among the Baptists, Williams o'r Wern with the Congregationalists. Each denomination cherished its own periodicals and magazines. When theological controversy broke out as it frequently did, each sect needed to have its own slant on the subject. The vitality of a certain kind of religious life was so great and it responded so swiftly to all the economic and social changes that it becomes almost possible to trace a direct correlation between the incidence of religious revivals and bursts of expansion or contraction in the economy. Certainly if a revival did not occur more or less in a seven year cycle, religious leaders were prepared to get worried and go out of their way to stoke up the fires, again in the manner of industrial furnaces, as if the end of the world was at hand. A revival became the only satisfactory sign of productivity, and it must be significant that as the century wore on, Welsh revivals tended more and more to originate in America.

John Elias nourished a deep suspicion of secular education, which was shared by many of the leaders of early nineteenth-century Welsh nonconformity. It smacked of heretical dissenting academies, of Jacobin atheism and American free-thinking. Whatever it was and wherever it came from, it felt alien to the unique spirit of revelation enshrined in Methodist and revivalist world views. Their attitude is perhaps more understandable now than at any time during the century and a half that has passed since their fervid reign came to an end. We no longer cherish the enthusiasm for education as a means of salvation, or as a guide map to the one far off divine event towards which late Victorian Wales felt itself to be travelling. The educational system has long since settled down into its well-meaning ancillary position in the all-powerful economic process. John Elias was no fool. When he took so much exception to the bright young Lewis Edwards registering as a student in London University, he was not being a comical obscurantist, standing in the way of the onward march of the noble army of Welsh B.A.'s. He knew that the power shift was about to take place, and that under the leadership of men like Lewis Edwards the sacred flame would be stolen from the altar of Methodism and be rekindled in the form of a utilitarian gas-jet in some infidel college classroom. Lewis Edwards became the Principal of Bala Theological College, and the editor of the best quarterly magazine in the Welsh language, *Y Traethodydd* (The Essayist) which happily is still with us. But the deeper fears of John Elias were fulfilled in 1872 when Lewis's son Thomas Charles Edwards became the first Principal of the University College of Wales, an essentially utilitarian institution, occupying a mock Gothic building in Aberystwyth originally intended as a railway hotel.

In spite of all the evidence amassing in front of his eyes, John Elias refused to believe in Progress. In his view, material changes were no kind of progress at all. All of the most important events in history had already taken place. The Bible was the supreme repository of wisdom and all the most important knowledge. The business of a religious organisation was to see to it that the seething multitudes should not escape the benefits of the arrangement for their salvation which had been made before the foundation of the world. There is a grim nobility reminiscent of King Lear in the way in which the old preacher stood up and shook his fist at the gathering storm.

16 Escape Routes

In the summer of 1818 a man called Edward Thomas walked from Merthyr Tydfil to the parish of Llangynyw in Montgomeryshire. He had a distressing task to perform. He had been tenant of a thirty-seven acre smallholding in the parish for seventeen years. There he and his wife had brought up a family of seven children until the agricultural depression after the Napoleonic wars forced them to leave and make their way to Merthyr to look for work. The landlord, the estate of Lord Powys, of Powys Castle, had made a 'distress' on Thomas's effects to recover arrears of rent before turning him out of possession. It was now harvest time and Thomas's last duty was to cut the corn, leave the straw on the ground and share the grain equally with the new tenant, a man called Davies. To carry out this work he carried with him his reaping hook, the stout sickle with which he had struggled to manage the crops of a sequence of wet harvests, which had contributed to his misfortunes. We can only imagine how much he brooded as he carried out the back-breaking task. He was in sight of his boyhood home and acutely aware of the disgrace attached to his situation. Davies came down to the field. A quarrel broke out which turned into a fight. A blow from the sickle cut through Davies's spine and he bled to death on the spot. Thomas was sentenced to a year's imprisonment for manslaughter. Almost at once the affray became the subject of an elaborate local legend. Garbled accounts appeared in Welsh and English newspapers. The murderer was said to have drowned himself in one version and to have fled to Merthyr in another. It circulated widely in rural Wales because it seemed to exemplify so vividly the terrible fate that could befall even the most pious and well-behaved chapel-going man when struck down by the hammer-blows of economic misfortune. Edward Thomas was the younger brother of the hymn writer Ann Griffiths.

The hillside smallholding had become the heartland of Welsh consciousness. From 1733 to 1832 ninety-seven Enclosure Acts relating to Wales were passed through a Parliament composed of landowners, which completely undermined those customs and practices of centuries which had literally provided the margin that allowed the peasant to make both ends meet. It was on the uplands that he had free grazing rights and unrestricted access to the benefits of cutting wood and turf. It was commonly believed that a young man who could erect a new hut within one night would have a legal right thereafter to the land that he was using. Enclosure threatened the way of life of an aboriginal population who were peaceable from age-old habit as well as 'God-fearing'; who were the privileged custodians of what poets like David Jones and John Cowper Powys would call 'deposits', the inherited wisdom of the ages reflected in the relationship between the humblest folk and the earth which sustained them. The peasants were perfectly aware of what was going on, and had been for a long time. The popular poetry of Glamorgan for example shows how acute their perceptions were. But they were scattered and helpless. They had no political power. The landlords became richer and more powerful and the landless peasantry became a reservoir of manpower ripe for exploitation by thrusting industrialists, particularly the ironmasters from England who established themselves on the bleak uplands of Gwent and Glamorgan.

In addition to their defenceless economic position, the monoglot Welsh were aware of being manipulated by an alien legal system and its devious operators in a language they did not understand. This was a frequent theme in the popular *Interludes* by the poet Twm o'r Nant and in the pamphlets of Jac Glangors, and Thomas Roberts, Llwynrhudol. They knew well enough that political power in a distant parliament was literally taking away from under their feet ground that had belonged to their ancestors since time immemorial. Unlike the Chartists in England later on in the nineteenth century they did not possess that assured half-knowledge that allowed them to speak of their ancient constitution or inalienable rights. The new religion to which they had responded so feelingly taught them the necessity of obedience to those set in authority over them. Their complaints were muted as a changing system prised open the floodgates of population reservoirs that began on that contour line where the water reservoirs now lie. With the ease of a neatly tapped raw material the surplus children of the landless peasantry and desperate smallholders flowed into the centres of economic activity.

These were years of acute rural distress. Any form of escape from the prison of poverty could become a picaresque adventure. The popular literature of the Welsh accounts of such escapes gave a particular form to the kind of memoir that developed into the novel. For example, in that remote parish where Ann Griffiths and her unfortunate brother lived, from a little farm across the fields to the scene of the manslaughter, John Davies, a weaver's son, managed to scrape together three months schooling for himself and then offered his services to Thomas Charles for work in the mission field. He reached Tahiti in July 1801 and continued for some time to correspond with Ann's family. John Davies died in the South Seas in 1855 having created a grammar and dictionary of the native language and having translated into it the New Testament, *Pilgrim's Progress*, and a whole range of religious works. His letters to John Hughes, Pontrobert, Ann's instructor in theology, were published in the denominational press. His life story was typical of the material featured in the ever-increasing output of Welsh magazines to be read avidly by candlelight in cottages and terrace houses all over Wales.

The autobiography of ap Vychan (Robert Thomas 1808–90) offers a grim picture of his parents' poverty during the depression after the Napoleonic wars. He was the third born of a family of ten. His father was a farm labourer who also wrote hymns and contrived to give his children the rudiments of education including the rules of Welsh prosody. When the father fell ill, the mother was forced to apply for poor relief. The Poor Law overseer took away the bed as the one thing of sufficient value in the house and the sick man was laid on straw. At the age of nine, Robert found work as a shepherd's boy and at twenty he set out for Dowlais, the Welsh Eldorado. But his mind was set on becoming a minister, and when he had saved a little money he moved to Oswestry to perfect his English. As befitted a hero in one more pattern of folklore, he eventually achieved his goal. He won eisteddfod chairs and became a professor of theology.

This could well have been the story of Dic Penderyn (Richard Lewis 1807/8–31). He too moved from a rural background in the Vale of Glamorgan to work as a collier in Merthyr. His sister was married to Morgan Howells, a rising star of the Methodist pulpit in Monmouthshire, famous throughout Wales for his imaginative preaching and fiery delivery. It has never been made clear how Dic became involved in the protest movement that came into being in Merthyr. Driven to desperation by the ruthless exploitation they were obliged to suffer, the workers, led by the redoubtable Lewsyn yr Heliwr (the Hunter) (Lewis Lewis 1793–?), attacked and destroyed the buildings in which the records of their Poor Law debts were kept. The whole episode can be seen both as a popular rising against the oppressive instruments of an alien government and the first stirrings of a new working class suddenly conscious of the possibilities of power. It only needed the rudiments of organisation to bring down the old order, achieve freedom for the people and the restoration of their dignity.

Merthyr was the largest town in Wales. It was also making rapid strides towards becoming the cultural and political capital of the Welsh people. Lewsyn yr Heliwr obviously had charisma and incipient military genius. The government paid him the compliment usually reserved for leaders of national insurrection. They sent in the Argyll and Sutherland Highlanders from the north (i.e. Brecon Barracks), the

Glamorgan Yeomanry from the south, cavalry from the west. From Beaufort to Nantyglo all work stopped. The red flag was raised and the workers held the town for four days. It took a thousand regular soldiers to recover it. More than 5,000 of the inhabitants fled the town. Lewsyn and Dic Penderyn were among the captured. They were sentenced to death, but Lewsyn's sentence was commuted to transportation.

The trial of Dic Penderyn became a *cause célèbre*. Nonconformist leaders organised petitions on his behalf. A weighty deputation travelled to London to wait on Lords Melbourne and Brougham. There was some delay and much doubt about the evidence. But in the end the Home Secretary refused to relent. The day Dic was hanged all the shops in Cardiff closed. Four ministers accompanied him to the place of execution in Cardiff Gaol. A great multitude joined the funeral procession through the Vale of Glamorgan. He was buried in St. Mary's churchyard Aberafan and it was his brother-in-law, the Methodist Morgan Howells, who gave an emotional funeral oration outside the churchyard wall. Dic Penderyn has been called Wales's first working-class martyr. He had died not so much for Wales or the working class as for that desirable quality of innocence which the pietistic strain in revivalist nonconformity had placed among the highest Welsh virtues. It seems certain that he was the victim of injustice, hanged for a crime he had not committed. In 1874 the Rev. Evan Evans in far away Ohio reported a deathbed confession made to him by an immigrant, who declared himself to be the man who had wounded the Scottish soldier and thereby committed the crime for which Dic had been hanged. This Rev. Evan Evans was highly regarded both as an author and translator. He was considered one of the experts in the Welsh press on both sides of the Atlantic on the problems of Welsh emigration and the need to preserve a network of Welsh institutions world-wide wherever Welsh people might settle. Evans's son, Beriah Gwynfe Evans, a schoolmaster in Wales at the time of the deathbed confession in America, became secretary of *Cymru Fydd** and one of David Lloyd George's right-hand men in the field of Welsh journalism. He was a playwright and his best known play *Owain Glyndŵr* was presented in a revised version at Caernarfon as part of the celebrations of the Investiture of the Prince of Wales, stage-managed by the Chancellor of the Exchequer, the Rt. Hon. David Lloyd George, in 1911.

There is no record that Beriah Gwynfe Evans ever contemplated writing a play about Dic Penderyn; although there is no doubt he would have done so had his hero Lloyd George required it. His *Rhamant Bywyd Lloyd George* (Romance of the Life of Lloyd George) appeared in both English and Welsh in the U.S.A. in 1916. It took the Depression to restore the legend of Dic Penderyn to a prominent place in Welsh

* *Cymru Fydd* (lit. the Wales that is to be), the Home Rule movement of the last two decades of the nineteenth century in which Lloyd George played a leading role.

consciousness. The grim reality of those years brought urgency to the business of re-examining the origin of working-class movements. After the second world war Dic's story provided the inspiration for Gwyn Thomas's novel *All Things Betray Thee* (1947) and his play *Jackie the Jumper* (1962). 'I tried to interpret the dreams of a people who didn't know they were asleep,' says Jackie the working-class leader who seems to resemble Lewsyn yr Heliwr much more than Dic. At the Cardiff national eisteddfod of 1978 the story was presented as a Welsh rock opera so that once again, a century and a half later, his last words reverberated through the town. '*O Arglwydd, dyma gamwedd.*' (O Lord, this is a great wrong.)

17 In the Eye of Light

The revitalised eisteddfod of the nineteenth century was Iolo Morganwg's public triumph and a fitting memorial to his genius. Of all institutions, this was the most peculiarly Welsh and for this reason alone the vicissitudes of its history can offer a most accurate record both of the condition of Wales and the condition of Welshness. Calvinistic Methodism was reasonably indigenous: but nonconformity was in origin and in essence an English concept, a pragmatic compromise within the framework of a nation state sufficiently strong to tolerate a limited degree of dissent. The Welsh were able to adopt it and adapt it to their own immediate religious and social needs. The eisteddfod, however, belonged to the Welsh and no one else and this would have been sufficient reason for it to become the conspicuous natural receptacle of the growing desire to express a national consciousness.

Men had other motives for encouraging this Cambrian phenomenon. Bishop Burgess of St. David's for instance. This learned English cleric came to Wales at the age of forty-six bent on ecclesiastical reforms that would stem the rising tide of nonconformity in the Principality. He gave particular attention to improving the quality of education of ordinands and launched a fund for building in Wales a college for the preparation of suitable candidates for Holy Orders that might equal and even surpass the dissenting academies. He found natural allies among the 'literary parsons' in his diocese who manfully carried on the literary and antiquarian tradition that had survived from the eighteenth century. He appointed the most enthusiastic of them, John Jenkins (Ifor Ceri) vicar of the parish of Kerry, south-east of Newtown in Montgomeryshire and the new vicarage Ifor Ceri built there was nicknamed Llys Ifor Hael by the circle of clerical bards in a romantic Welsh-Anglican echo of the lost splendour of Dafydd ap Gwilym's patron. For the first week of every new year it was open house 'for all who could compose an *englyn*, give voice to an air or set a harp'. In August 1818 Bishop Burgess visited Kerry and together the two men decided 'to make an effort to revive the gift and genius of poetry of the

Principality . . . by maintaining eisteddfodau in circuit in the four ancient divisions of the country'.

Conservative elements in nonconformity were particularly wary of this development. An eisteddfod movement, they felt, could be used to win back the affections of the multitude for the *hen fam* (the old mother church) at the very moment when they were turning in their hundreds to one dissenting conventicle or another. Unlike so many of his Anglo-Welsh predecessors in the eighteenth century, Burgess showed an acute awareness of the historic rhythms that had made the Welsh the awkwardly complex and self-conscious people that they were. In 1815 he had published *Tracts on the Origin and Independence of the Ancient British Church* in which he set out afresh the theory of the independent and 'protestant' Cambro-British church that had flourished among the ancient Britons and the Welsh: a repetition of the argument prepared by Bishop Davies of St. David's for Archbishop Matthew Parker in 1567. And in the autumn of 1818 in that same place of Abergwili where two and a half centuries earlier William Salesbury had worked with Richard Davies on the translation of the New Testament and the Book of Common Prayer, Bishop Burgess assembled his literary parsons to draw up a work programme for the Cambrian Society in Dyfed. This society would prepare a catalogue of all ancient Welsh manuscripts in private and public hands in Wales, in England or anywhere in the British Isles or on the continent. They would be copied by skilled hands and studied. They would as far as possible be prepared for publication. Some attention would also be given to printed books and no less a person than Iolo Morganwg, Old Iolo himself, would be employed to supervise the society's publication and to instruct promising young students in the strict metres and all the bardic arts. This was not a new programme. It was in effect a continuation of the pioneer efforts of Edward Lhuyd* and Evan Evans the curate (Ieuan Fardd), and it was a significant staging post in the halting journey of Welsh scholarship from the Renaissance to the late nineteenth-century ideal of a national library and university.

The agreeable collaboration between the English bishop and the secretive Unitarian stone-mason reached its mystic climax on an afternoon in July 1819 in the garden of the Ivy Bush Hotel in Carmarthen when the old sorcerer slipped a white ribbon over the bishop's arm and declared him to be a member of the *Gorsedd* of the Order of Druids. This could almost have been one of those quiet moments in history when a delicate and unspoken compromise lays down the direction the future should take. But there were other elements at work. The musicians for example were poised to move in.

* Edward Lhuyd (1660–1709), philologist, antiquary, botanist and geologist, Keeper of the Ashmolean Museum and the founder of modern scientific Celtic scholarship.

They had much to offer in the way of innocent entertainment to a growing audience eager for undenominational emotional release. There was choral music to develop and exploit, and grand concerts of miscellaneous but preferably sacred music soon reached large-scale proportions. These harmonised happily with the perennial impulse of the prosperous to parade rank and fashion. The upper classes would need no Welsh to listen to music and the social prestige of the eisteddfod reached dizzy heights at Beaumaris in 1832 when it came within an ace of being visited by the Princess Victoria and her mother. The inclement weather prevented the princess from being present at proceedings in Beaumaris Castle. But Sir Richard Bulkely was as quick to serve her as his ancestor Sir Richard 'the old courtier' had been to attend on Queen Elizabeth, and all the eisteddfod winners were invited to Baron Hill to be presented with their prizes by the princess herself.

Iolo's primary and secondary aims, and for that matter the good bishop's, were to find more effective expression in a series of remarkable eisteddfodau that were held in Abergavenny between 1834 and 1853. The geographical location is of some importance. The valley of the Usk is the last outpost of a lowland Celtic world, a rural Siluria, that includes West Herefordshire and the potent myth-making centre of Erging. Westward begins the climb towards the open plateau and moorlands that from the beginning of the nineteenth century provided the industrial backbone of what was in effect a new Welsh identity. Abergavenny was the natural meeting place of the old and the new. It was a market town that in times of prosperity could call on the wealth being forged in the furnaces from Merthyr to Brynmawr, and the flourishing agriculture of a fertile area stretching far into the border country. When certain leaders in the town decided to found a society 'for the wellbeing of the Welsh language' they knew they could turn easily for support on the one hand to Taliesin Williams, Iolo's first-born, the Unitarian schoolmaster of Merthyr Tydfil; and on the other to the Rev. Thomas Price, vicar of Cwmdu and Llangadog in rural Breconshire, who was known throughout Wales by his Breton-sounding bardic title, Carnhuanawc.

Somewhat in the traditional manner of Brân the Blessed this Anglican parson possessed that bridge-building capacity which has to be cherished in any society that is by nature fissiparous and contentious, given to sectarian arguments, easily divided but not so easily ruled. As a boy at Christ's College, Brecon, Price had learnt French from prisoners of war and he had assisted Theophilus Jones, the historian of Breconshire, and grandson of the celebrated Theophilus Evans, to complete the second volume of his work. Thus when he took Holy Orders Carnhuanawc placed himself in what was virtually an apostolic succession of Anglican clergymen passionately concerned with Celtic antiquities, Welsh literary remains, and the fostering of the Welsh language. He did not possess the wayward literary genius of Iolo Morganwg, but he was a noted orator in an age when public speaking was taking on a new significance. He established a following which cut across barriers of class and sect and language. He was a man of many parts. He had some skill as a draughtsman and illustrator. He could make and play a Welsh harp (*y delyn deirres*). He travelled extensively on the continent in pursuit of Celtic antiquities and his Breton was so good that he gave much assistance in the translation of the Old Testament into that language. His Welsh prose style however was awkward, contorted both by Welsh philological quirks of the period and the over-blown English-influenced style that had come into vogue. Nevertheless between 1836 and 1842 he brought out, in fourteen parts, a *History of Wales from earliest times to the fall of Llywelyn ap Gruffydd*, which led the field for several decades. He opened a country school at his own expense for teaching through the medium of Welsh and he was remarkable in his day for the affection in which he was held by both the ordinary folk, the dissenting ironworkers and coal-miners of Merthyr, and the upper classes, British and continental, well to do aristocrats, and pillars of the established church. He made passionate appeals to the landed gentry, people like the Morgans of Tredegar, the Guests and even the Crawshays, Rolls of Hendre (and later of Rolls Royce), and the Duke of Newcastle, to support Welsh culture in all its manifestations and particularly the Welsh language. When they were most attentive to his message the rich responded by endowing the eisteddfod competitions with very substantial prizes: prizes big enough to attract continental scholars, and there were heady moments at Abergavenny and Llanover Hall when the academic side of the Celtic vision seemed about to take off.

Like Old Iolo he was a myth-maker, but he worked in the open. His platform eloquence moved his eisteddfod audiences to strive to live up to the flattering picture he painted of the Welsh *gwerinwr* (peasant) and *gweithiwr* (worker).

> Show me another country in the world in which the peasantry and the lower classes feel such an interest in literature and intellectual pursuits as the people of Wales do . . . show me another race of men on the face of the earth among whom the labouring classes are the entire patrons of the press.

As early as 1822, Carnhuanawc was given to naming the Welsh language periodicals and newspapers that came from the multiplicity of printing presses and publishing houses that had mushroomed in the Principality. 'These are the property of the common people, without patronage and without support.' The political lesson he drew from this Welsh appetite for printed matter and culture was resolutely conservative. It was their attachment to the things of the spirit such as eisteddfodau, choral singing, and literary and religious publications that had preserved Wales from the revolutions and riots that had shaken the foundations of so many countries after the Napoleonic wars. The Merthyr riots were yet to make this view seem naive.

At Abergavenny the primary organisers were bourgeois burgesses anxious to give some colourful encouragement to the flagging woollen industry of the town. Through Carnhuanawc they were able to turn to the gentry of a wide area and particularly to the enthusiastic support of Augusta, Lady Llanover, and her husband Benjamin (the original 'Big Ben'). Augusta, an energetic little woman who lived to be ninety-four, had access to royalty through the friendship of her great aunt Mrs. Delany with Fanny Burney. Her own pedigree gave her pretensions to Celtic royalty since Lord Lansdowne was one of her ancestors. On her estate at Llanover she literally surrounded herself with Welshness. By so doing she unwittingly elevated herself to the status of a folk heroine. The fashion of her time inclined even more sharply than usual towards the disparagement of things Welsh. Both the people and the language were in an exposed and unprotected condition and therefore inclined to tiptoe through the harsh wilderness of an industrialised world in the hope of not attracting too much notice. The mere idea of Carnhuanawc, strikingly handsome in his habitual Welsh tweed, and of Lady Llanover calling herself Gwenynen Gwent (the Honeybee of Gwent) and lending so much of her wealth and energy to the propagation of Welsh culture, encouraged the faint-hearted to cherish the eisteddfod as an institution out of which all manner of unexpected benefits and blessings could flow.

It was in Rome at the Prussian Embassy that the Breton savant, François Rio, met Gwenynen Gwent's older sister Frances, the wife of the amiable and learned ambassador, Baron Bunsen. She urged Rio to visit Wales where he made a romantic marriage with the daughter of one of the leading families, the Joneses of Llanarth Hall. This former Chouan also established a firm friendship with Carnhuanawc. Between them they determined to transform the Abergavenny eisteddfod into a Celtic academy. At the fifth eisteddfod in 1838 a Breton deputation 'approuvée par le roi Louis-Philippe' included the twenty-three-year-old Count Theodore Hersart de la Villemarqué who proved to be a greater public and social success in Gwent than even Rio himself. At the eisteddfod of 1834 Rio had caused a stir by declaring at the end of his speech 'King Arthur is not dead!' When la Villemarqué took off his boots and in his stockinged feet entered the circle of stones to become a fully-fledged bard according to the rights and customs of the Bards of the Isle of Britain 'in the face of the sun and in the eye of the light',* it seemed as if the invisible threads of history were being drawn tight and the old link between Arthur's scattered Britons firmly re-established.

* The roof of a large building had been removed for the occasion.

One of his companions read a poem written for the occasion by Alphonse de Lamartine. La Villemarqué followed with a composition of his own, Breton spiced with Welsh. He vowed on the spot to devote his life to collecting the scattered remnants of the songs and stories of Brittany. He would dedicate his collection 'to Brittany, to Wales, to the whole of Europe and to the generations yet unborn, for ever, for ever, for ever'. It was in fact an emotional occasion of some importance. Villemarqué visited Charlotte Guest and learnt that, with the help of Carnhuanawc and Tegid, she was launching her English translation of *The Mabinogion*. A new chapter in the influence of Celtic art on European culture had begun. In his excited report to the French Minister of Education, Villemarqué claimed that the language of Aneirin and of Taliesin, of Myrddin and Llywarch Hen was in fact the language of the druids. Indeed he went into greater detail. He claimed that the peasants of Basse-Bretagne were in fact in their dialect using the very tongue in which Taliesin had sung and prophesied. Villemarqué was infected with the spirit of Iolo in more ways than one. His collection *Barzez Breiz* published in 1839 was much praised. It gained him an Academy prize and gave a new impetus to Celtic studies in France and on the continent. But before long he was accused of forgery along the lines of Macpherson. He confessed to some alterations. His aims were literary rather than scientific. Again somewhat in the style of Iolo's adulation of Glamorgan, he devoted the rest of his long life to the preservation of the ancient glories of his native Brittany.

The sequence of eisteddfodau held at Abergavenny became a showcase for the worthiness of Welshness. When the last in the series was held in 1853, the procession through the town was two miles long. No expense was spared. Wagonloads of harpists played their way towards the specially built eisteddfod pavilion, and behind them came Welsh woollen looms in action, with weavers plying their shuttles; and even printing presses on parade churning out copies of loyal greetings to the eisteddfod president before the eyes of the enthusiastic multitudes lining the streets. There was a splendid turnout of gentry attended by retainers in Welsh livery of green and silver. The Rolls equipage was naturally conspicuous: 'The post boys having Cymreigyddion jackets of Gwenffrwd woollen and the four horses . . . elaborately ornamented with national emblems.'

18 The Glass of Fashion

Carnhuanawc had some reason to be proud of his people. Their Welshness functioned with considerable success as a shield and a bastion against the brutalising effects of hectic industrialisation. It offered them the protection of their own unique kingdom in a world which otherwise showed little respect for the basic requirements of their human dignity. Like the chapel, the eisteddfod was a civilising influence and both these indigenous institutions were at their best when they were structured by the culture inherent in the language the people used. To cherish the language was no more than a necessary act of self-respect.

Carnhuanawc's eloquence and his industry never allowed the wealthy aristocratic patrons of the eisteddfodau of this period to forget the value of the Welsh language as a social lubricant and agent of industrial peace. In the spirit of nineteenth-century cultural national-ism, the Welsh language would expand in order to sustain a national university which would foster the whole range of subjects from science, engineering and agriculture to the rehabilitation of manuscripts, myths, and a popular culture that so subtly enshrined the deposits of the more glorious past: body forth in fact the whole range of Old Iolo's dreams when his mind was at its least flawed and most fertile. Carnhuanawc may have offered the Welsh working class the enticing spectacle of the common people reaching for the stars and ascending the slopes of Parnassus on their knees. This was a myth they were very ready to accept and they were prepared to go as far as they could, within the limits of enlightened self-interest, to make it manifest in their own history. Indeed the concept of the culture-hungry worker and the intellectual *gwerinwr* became a dominant theme in Welsh affairs from this time forward. But the choice of language was crucial. As choice became an increasing possibility, the act of choosing quietly took over the dynamic role of Carnhuanawc's dream; and this act of choosing was invariably part of a greater act of social climbing. And this state of affairs can be seen to have existed right from the moment when choice became a possibility.

English poetry at that time, like the more expensive forms of orchestral music, and in spite of the fierce romantic radicalism of a Shelley or the deep sympathy with the sterling qualities of simple peasants of a Wordsworth, remained unshakeably elitist and aristocratic. The prevailing mode of English culture may have grown more and more romantic in reaction to the grim realities and spiritual hammer blows of industrialisation, but it never grew less aristocratic. Even in the bourgeois novel a sprinkling of titles was always a necessary ingredient for any form of commercial success. It was at this same period that the English obsession with class tightened its grip on the burgeoning imagination of a whole people. Whereas the concept of a miner or his son winning an eisteddfod prize had already become endlessly beguiling for the Welsh, even before the eisteddfodau of Abergavenny, in the world of English letters such a feat would have had little appeal. (Not until the twentieth century could a D.H. Lawrence make his savage kick at the door of privilege, subconsciously on his father's behalf.)

English literary criticism could hardly interest itself in the degree of competence in the strict metres exercised by Welsh workers and peasants, or take the trouble to learn something of the intricacies of *cynghanedd* in the manner followed by Gerard Manley Hopkins in his North Wales retreat a generation later. The Welsh language was an insuperable obstacle and the only practical course was to continue the long established official policy of progressive devaluation. From the point of view of government and the exercise of power it continued to be an outlandish survival that made a corner of the island more difficult to understand and ultimately more uncertain in its loyalties: and since power continued to create leisure and leisure sustained culture, the ordinary flow of literary activity could do little else than reflect the preoccupations and predilections of the class which exercised the most power.

Old Iolo had been able to evoke a brief but intense interest among the romantics in the work songs and the Arcadian magic of the peasant culture of his native Glamorgan. The landscape of Wales from Tintern Abbey to the moonlit slopes of Snowdon had given Wordsworth important inspiration. Shelley, Peacock and their friends transformed Ardudwy and Eifionydd into useful sources for English romanticism. But as Wordsworth rather wearily put it,

> . . . all things swerve
> From their known course, or vanish like a dream:
> Another language spreads from coast to coast:
> Only perchance some melancholy stream
> And some indignant Hills old names preserve
> When laws, and creeds, and people all are lost.

Wordsworth had a remarkable sense of history. His outlook and his attitude were resolutely bardic. But the language barrier was too much for him. Wales after all was not his responsibility. He was a man of the Old North and all he could see in Welsh Cambria was a mystical, topographical prefiguration of what his Cumbrian Lake District had once been. Another mighty man of English letters of the same period had the same problem. Wales fascinated Sir Walter Scott as a romantic alternative to Scotland.

> I will own that the idea of taking a Welsh subject, and even the very topic of Glendower . . . crossed my imagination . . . the gallant resistance made by the Welsh to their engrossing neighbours affords as many grand situations as the romantic country which they inhabit contains beautiful localities . . . The mere knowledge of facts might be acquired by study, but [what of] the far more indispensable peculiarities of language habits and manners?

The language barrier again. And it was a parallel imbalance of cultural gravitational pull that cooled off the interest of the Anglicised upper classes in Welsh language and culture. It really was too much of a sweat to bother to learn a language hardly at all in use in the highest circles of polite society and only too often the vehicle of sullen work folk and disaffected dissenters.

When Carnhuanawc and Sir Charles Morgan of Tredegar Park, who in so many ways saw himself as the spiritual heir of Ifor Hael, died, much of the essential Welshness of the Abergavenny eisteddfod died with them. The customary 'engrossing' power of cultural expansion made itself felt. The proceedings became increasingly anglicised and this process in itself was sufficient to wither the sensitive plant at the root. Courageous individuals like Lady Llanover were shunted off into the sidings that the expanding railway culture of Victorian England provided for colourful eccentrics. For the next hundred years the position of Welsh in the eisteddfod, an institution which had come into being primarily in order to celebrate the Welsh poetic tradition, resembled that of the owner of a country house who chooses to masquerade as a butler in order to confuse and mystify his guests. At one moment it would enjoy a ceremonial enthronement and at the next find itself in the scullery, its hands red and chapped at the steaming sink where it washed the dishes used by distinguished English visitors.

An inclination towards servility is perhaps inevitable in a cultural mode which is merely tolerated by the occupying power. The Welsh language had continued to thrive through a combination of the loyalty of the lower orders and the grace and favour of cultivated clerics. Could it now take a more virile stance in the new industrialised society that was emerging? Something of the problem can be discerned in the situation of the important group of Unitarian radicals in the boom town days of the expansion of Merthyr Tydfil. Like Taliesin Williams, the president of the first assembly of the Abergavenny eisteddfod in 1834, they were conspicuous supporters of the eisteddfod movement. They saw in it an unique opportunity to bring secular education and political enlightenment to the people. They were almost by definition in favour of the democratisation of literature. Through the eisteddfod the Welsh language would provide the means whereby a glamorous past, which stretched back into the mists of time beyond the mediaeval aristocratic tradition, could be recovered and refashioned to cope with the stern realities of the industrial present. These eisteddfodic Unitarians were also among the first apostles of Chartism in Wales. They published newspapers for working men in both languages. They were in the forefront of the struggle to improve the appalling conditions that prevailed in a town whose population had multiplied seven times in less than fifty years.

The most able man of letters among the Unitarians of Merthyr was Taliesin Williams's friend, Thomas Stephens the chemist. At the age of twenty-seven Stephens won the prize for an essay on Welsh literature at the Abergavenny eisteddfod of 1848. The adjudicating critic was a notable classical scholar, John Williams, recently created Archdeacon of Cardigan and formerly the close friend of Sir Walter Scott and his biographer, Lockhart, and tutor to Sir Walter's son. Williams described the essay as a work of genius and it remains true that it was the first step towards a combination of scientific scholarship and enlightened literary criticism in the treatment of mediaeval Welsh poetry. Unlike the bardic enthusiasts, whether of Wales or Brittany, Stephens did not go in for hyperbole or unrestrained enthusiasm. He was firmly wedded to the scientific method, and his prose style had that touch of iconoclastic arrogance which was to become the hallmark of readability in English criticism from this time forward. But it was symptomatic that this assiduous eisteddfod competitor chose to send in his efforts written for the most part in English. (At Abergavenny the competitions were usually advertised separately 'by his Royal Highness the Prince of Wales, a prize of twenty-five guineas, a critical essay . . . accompanied by specimens both in the original and in a close English or Latin translation' . . . 'A prize of sixty guineas including a ring valued at ten guineas . . . the essay to be written in either Welsh, English, French, German, Italian, or Latin; or with a translation of one of these languages.' This latter prize was won by Carl Meyer writing in German.)

When the young Stephens came up to the platform to receive his prize, Sir John Guest, the industrialist, made his offer to pay for the publication of such an important work. The crowd roared their approval in a manner now reserved for young fly-halves scoring their first try in a rugby international. The contrast between the cool head of the 'individual talent' and the seething warmth of approval of the society from which it emerges is very significant. A numerically small people who persist in regarding themselves as a nation in spite of the defeats and setbacks of history, need to imagine themselves as in some sense 'chosen' in order to carry on a struggle that would otherwise appear hopeless. Every small success is in a sense a form of reassurance. The trek through the wilderness won't last for ever. When that small nation is for the most part sustained by dissenting denominations that are in themselves congregations of the elect, a great pressure of resentment can be built up and demand some emotional release. Stephens belonged to one of the smallest denominations, a minority among minorities. He understood that the cool-headedness of the chosen person needed to operate in inverse ratio to the emotional pressure of the chosen people thrusting him towards the limelight.

The book appeared in the following year under the imposing title *The Literature of the Kymry*. Like Lady Charlotte Guest's *The Mabinogion* it was printed in Llandovery and published in London by Longman's. It was soon translated into German and French and it made a deep impression in the world of Celtic scholarship. In his introduction, Stephens sets out his reason for writing his book in English.

> This is the way in which the Kymry can best serve their country, as the preponderance of England is so great, that the only hope of obtaining attention to the just claims of the Principality, is by appealing to the convictions and sympathies of the reading part of the English population . . .

It is of course always possible to do the right thing for the wrong reason; but Stephens's introduction unconsciously draws attention to the inherent feebleness of the Welsh position. 'The just claims of the Principality' presumably refers to the recognition of the Welsh as a distinct nation on the strength of the glories of their distinguished past, set out in authoritative English by a recognised expert. The critical essay would prove the value of Welsh language and Welsh literature. But 'the just claims' would only be met by the grace and favour of the English – 'the convictions and sympathies of the reading part of the English population'. In other words decisions concerning the life and death of the language and therefore of the Welsh identity would be taken by 'the preponderance of England' and not by the Welsh themselves. Stephens, the rational Unitarian and apostle of scientific freedom, was in fact laying down the ground rules of permanent servility.

Stephens had little appetite for the more flamboyant aspects of the eisteddfod as a public institution. Although he could see clearly that it responded to a real and urgent need among the Welsh people, he was suspicious of its claims to unbroken links with the remote past, of its druidical pretensions, of the hopes it seemed to offer a once pastoral people of a renewal of ancient Arcadian ways. What interested him was the progress of academic scholarship and this was the aspect of eisteddfodic activities he sought to support and foster. The busy chemist had all the natural instincts of a first class scientific critic. Characteristically, like any other mid-Victorian hero, he carried on his essential studies and did all his writing at night when the shop was closed. In Merthyr Tydfil he was a model citizen. He served on committees concerning education, the town library, temperance, and public health. Among the unruly poor he was a missionary of self help and sobriety, 'the only remedy for distress'; and every Sunday he tutored a class of boys in the Sunday School of his chapel and gave them free access to his books.

Stephens was one of the first nonconformists to advocate openly in Wales an English education financed by the state. It is important to realise that in those days this was unpopular on two counts. The nonconformist religious bodies had vivid memories of the many disabilities imposed upon them by a state that disapproved of their mere existence. And among the mass of the people a newly awakened sense of national pride could not easily reconcile itself to what appeared to be only a newly-fashioned yoke imposed on its neck in the shape of the language of the oppressor. By this time the Welsh language had been elevated among all the nonconformist bodies to a semi-sacred status. It was both a banner and a battle-cry. (Many decades were to elapse before the sophisticated Welshman could refer to it in after-dinner speeches as 'the language of Heaven'.) On more than one occasion Stephens dared to use the eisteddfod platform to put across his unpopular message. His argument was utilitarian. The Welsh should learn English in order to improve their chances in the material world. They could still cherish their own tongue in chapel and in harmless eisteddfodic pursuits like writing poetry. Many nonconformist leaders accused him of treachery; but as time went by, almost by stealth, Stephens's view prevailed. The Welsh condition of the twentieth century was largely the making of men who shared his social vision.

The defining experience of the Welsh in the nineteenth century arose from the simultaneous discovery of a national identity and an appetite for freedom. Both these discoveries were made articulate by the phenomenal expansion of industrial capitalism and a world-wide British Empire. In an area like Merthyr Tydfil there was an awareness from the beginning that the pains of industrial growth would give the Welsh identity another chance in history. It is no accident that Iolo Morganwg spent so much of his time there in his declining years, lecturing in engineering as well as weaving his irresistible myths. He knew furnaces could be cauldrons of rebirth. Even mines could be caves where giants from the past dozed over their treasures. He understood that a communal life would flourish under siege conditions. Centuries of Welsh life demonstrated this fact. When people learnt to stick together in adversity, comradeship could flourish, and a life-style could emerge in which a desperate idealism could fuse with a new resourcefulness and confidence. It is not difficult to discern something of Old Iolo's magic in both the myth and the reality of the industrial valleys of South Wales. Thomas Stephens came into prominence in the life of Merthyr under the benevolent patronage of Iolo's son, Taliesin Williams. His relationship with the development of the eisteddfod movement is both sad and instructive because it illustrates an unhappy polarisation taking place at the heart of Welsh life. It is almost as if the flaws inherent in Iolo's character and in his vision were impelled to work themselves out in the lives of the people who most ardently cherished the institution to which he had given a fresh lease of life.

By the late 1850s the eisteddfod in its national form fell into the hands of a group of North Wales clerics led by the rector of Llan-ym-Mawddwy, John Williams ab Ithel. Ab Ithel was what was called in those days 'an Oxford man', and by publishing rehashes of Welsh ecclesiastical history he had somehow acquired the reputation of being a scholar. (He was even considered a likely candidate for the new chair of Celtic that was to be set up at Oxford at Matthew Arnold's suggestion.) His most notable qualities however were a passionate and undisciplined Welsh patriotism, gullibility, and a gift for organisation that would have made him a fortune running a circus or selling patent medicines in the American Middle West. The good people of Abergavenny had published Taliesin Williams's selection of his father's papers in 1848 under the title *Iolo Manuscripts* and this caused a fresh outbreak of antiquarian fever. Ab Ithel already believed that the Welsh bards had inherited the secret learning of the druids; and that the first Welshman was Gomer, the grandson of Noah. Now Iolo's manuscripts demonstrated conclusively that the *Gorsedd Beirdd Ynys Prydain* was a druidic institution and held the ultimate responsibility for the moral, religious, and cultural life of the nation. According to Iolo this inevitably included an overall responsibility for every imaginable branch of learning. All this was very good news to a people long oppressed who fancied their chances of becoming a chosen race. To ab Ithel, the ambitious and enthusiastic organiser, there was an inevitable logic in the situation. In order to organise an eisteddfod on an impressive scale he had to become a member of the *Gorsedd*, of Iolo's *Gorsedd*, and to do this he needed to travel to South Wales and present himself to the reigning archdruid, the man who had the most genuine claim to be Iolo's successor. *Mutatis mutandis*, it was a clear case of apostolic succession.

By this time the druidical traditions of Gwent and Morganwg had become a minefield of eccentricities. There were two outstanding claimants to the archdruidical role, a Pontypridd watchmaker, Myfyr Morganwg, and the celebrated Dr. William Price of Llantrisant. Dr. William Price was accustomed to receiving his patients dressed in a green uniform which he claimed had been worn by the victorious Welsh soldiers at the Battle of Bosworth. There is some suggestion that his gruesome experiences in the dissecting rooms of St. Bartholomew's Hospital might have affected his sensitive spirit; on the other hand his oddness may well have been hereditary. His father, William Price the Elder, was a fellow of Jesus College, Oxford, who declined to take any living after being ordained on the grounds that it was 'too serious an undertaking'. He married his domestic servant and brought up a large family in a gloomy house under the shadow of Caerphilly Castle. He seems to have been obsessed with snakes and water. It is not recorded that he ever did a day's work and he resented having to pay anything towards his son's education. Having to work his way up certainly contributed to the horrors of young Price's London training. By 1827 he was in practice at Nantgarw and medical adviser to the Crawshay family. During his long life he was a Chartist, and also indulged indefatigably in litigation. At the age of eighty-three he married for the third time, christened the first-born of the marriage Jesus Christ, and when the child died of convulsions, attempted to cremate him on the mountainside in a barrel filled with petroleum jelly. Price clearly admitted no limit to his druidical powers. But he was not a respectable person. He had been a Chartist leader and had fled to France in order to avoid arrest after the attack on Newport in 1839.

For the rector of Llan-ym-Mawddwy, bold man though he was, the much milder Myfyr Morganwg was the only possible choice. This was the man with the best claim to the archdruidical succession. Ab Ithel knew this because he had spent the best part of two years at Llanover Hall poring over Iolo Morganwg's papers and copying them out with the unquenchable zeal of a convert. In 1856 in the *Cambrian Journal*, one of several magazines that he founded, one may still sense the exultation with which he contemplates the awesome antiquity of the Welsh poetic tradition as envisaged by Iolo Morganwg.

> The Cymry . . . are a favoured people, for they alone, having to the latest times been able properly to read and understand the Great Book of Nature, can now boast of ritual connection with the type and anti-type . . . Other nations had more or less corrupted the primitive truth so that when they embraced Christianity, their former systems, scarcely presenting any elements of a kindred and general character, were necessarily abolished.

Ab Ithel saw no reason to disagree with the convenient simplification formed by Myfyr Morganwg (in civil life, if one may use the phrase, Evan Davies, a one time Congregationalist lay preacher) that Christianity was no more than druidism dressed in Jewish gaberdine. And of course this notion was not without respectable intellectual antecedents. Old Iolo had not just snatched it out of the air. The longing for a universal religion and a belief in its existence in remote antiquity is a theme of the Renaissance which can be traced through the literature of most Western European countries, and once again provides a glimpse of the parallel roles played by Dr. John Dee and Iolo Morganwg in the cultural life of their time. Much to the distress of the nonconformist ministers of the district, Myfyr Morganwg, the Pontypridd watchmaker, conducted druidical religious ceremonies in the shadow of Maen Chwyf (the Rocking Stone) at each solstice and equinox. Giordano Bruno was burnt at the stake for doing far less. The Anglican rector of Llan-ym-Mawddwy was in no way deterred. Like one of the Illuminati he had become a man with a mission. His role was to establish the authority of the druidical *Gorsedd Beirdd Ynys Prydain* over the eisteddfod and transform it into a vehicle for the cultural and ultimately the political salvation of the Welsh people. He would provide them with a secular Feast of Tabernacles to celebrate their emergence as a people from an historical wilderness. It is clear that in spite of his shortcomings as a scholar, he had a shrewd enough notion of the Welsh psychological condition. 'Deprive him of these [i.e. a pride in the Welsh poetic tradition etc.] and he is paralysed: he becomes a gloomy slave to the Saxon, regardless of his country's fate.' It is worth remembering that ab Ithel was not alone in his beliefs and enthusiasms. A whole range of Celtic scholars from England, France, Ireland and Scotland contributed to his *Cambrian Journal*. Even Archdeacon Williams who lavished so much praise on Thomas Stephens at Abergavenny could write in 1857:

> Let us, who represent the remnant which God in his mercy has spared, endeavour to save from the ruinous edifice of the druids whatever may be regarded as more precious and spiritual, and show the world that there once prevailed a better philosophy and a holier teaching than was ever taught by spurious Christians, who smothered all true development of the religion of Jesus by the grossest materialism of the epicurean school. Pray therefore supply me with all the information you possess respecting 'The True *Cyfrinach y Beirdd*.'

Once ab Ithel had been received into the *Gorsedd* by the archdruid Myfyr Morganwg at a ceremony under the Rocking Stone he felt himself in a strong enough position to organise what has been described as the most extraordinary eisteddfod of all time, *Eisteddfod Fawr Llangollen* 1858.

In close concert with two other notable eisteddfodic clerics, ab Ithel made what was virtually a take-over bid for a chapel eisteddfod at Llangollen, and by an advertising campaign on an American scale turned it into a major national event. His posters appeared in the new waiting rooms of railway stations in England and Wales, wherever the wandering Welsh would be likely to see them. They even reached America. There were house-to-house collections. Ab Ithel was resolved to free the event from the tyranny of upper-class patronage. The Llangollen eisteddfod would be run by the *Gorsedd*, of which he was now the moving spirit, for the edification and entertainment of the whole people. The keynote would be patriotism, and the subject set for the chair poem was 'Bosworth Field', and for the *pryddest* (ode in free metre) 'The Cymry under Brân occupying Rome'. In the shades of the megaliths, Merlin, Geoffrey of Monmouth, John Dee and Old Iolo must have been silently applauding and even joining hands in readiness to execute a new Giant's Dance. For once the Welsh people would be given an occasion to celebrate their own unique existence. The pavilion tent was designed to hold 6,000 people. Ab Ithel conducted his preparations like a military operation, riding roughshod over local objections and treading on episcopal and nonconformist toes with manic impartiality. The nonconformists thought the *Gorsedd* smacked of paganism, and the Anglo-Welsh bishops, true to form, thought the whole thing too subversive and too Welsh. It was the railways that held the key to the festival's success. The canals helped too. When September came the people arrived in their thousands, and they were diverted by extraordinary spectacles. The paper *Seren Gomer* reports a procession over Llangollen bridge. It was led by none other than

> . . . Dr. William Price of Pontypridd, who, with his most reverend and patriarchal beard was dressed in green edged with scarlet and on his head a fox-skin cap according to the custom and practice of ancient days. Miss Price, the doctor's daughter, sat upon a war-horse and she was dressed in a scarlet riding habit, and a head-dress of fox-skin on her head. Certain gentlemen wore multicoloured waist-coats on which were woven sacred utterances in the ancient letters of the Alphabet of the Bards. It was a most strange sight to behold the procession wend its way over the old bridge to a meadow near the town where it had been decided to assemble the *Gorsedd*.

Ab Ithel had set out his purpose clearly enough in a pamphlet he had published and distributed widely beforehand. The purpose of the eisteddfod was to promote the study and the cultivation of poetry, music, and Welsh literature in general; to preserve and enhance the status of the Welsh language; to encourage native arts and manufactures and to rescue from neglect national usages and special characteristics of the Principality. The eisteddfod existed in order to promote a spirit of loyalty and patriotism among the people; of mutual confidence between rich and poor, and of social harmony among all classes in Wales. This festival of the people would be conducted in strict accordance with the forms and usages of ancient times. All this seemed acceptable enough and if there were differences they would only be minor points of definition.

The inevitable clash came on the last day of the eisteddfod, and it came in the form of what appeared to be a dramatic encounter between myth and science. The bone of contention was an essay by Thomas Stephens. In Welsh history this was an important moment because it seemed to dramatise an unfortunate polarisation between two aspects of a national revival. It could not have occurred at a more unfortunate time. This was the age of fierce controversy between the new certainties of science and religious belief. The pragmatic English were shaken by the ape versus angel debate. But even at its height, the well-being of the nation and its manifest destiny were never in doubt. It could amuse a Tory leader to declare himself on the side of the angels to win a few votes. The fragile vessel of Welsh nationality was not built to withstand anything more than a storm in a large sized teacup, such as the scandal concerning Thomas Stephens's essay on 'The Discovery of America in the Twelfth Century by Prince Madoc ab Owen Gruffydd'.

For their great eisteddfod ab Ithel (and his pliant committee) had prepared a list of subjects for literary competition that read like an anthology of the myths, fantasies and superstitions that had sustained the precarious sense of a Welsh national identity down the centuries. These had become the vague pillar of cloud that had gone before him in all his efforts and the Llangollen eisteddfod was clearly designed to be the consummation of everything he desired for his people. It would be the gateway to a cultural promised land. The evidence also suggests that the sheer size of his enterprise and the uncritical confusion with which he struggled to absorb Iolo's most extreme flights of fancy, finally disturbed the balance of his mind.

The Madoc legend was already discredited in realistic terms. In spite of George Catlin and his remarkable pictures of life among the Mandans, it was widely known that no such thing as a tribe of Welsh Indians existed in North America. But ab Ithel and his supporters were never too much constrained by reality. Their concern was to colonise all the uncharted continents of the remote past with the theories and fantasies they needed to sustain themselves as they moved into an ominously uncertain future. The very intensity of their efforts carried an undertone of hysterical desperation. Their instincts and their emotions warned them that an old Wales was dying and all their

Dr. William Price (1800—93), surgeon, revolutionary and eccentric disciple of Old Iolo; this druidical Chartist fathered three children in his eighties and pioneered cremation by attempting to burn the body of his infant son, Iesu Grist (Jesus Christ), in 1884. (National Museum of Wales, Welsh Folk Museum)

intellect seemed capable of doing was shoring up fragments against their ruin.

Thomas Stephens's essay was a masterpiece of historical criticism. He proved conclusively that the Madoc story was without verifiable historical foundation. In spite of the adjudicators' praise for the work, ab Ithel's committee intervened to disqualify the entry on the grounds that it was not on the given subject. They had asked for an essay to prove that Madoc had discovered America and not a remorselessly sustained and scientific argument to demonstrate that this was not the case. When this was announced, Stephens marched up to the platform and demanded a hearing. As he began to speak, Môr Meirion, one of ab Ithel's fiercer druidical clerics and a great hater of bishops, ordered the band to strike up and drown the voice of the protesting heretic. The crowded audience would have none of this. On one level they scented a first class row and on the other they dimly perceived that this was an occasion when two crucial views of the nature of Welshness had come into open conflict. It was no mere academic quarrel. The nature of the argument bore directly on a pressing problem which occupied all their minds. What kind of a remnant were they, and to what kind of identity were they entitled? In such a rapidly changing world, how were they to sustain their position and what methods were they to adopt in bringing up their children? What were they to tell them, and what were they to allow them to be told? What chances were there of transforming the yoke of Welshness into some more comfortable mode of apparel that would give them a respectable place in the splendid new vehicle called Progress?

Stephens seized his chance and demonstrated unexpected eloquence. He carried the war straight into the enemy's camp. The eisteddfod, he said, was a place to publish the truth. Making claims that could not be substantiated would only lower the standing of the Welsh as a nation in the eyes of the world. His mission as a scholar and a writer was to advocate the true merits of the literature and the language of Wales. Judging by the enthusiastic response of the audience, he had put his finger on the most exposed nerve in the Welsh anatomy; the haunted preoccupation with what other people would think of them, particularly the English, who occupied all the positions of authority in the circumstances which governed their lives. He stood before them as the advocate of the unquestionable virtue of simple truthfulness and in this impeccable uniform he won them over. He said that the committee had no right to overrule the judges and they agreed with him. In full public view the committee was forced to back down. Carn Ingli, the most conciliatory and level-headed of the trinity of druidical churchmen, stepped forward to announce that the whole matter would be reconsidered and he managed to persuade Stephens to withdraw his protest. But the controversy went rumbling on in the Welsh press long after the eisteddfod was over. Stephens's thesis on the Madoc legend had to wait another thirty-five years for publication, that is eighteen years after his death. But there was no question of his moral victory. Somewhat in the manner of another populist and fundamentalist, William Jennings Bryan, in the United States, ab Ithel's reputation went into rapid decline after an eisteddfod which was both a triumph and a disaster. His controversy with Stephens was like the celebrated monkey trial at Dayton, Tennessee, in 1925, in which Bryan so clearly won the battle and lost the war. Stephens's rational arguments, like Clarence Darrow's, had a permanent effect on Welsh public opinion and even on the course of eisteddfod history. Llangollen established the national eisteddfod as an institution to be cherished by all the Welsh people. But its wilder aspects and colourful disorders brought blushes to the cheeks of the new Welsh middle class and prosperous men who felt it was their duty to give their country a lead in more sober and respectable directions. They could not tolerate the eccentric antics and exaggerated claims of bards like Dr. William Price and Myfyr Morganwg who solemnly paraded the platform with an egg on his chest, suspended from his neck by string and cosmic significance. Ab Ithel, in spite of his herculean efforts, was openly accused of peculation and arranging competitions in order to award prizes to members of his family. Through the breach which Thomas Stephens had made the business men and administrators moved in. So did the nonconformist establishment. At the next national eisteddfod, held at Denbigh in 1860, the presiding spirit was Thomas Gee, Calvinistic Methodist printer and newspaper publisher, and ardent supporter of radical liberalism. The eisteddfod was reflecting with seismographic accuracy the change in the balance of political power in Wales.

19 Unarmed Insurrection

The cultural activities of the Welsh, however colourful, were of little interest to a central government absorbed in the problems of an expanding economy and an expanding empire. Even after the Reform Bill the franchise did not oblige the ruling class to curry favour with any section of the lower orders. 'Politics' was still the professional preserve of gentlemen. Eisteddfodau were a comic combination of eccentric antiquarianism and harmless romanticism. But unrest in Wales was a different matter. The normal imperial reaction when natives grow restless is to send in detachments of well-armed troops. In Wales as in Ireland this happened several times in the hungry forties. The pattern of even economic growth over all the thirteen counties had been broken by the phenomenal industrial expansion of the south-east. The frontier town excesses of the first phase of the development of Merthyr were replaced by the uniform squalor and haphazard development of industrial communities spreading down all the valleys. This made them particularly fertile recruiting grounds for the Chartist movement. Among the Chartists, Dr. William Price was as conspicuous as he had been in the demoralised streets of Merthyr and would be later in eisteddfodic processions. His strange figure has a way of flickering through all the more shadowy pages of nineteenth-century Welsh history.

The unrest was not confined to industrial areas. The spirit of rebellion and the appetite for reform both flowed most easily through the channels of communication that had been established by the increasingly self-confident nonconformist denominations. In rural West Wales there were close ties between this network and the forces of Rebecca, those bands of farmers and farm labourers who tore down toll-gates and destroyed toll-houses. While they blacked their faces and wore women's clothes, these men demonstrated their familiarity with William Morgan's Bible by spattering their proclamations with biblical quotations.

In 1843 a journalist from *The Times* gained the confidence of the

'Daughters of Rebecca' in West Wales and was able to give an English version of their grievances in a series of vivid reports to his newspaper that read like despatches from the front. There had been an attack on the Carmarthen poorhouse by two thousand persons led by their own cavalry of four hundred mounted farmers. The workhouse had been destroyed and the insurgents driven back by detachments of cavalry and seventy mounted London policemen. Accompanied by an inter-preter, the man from *The Times* attended secret meetings in noncon-formist burial grounds. The agitation was not only against toll-gates. It was against all the forms of oppression which had accumulated over the heads of the native peasantry in the centuries since the incorporation of the dominion of Wales in the anglicised Tudor nation state, the absence of native and natural justice in the law courts, the imposition of tithes to support an anglicised church to which the people did not belong; rack-rents, harsh game laws, the appointment of alien stewards, the manifold oppressions of an anglicised and unsympathetic landlord class. All forms of authority were tinged with the same attitude, an inclination, as the *Times* man wrote, to treat the people 'as if they were beasts and not human beings'.

There were hidden links between the Rebecca riots and the Chartist movement, just as there were between the eisteddfodic eccentricities of men like Iolo and William Price and the spirit of Jacobin rebellion. The furnaces of the south-east were melting-pots in more senses than one and they re-activated cauldrons of rebirth that had lain dormant since the middle ages. But perhaps the most astonishing and influential Welsh eccentric of the period came from a smaller industrial com-munity in mid-Wales. The career and the social theories of Robert Owen of Newtown made their impact outside Wales, but Owen was as much a product of the Welsh condition as Iolo or Dr. Price and in his own way he was just as creatively colourful. He escaped from the all-pervading influence of the language and druidism and the revival of national consciousness by leaving Newtown before he was twelve years old and joining his brother in a draper's shop in London, several years before Old Iolo assembled his choice selection of London Welshmen to hold the first *Gorsedd* on Primrose Hill. Robert Owen was virtually a millionaire before he was thirty in 1800 – the year that William Price was born – and the scene of his revolutionary experiments moved to Scotland. At New Lanark, in the Old North, among the 2,000 work people who were connected with his mills, five hundred were children from Scottish poorhouses. For these Owen opened a school. He also initiated model housing and sanitation improvements which drew visitors from all over Europe. All his energies and his considerable intellect were concentrated on social problems, and he has a good claim to the title of being the world's first socialist. Like every reformer of his time, and indeed well within the Welsh tradition, he looked towards the virgin territories of the United States as the most suitable laboratory in which to conduct experiments in the human spirit that would produce a new society and thereby engender a new and better race of men. It is at this point that a wide range of 'other people' begin to accuse Owen of eccentricity. The experiment at New Harmony in Indiana contained incongruous elements that could be held up to ridicule in exactly the same way as Dr. Price's fox-skin cap and stockingless feet. Indeed, Price himself had his own version of New Harmony. This was a centre of druidical learning and social improvement that was to be built at a precise angle to the Rocking Stone on Pontypridd Common. A subscription list had been opened, and the Doctor had collected £137. 17s. 11d. in 1838, before his energies were caught up in the rising tide of the Chartist movement.

In chronological terms the Chartist movement sprang from widespread dissatisfaction with the Reform Bill of 1832 and the Poor Law of 1834. Owen himself played a central role in the genesis of this dissatisfaction. When he returned home from America he found himself in London the leader by popular acclaim of what was in effect the first mass movement of the working class in Great Britain. He made the attempt to unite all the workers of the country in a national trades union. He came so near success that the government sensed a challenge to its own position of authority and power. Matters had reached a pitch that would in any other country have threatened civil war. It seemed a classic revolutionary situation. The working class were poised to make their first bid for political power. Owen drew back. Violence was not part of his creative nature. A man who would not say 'boo' to an Indian in Indiana was even less likely to say 'bah' to the reactionary government of Great Britain. This sad Tolstoi of the woollen mills was forced to dissolve his mass movement in 1834. He retreated from practice into theory and nine years later Marx and Engels were able to pour scorn on his head in the Communist Manifesto. His socialism was 'Utopian', an eccentric fantasy, a dream as inconsequential and irrelevant as any druidical notion of resurrecting elements of a remote Arcadian past in order to reconstitute them in the new earthly paradise. This was 'soft' socialism as opposed to their own scientific doctrine and the unshakeable analyses of historical materialism.

1834 was the high-water mark of Owen's intervention into the world of *Machtpolitik*. For the next quarter of a century he devoted himself to voluminous writings on behalf of his various theories. His influence made itself felt in the growth of the Co-operative movement and in educational practice both in Britain and America. But his behaviour grew more eccentric as he grew older. He took up with Spiritualism and, in the last year of his life, returned to Wales apparently determined to communicate directly with the spirits of his ancestors. This was 1858, the year of the Llangollen eisteddfod. Outside Merthyr, there was still little inclination in nonconformist Wales to listen to the theories of 'Mr. Owen the atheist'. In comparative poverty, he died in Newtown in a cheap hotel bedroom, which was no more than a few feet from the room above the saddler's shop where he was born.

'The People's Charter' was a legislative programme drawn up by an association of London working men, and submitted to parliament in 1837. It contained six specific demands, the most important of which were the right to vote for all male citizens of twenty-one years of age and over, and elections conducted by secret ballot. These demands, which seem mild and reasonable enough to us, were rejected out of hand by the House of Commons. This became a signal for nationwide agitation. Chartism became the burning political issue of the day. In spite of its urban origins, and the fuel of industrial discontent, Chartism first took root in Wales in the countryside and the small market towns. As a moral force it was also welcomed by a new generation of radical leaders among the non-Methodist nonconformists. Particularly prominent was the Rev. David Rees of Llanelli, editor of the monthly periodical *Y Diwygiwr* (The Reformer). Rees was a Congregational minister. It is incidentally of some significance that the Welsh Congregationalists have persisted in calling themselves *Annibynwyr* (Independents) in a way that preserves their link with their politically active predecessors of the seventeenth century. For his magazine Rees took as his motto Daniel O'Connell's 'Agitate, Agitate, Agitate.' In Welsh with exclamation marks (*'Cynhyrfer! Cynhyrfer! Cynhyrfer!'*) it took on even more emotional overtones. The renegade Baptist, Brutus (David Owen 1795–1866), who edited the Anglican magazine *Yr Haul*, accused Rees of inciting people to violence and encouraging disorder and anarchy. When the Chartist disturbances and the Rebecca riots in rural Dyfed broke out, it appeared that there was some substance in the charge. Brutus was a skilled and witty publicist, and David Rees's oratorical style with its sanguinary Old Testament flourishes (much appreciated by a people whose chief and almost only reading was still the Bible) left him as wide open to the thrusts of this literary matador as a wounded bull. When the going got really rough, David Rees became a firm advocate of restraint. The motto was removed from the front page of the magazine and Rees concentrated his attention on such matters as temperance, public health and public morals and the propagation of the political liberalism which was to become the hallmark of Welsh nonconformity.

In Wales the dividing line between moral force and physical force became increasingly blurred. For the conscientious historian it is just as difficult to make this distinction as it is to decide whether a particular leader spoke in English or Welsh, or a mixture of both, and to what extent he was understood by the great mass of his followers. Everyone, whatever his language, understood the meaning of hunger and economic oppression. But when he came to the fine print of parliamentary resolutions and when there were principles and practices to be spelt out, the working man needed to go through the matter in his native language. Throughout the disturbances additional confusion could always arise between English and Welsh instructions. The historian David Williams in his book on the Chartist leader and former mayor of Newport, John Frost, described the founder of the Working Man's Association of Newport, William Edwards:

> . . . a baker by trade. He was forty-one years of age and claimed he had been a radical since 1816. He was a man of huge stature and colossal strength, and was accused by his opponents of preaching violence. 'Mad Edwards the Baker' was how he was invariably characterised in the local press. Yet he himself claimed to be a 'moral force' man, and the only literary production of his to survive, 'An Address to the People' (written, it is true, within the sobering precincts of Monmouth gaol) is moderate enough. It is, however, full of scriptural allusions . . . Edwards addressed a meeting of about 150 persons at the Bush Inn . . . he attributed the grievances of the working class to the lack of representation in Parliament. Another speaker then proceeded in Welsh to explain the principles of the Charter.

The most serious outbreaks of Chartist violence took place at those points in Wales where the intermingling of the two languages and to some extent the two cultures had reached an advanced stage because of the progress of industrialism. In the woollen towns of mid-Wales, suffering acutely from the rise of 'King Cotton' and Japanese-style competition from Yorkshire, Chartism made rapid strides. London policemen sent down to arrest the ring-leaders declared that the fury of the Welsh mob exceeded anything they had ever seen before. The town of Llanidloes was in the hands of the Chartists for a week. The cavalry and infantry were sent for and the Chartist leader, Charles Jones, went into hiding. Every effort was made to apprehend him. The rumour was that he had fled to Merthyr and that he was dying of tuberculosis. As the druidic movement, to which Welshmen like Dr. William Price attached so much importance, made its appeal to the historicity of a form of primitive Celtic democracy, so the unenfranchised working men of London demanded the restoration of the ancient rights they believed their ancestors had enjoyed in the Anglo-Saxon witenagemot. In the industrial valleys of South Wales these mythologies interacted and influenced each other in potent if confused form. The Chartist demands seemed simple and reasonable enough. They were asking for forms of democracy that would bring to the people forms of social justice. In the valleys, the suffering was there in plenty and the indifference and the injustice. But the desire for open rebellion, like the urge to expressions of violence, had to be structured. Discipline was called for and the voice of authority.

Chartism came like a message from a greater world. Workers everywhere were on the march. They were about to witness the birth of a vigorous, new, universal faith, and birth was always a bloody business. Out of this would come at last the foundation of a new and better world, and a myth that was wide enough to provide room for druids and dissenters, for Welsh-speaking and English-speaking, for Owenites and Unitarians, for moral force and for physical force, for Dr. Price with his fancy fox-fur and for the bull's head of the dreaded 'Scotch Cattle', the indigenous Welsh worker's own flying pickets and unofficial agents of vengeance. These were heady days and in the mirage that went before the would-be military minds of the conspirators, men like John Frost, Zephaniah Williams the free-thinker of Bedwellty, William Jones the watchmaker and Dr. William Price, the map of western Monmouthshire displayed narrow valleys pointing like arrows at the heart of Newport. Verses rang out from even the most respectable pulpits. 'Put yourselves in array against Babylon round about: all ye that bend the bow, shoot at her, spare no arrows: for she hath sinned against the Lord!'

The Old Testament became the textbook of the oppressed and the People of the Book knew how to read it. In the taverns where the committees met, and at the mass meetings, there was eloquence and alternative modes of intoxication. In both languages it was the age of verbosity. The leader in London, Feargus O'Connor, once an ardent Irish nationalist who had learnt his eloquence at the feet of the great Daniel O'Connell, was much given to theatrical gesture. Events proved him to be no more than a player king. But during those fateful days in the late autumn of 1839, his was the voice of authority, anxiously listened to in the valleys of South Wales and by the industrial centres of the Midlands and the North of England.

The plan was formed to attack Newport with working-class forces drawn from the reservoirs of human courage and endurance hidden in the bleak valleys of western Monmouthshire. Frost, Williams and Jones became captives of the pressure of the forces behind them. Dr. William Price was more adroit. He was reputed to have bought 'seven pieces of cannon' and in later years he was to claim that he had been appointed leader of the best disciplined force in the movement, the men of Pontypridd and Merthyr. On the night of the attack, they never moved. In the other valleys the Chartists assembled on the mountain-side. There were among them monoglot men from the hills who believed they were joining a march on London to capture the kingdom. Echoes of the old poets and even of Geoffrey of Monmouth were still ringing in those heads. Zephaniah Williams addressed them in English and in Welsh. They were going down to Newport to show their strength and to show that they were determined to get the Charter made the law of the land. In spite of the storm which was rising he promised them that they would be there by two o'clock in the morning and that the soldiers would not touch them. There was to be no shedding of blood. On the morning of November 9th, Frost led a rain-soaked mob in an attack on the Westgate Hotel in which the magistrates were assembled. Frost himself had been deprived of his seat on the bench by Lord John Russell because of his Chartist activities. Unknown to the mob special constables and soldiers guarded the building. It was their fire which killed several mud-spattered protesters and put an end to the doctrine of physical force.

Frost was arrested. Williams and Jones failed to escape, but Price claims to have escaped to France dressed in women's clothes. The three active leaders were condemned to death but, as in the case of Lewsyn yr Heliwr, their sentences were commuted to transportation for life. In Tasmania Zephaniah Williams lived to make a fortune in coal. His son Llywelyn remained in Wales and became a celebrated eisteddfod harpist with the bardic name of Pencerdd y De (Singer of the South), almost as if the story of one family was designed to encapsulate the history of nineteenth-century Wales. Dr. William Price retreated into litigation and the universe of his own ego protected by a thick wall of eccentricity. Feargus O'Connor lived to place himself at the head of moral force Chartism and enter the House of Commons with a petition he claimed to have been signed by 6,000,000 people. That too was rejected. O'Connor, whose personal behaviour had become increasingly erratic, was declared insane in 1852.

It seemed as if the Welsh people had been bruised by yet another ignominious defeat. They had been misled and misused. There were dark mutterings of treachery and of the presence among the marchers of police spies and agents provocateurs. Their own leaders had failed them because they lacked an independent sense of direction. They were incapable of originating their own strategy because they were listening to a distant voice and an indistinct message. They were caught up in the confused nervous frenzy that characterises the front runners in the stampede of a herd. Fifty years later in an interview with a reporter from the *Cardiff Times*, who modelled his patronising style on George Borrow but used the odd pseudonym of ap Idanfryn, the eighty-eight-year-old Price stated that he had never held a good opinion of Frost. He had found the Mayor of Newport a nervous and undecided man. As far as he was concerned he was prepared as always for battle; but he had been warned by a friend on the other side that a military sharp-shooter had been hired to pick off 'the Doctor with the long hair' when the marchers arrived in Newport. Judging by the costume still on exhibition at St. Fagan's Museum, there can be no doubt that Price would have been a conspicuous target.

In May 1848, the year of revolutions, a public meeting was held in Merthyr Tydfil, to oppose the Chartist movement even in its more mild and respectable forms, and to express the undeviating loyalty of the people of the town to the queen of England. Among the speakers was Thomas Stephens the chemist, a young man of twenty-seven, who must at that time have been preparing his *Literature of the Kymry* ready for entry at the Abergavenny eisteddfod in the autumn. As always, his argument was characteristically lucid. He made his appeal to history in a way that was oddly parallel to the analysis being developed at that time by Marx and Engels. Power had once belonged to a landed aristocracy descended from a warrior aristocracy. Their power had been curbed by the crown and by the rise of a mercantile class. Now the growth of industry was pushing forward the claims of an expanding middle class. The best hope of progress for the workers was to attach themselves to the growing power of the middle class because their political, economic and social interests could be made identical. All that was needed was time and patience, sobriety and self-help, and eventually the workers would become part of the middle class themselves. There were Chartists present and they made two attempts to capture the meeting. For Stephens it must have been an embarrassing occasion, since the leading voices among the Chartists present belonged to the minister of his Unitarian chapel, and the minister's son Matthew. The attachment of the minister and his three sons to the Chartist movement had caused split after split in his chapel.

What Stephens and those who thought like him in Wales were doing was heading off the development of working-class consciousness in precisely the same way as they were heading off the development of the Welsh language as an organic and all-encompassing medium of social life, education and communication. They dangled in front of the noses of peasants and workers alike the dream of an English education and an escape route to the middle class. The path was narrow and perilous, but a mountain people, like sheep and goats, have a special skill in negotiating such hazards. In England the working class were able to make more realistic use of the political lessons from the Chartist movement, because their sociological and cultural development were not obliged to be linked so closely or to have such a total effect on the national psyche. In Wales there had been a disastrous gap in the chain of inheritance. Aristocratic Welshness had virtually died before the birth of a new Welsh nation so that the life of the new nationality was obliged to hang on the delicate albeit amazingly tough thread of language. In the absence of the traditional political lead from a native aristocracy and the inability at this stage of a new working class to provide an alternative leadership, it fell to the lot of nonconformity with its residue of rural strength to lead the emerging nation in the direction of middle-class radical reform. Between 1848 and 1868 Welsh nonconformity effected the transformation with astonishing speed and efficiency. The Welsh working class were to need Dic Penderyn and the pathetic anonymous victims lying in the mud outside the Westgate Hotel as martyr figures. The comfortable road towards a middle class identity had no need of such sacrificial figures.

20 The American Alternative

On April 19th, 1839, a week before the Chartists enjoyed their brief reign over the town of Llanidloes, a great public meeting was held by the Calvinistic Methodists in Liverpool to bid Godspeed to the Rev. Henry Rees and his loyal companion, the Rev. Moses Parry, before they set out on their mission to survey the condition of the scattered Welsh Calvinistic communities in the United States of America. The great John Elias was expected to attend, only to be prevented at the last minute by illness. His place was taken by an alternative heavyweight of the Connexion, who was seen to make hurried notes with paper and pencil and then, in spite of the short notice, succeeded in reducing many in the packed audience to tears. The following day Henry Rees, a prince of the church at the age of forty-one, stood on an improvised bridge on board the *Liverpool*, one of the latest paddle-wheel steamers, and shook hands with 160 prominent Calvinistic Methodists as they passed before him. They had hired a special steam boat in order to make these last salutes. Before he left, Rees had written to John Elias in Anglesey and to Lewis Edwards at Bala, the eldest and the youngest member of what was in effect an informal but inflexible spiritual praesidium. The Connexion had its assemblies, courts, and governing bodies, for the most part elected in democratic fashion, but the important decisions were made by the accepted leaders, 'the eight-inch nails' as the pulpit giants were called, and then handed down for grateful acceptance among the faithful. Their authority sprang from a sophisticated combination of eloquence and orthodoxy, and an unspoken recognition of acknowledged merit. In this the Connexion offers a notable contrast to the Chartists, moral or physical. It never lacked for leadership. As long as that leadership lasted, which was in effect up to the end of the first world war, the Calvinistic Methodists flourished in and outside Wales as a most Welsh and influential nonconformist body.

As a body they had been slow to appreciate the importance of America. From the end of the seventeenth century all the older nonconformist denominations had sent a steady trickle of their membership across the Atlantic in the wake of the Quakers and the Baptists. Even the Welsh Anglicans had shown some concern, poaching and proselytising among the Welsh Quakers and Baptists in Pennsylvania and elsewhere. After the American and French Revolutions, the idea of emigration was frowned on by the conservative element in all the denominations. Christmas Evans, the one-eyed pulpit star of the Baptists, pilloried a light-headed and unreliable character called Mistir Mynd-i-'Merica (Mr. Going-to-America). While John Elias became so enamoured of the notion of quietistic submission to the civil authority that a good Methodist would need the written permission of both the Marquis of Anglesey and the Duke of Wellington before daring to cross the ocean. Nevertheless they went. The economic motive became increasingly pressing with each succeeding decade after the Napoleonic wars; so that by 1839 even John Elias saw that the scattered flock in America would be taken over by other shepherds, unless the Connexion took steps to arrange for their regular feeding inside properly arranged Calvinistic Methodist pastures and sheepfolds.

Henry Rees kept a diary and wrote an account of his journey which appears in the eighth chapter of his massive two-volume biography written by his friend and admirer, Owen Thomas of Liverpool. (Thomas was the outstanding practitioner of the art of biography in an age when this was the most popular literary form in Wales. He was also the maternal grandfather of Saunders Lewis.) Rees found New York a pleasant town where you could go to chapel or go to bed without locking your door or closing your windows – so unlike Liverpool. Water was the popular drink and every man had a right to it on any form of public transport or in any public place, for nothing. There was no class distinction, rich and poor alike were ready to eat at the same table. Great respect was shown to women everywhere, far more so than in the old world. The weather was unbearably dramatic. On their trip down the Ohio, they witnessed tornadoes and hurricanes, and when they were lost in the forest they resorted to prayer meetings before finding their way out. They travelled as far as Cincinnati, where the country was full of Welsh people. They did everything they could to live up to the alternative name of their denomination *Y Trefnyddion Cymraeg* (the Welsh Organisers or Arrangers) and warned their people against crossing the river, since Kentucky was a state which permitted the abominable custom of slavery.

Once the Methodists had brought themselves to accept the fact of emigration, their natural inclination towards order and discipline drew them into the business, and Henry Rees's account was published as a pamphlet in 1841. Methodists had to realise that America was a daunting wilderness and that it could only be transformed into a place worth living in by healthy people who were prepared to make a superhuman physical and spiritual effort in the best Calvinist tradition.

An expanding world and the growth of industrial capitalism was offering the Protestant poor the unexpected illusion of choice. The wilderness of this world was turning out to be much bigger than John Bunyan had imagined. Among the nonconformist sects the allegory of a pilgrimage transcended doctrinal differences. Indeed in one sense it had facilitated them. Time and again, examples occurred to suggest such a thing as an intellectual pilgrimage from High Calvinism via Fullerism to Arminianism and the delectable mountains inhabited by Arian shepherds in sight of the Celestial Unitarian City. And again in parallel with this was the pilgrimage to prosperity, where the practice of such virtues as self-restraint, thrift, chastity, honesty, industry, discipline, could lead to the accumulation of capital as well as merit. For the Protestant poor or hard pressed, there occurred within this framework the choice between a pilgrimage to Merthyr or emigration to America. 'The Colonies' in this context were a second and later choice, because they still had something of a penal stigma. They came directly under the crown and therefore did not offer so much theoretical freedom to those Welsh nonconformists determined enough to go looking for such a thing. The United States of America still offered the alluring prospect of a nonconformist state.

Even among the members of a denomination as small as the Unitarians there were distinct differences of emphasis and attitude. The Unitarians of Merthyr were varied enough in themselves, people like Taliesin Williams, Thomas Stephens, and the family of David John, the Chartist minister; but they had all opted for the progress of industry as the best hope both for a new society and for the progress of the soul. Yet in the 'Black Spot' back in rural Cardiganshire there was still a strong inclination to cling to the ideal of a rural Arcadia. The Garden of Eden was after all a garden, and by the sweat of his brow and the disciplined cultivation of his soul there was always a hope that some corner of it could be reclaimed. In 1841, Richard Lloyd Jones, a hatter and a Unitarian preacher, and a grandson of David Lloyd (Dafydd Llwyd, Brynllefrith) the poet and Arian, decided that emigration to the New World might well solve many of the problems which beset him and his family. Like most Welsh emigrants he did not take the decision lightly. Richard was in his early forties, the father of six children with another on the way. He sent his bachelor brother Jenkin first, and he worked as a lumberjack in the forests of Wisconsin for almost two years until the time was ripe for the family to move. Wisconsin was the place. A true frontier where the family could escape from the growing hostility of the larger denominations in Cardiganshire and the ignominy of scratching an inadequate living on an upland smallholding. Richard and his wife Mary were both poor relations in a family which took particular pride in its pedigree. In the New World they would find the means through their own efforts to recreate an ancient family glory in an improved Unitarian fashion: a new and better Wales of their own making.

The journey was a memorable nightmare and became transformed over the years into a family saga. Their ship was wrecked. In New York Richard, who spoke no English, was cheated. A child died on the journey and had to be buried on the roadside. In the forest they suffered malaria, and brother Jenkin died. On his gravestone was carved 'Though he slay me yet will I trust in him.' At the end of many vicissitudes the family established itself in what Richard's grand-daughter was to call 'The Valley of the God-Almighty Joneses'. More relatives came over. The hills were given Welsh names: Brynmawr, Bryncanol, and Brynbach. This would be a place where the Welsh Unitarians could live in harmony, preserve the old customs and speak the old language. Part of their Unitarian inheritance was the druidical lore of Iolo Morganwg. Their vision of Wales and the antiquity of Welshness was entirely his; and it remained with them to the second and third generation when memory of the language itself had begun to grow dim. In his autobiography, published in 1940, Richard's grand-son, Frank Lloyd Wright, gives a vivid description of life in the valley as he remembered it as a boy. To him his grandfather was an awesome combination of an Old Testament patriarch and a druid. He assumes that Iolo's symbol was the family crest, and Iolo's motto 'Y Gwir yn erbyn y Byd' the family motto (The Truth against the World). Frank Lloyd Wright adopted the motto as his own and had it carved on the oak beam above the fireplace of the first home he built for himself and his own family in Oak Park, Chicago. Of his grandfather he writes:

> He was in league with the stones of the field and he taught his children to work hard until the valley blossomed like a garden. His New Wales. He planted a small world within the world that is again within other worlds, without end.

It is the druid as much as the Unitarian that seems to blossom forth in the astonishing career of Frank Lloyd Wright; so that Iolo would have more than a small claim to be a part of his inspiration. And if we may allow ourselves to succumb to the charm of a more ancient magician, it seems appropriate that a great shape-shifter should give his name three times to the home of a great architect. Wright makes a great deal of this:

> I began to build Taliesin to get my back against the wall and fight for what I saw I had to fight . . . Taliesin was the name of a Welsh poet, a druid bard who sang to Wales the glories of fine art. Many legends cling to that beloved reverend name in Wales.

In a filmed interview in 1953 he gives a characteristic extempore version of his background. He says that his people were Welsh and that his old grandfather came to the region when the Indians were still there, 'about 125 years ago'. In the autobiography he is quite proud of the good relations that prevailed between his family and the remnants of dispossessed Indians still hanging about the place. As Unitarians they were fundamentally humanitarian. As druidical Welsh they had a certain sympathy for any form of aborigine. The interviewer was intrigued by the name Taliesin.

> All my people had Welsh names for their places – my sister's place was called Tan-y-deri (Under-the-Oaks). So I too chose a Welsh name for mine and it was Taliesin. Taliesin, a druid, was a member of King Arthur's Round Table. He sang the glories of fine art – I guess he was about the only Britisher who ever did – so I chose Taliesin for a name – it means 'Shining Brow'.

When regular services were established by steam-powered vessels across the Atlantic in the late 1840s the pace of emigration quickened. In the case of Wales it was a two-way traffic and nonconformist ministers particularly divided their time between two continents. An outstanding example would be Benjamin Chidlaw, born in Bala. His parents emigrated in 1821 when he was ten years old. He was educated in America and spent ten years as minister to the Welsh Independents at the curiously named Paddy's Run, near Cincinnati. Later he became the first 'missionary' of the 'American Sunday School Union', and established so many of them that he came to be regarded as the father figure of the movement. But he also found time to visit Wales and tour the country as an evangelist. Here again his record was notably successful. One of his sidelines was to advise on emigration and his activities throw light on what was in fact a constant factor in the process of emigration from the time of the Quakers to the twentieth century: a denominational network. Wherever he went, London, England, or London, Ontario, the Middle West or Australia, the first thing the well-brought-up Welsh nonconformist did was to contact the nearest appropriate chapel or, if it did not exist, take steps to assist in its creation.

The possibilities of choice could sometimes be an embarrassment. S.R., the Rev. Samuel Roberts of Llanbrynmair, Montgomeryshire, minister and son of a minister, farmer, magazine publisher and editor and radical reformer, had been in love with America and Liberty all his life. S.R. was a successful publicist with an unquenchable interest in all forms of communication. He was the first to advocate the penny post, a pioneer of paperback publishing, and an enthusiastic believer in the economic and social benefits of an extended railway system. When his father died S.R. succeeded him both as tenant of Diosg Farm and as minister of the Independent Hen Gapel in Llanbrynmair. As editor of *Y Cronicl*, a three-halfpenny monthly magazine, he became a household name in Wales. The magazine was reputed to have sold a million copies in the first twelve years of its existence. It was unrelentingly progressive and yet respectable. It advocated votes for women, but frowned on the physical force element in both Chartism and the Rebecca riots. S.R. was the first influential pacifist in Wales and became the most prominent voice raised against the more outrageous imperialist adventures of the British government such as the punitive military expeditions against the native populations in Abyssinia, Afghanistan and China.

All his life, he and his brothers had conducted a steady stream of correspondence with their relatives across the Atlantic. In 1855, an American cousin arrived in Llanbrynmair, Governor William Bebb of Ohio, 'the first white child to be born west of the Miami river'. He brought with him an attractive plan to purchase 100,000 acres in East Tennessee for sale to Welsh settlers. Governor Bebb's motives were clear enough. He argued that land prices in the western states had reached too high a level and that they should take action to direct the flow of immigration southward, use Welsh settlers to tame the wilderness of East Tennessee, do the country a bit of good and make a reasonable profit. A brochure was issued with S.R.'s name on it. Now he was committed. At the ripe age of fifty-seven he became an emigrant. He also sent a younger brother ahead. (There were three brothers known as S.R., J.R., and G.R.) G.R. was the farmer and accustomed to hard labour. Accompanied by his wife and little daughter, he led a small advance party into the wilderness, and they spent a year clearing the land. They called the settlement Brynffynnon. S.R. made a leisurely preaching tour around the Welsh communities in the north-east and middle-west, visiting relatives, arranging for the American publication of some of his writings, and advertising the attractions of the new settlement in East Tennessee. It was to be a haven of Welshness, where there would be no oppression, injustice or violence; where each family could rest after the day's labour in the shade of its own fruit-bearing trees.

He could not have chosen a worse place at a worse time. The land was improperly surveyed and the titles were unclear. Bebb was more than ready to answer the call when Abraham Lincoln summoned him to manage his election campaign in the Middle West. The brothers were left the victims of unscrupulous land sharks and in deep financial trouble. Then like a final blow to the delicate edifice of their hopes, the Civil War struck. S.R., the convinced pacifist, and delegate member of the European Peace Society, found himself trapped between the front lines of contending armies that were equipped to give the world the first exhibition of the enhanced destructive power of modern warfare. East

Tennessee remained loyal to the North and the Union. But the rest of the state was Confederate. Before hostilities broke out, S.R. had gone to press advocating a railway from Cincinnati to Chattanooga as the short answer to the economic problems of East Tennessee. It was not a railway he saw coming through the settlement, but the unruly troops of the flying columns of two opposing armies. Soon the settlement was isolated. Its work ground to a halt. Their stores were invaded by troops of both sides. Two of their friends were killed near the log cabin. S.R. was forced to watch the execution of another by a firing squad.

Soon his financial misfortunes gave rise to ugly rumours that were inflated by wartime propaganda. The vast majority of the Welsh were fervent supporters of the Union. S.R. was accused of changing sides when all he did in fact was stay in the same place as the tide of war ebbed and flowed around him. In the North he was accused of being a slave-owner and writing articles in favour of splitting the Union. In the South he and every member of his family were suspected of being fifth columnists, working secretly for the North. The more he wrote, the more his words were misinterpreted. This pioneer of controversial journalism and the importance of the press as a power to mould public opinion himself became the victim of the basest practices of the profession. In Tennessee all his optimism and energy and inventiveness came to nothing. In the end all he was left with was the habit of pulpit eloquence. He lost his battle with the wilderness. At the end of the war, Governor Bebb was able to recharge his private store of American enthusiasm in the security of his Washington office. He sent a cheering telegram to his cousin in Tennessee, 'Mr. Lincoln's railway is coming!' It came too late to save S.R.'s settlement. The prophet of progress was obliged to retreat. His American dream had come to nothing. After ten years of suffering in the wilderness, S.R. returned to Wales. His friends rallied round him and his position was to some extent restored by the largest collection ever made in nineteenth-century Wales for a private individual. The Independents and the progressives could not allow one of their champions to lie prostrate in the dust, an object of ridicule to conservative poets and denominational enemies. For the remainder of his long life, somewhat in the manner of a king in exile or a politician out of office, he held court in Conwy justifying his past, writing endless letters and trying to salvage what he could from his American disaster.

The origin of the intense interest of the Welsh Independents in emigration and in the possibilities of the New World sprang from their growing attachment to the idea of religious freedom. In times of economic depression this was underlined and reinforced by the prospect of material improvement and a higher standard of living. In 1848, Michael D. Jones was ordained minister for the Welsh church in Cincinnati at the age of twenty-six. He was the son of the first Principal of the Independent College established at Bala for the training of candidates for the ministry. The line from North Wales in particular to the frontier of the Middle West had alternative routes; one ran through upstate New York and the other, more direct, through Pennsylvania. In Cincinnati, the young Michael D. Jones came to the river bank each morning to watch the flat-boats unloading immigrants from the east. It distressed him to see the monoglot Welsh being badly treated and pushed aside to wait for interpreters. He knew that they were not illiterates and he also knew that they were the victims of the oppression of absentee landlords and the relentless poverty of the hungry 'forties. It was here on the banks of the Ohio that he decided on a single solution to the problems of Welsh poverty and the preservation of the Welsh identity: a politically independent second homeland for the Welsh across the sea.

It was in Welsh-American magazines that he first outlined his schemes. His proposals were a new Welsh society where the farmers would own their own land and the workers would own all the forms of industry on a co-operative basis. The site for this settlement would be somewhere on the new frontier by agreement with the governments of the United States and Great Britain. This was the logical development for any scheme to nurture the Welsh identity inside the twin spheres of influence of the two expanding English-speaking empires. The historic parallel with the attempts of the Jews to maintain their identity under the ancient empires was not lost on a reading public who had, so to speak, cut their mental teeth on the Old Testament. Michael D. Jones was a pioneer in several senses. He was the first in modern times to offer the Welsh a rational political solution to the age-old dilemma of preserving their identity. In accordance with the spirit of the age in Europe, the temperature of Welsh nationalism was rising. From the middle of the century onwards it became a matter of some urgency to forge new political forms to contain its growing intensity.

Within two years Jones abandoned the notion of a Welsh homeland established in the American West. He was enough of a realist to notice the dangerous resemblance to the westward moving mirage of the Welsh Red Indians. Even before the Civil War, the United States of America was shaping itself into a great melting-pot and the unifying ingredient for the great diversity in the stew would be the living waters of the English language. For those whose aim it was to preserve the essence of Welshness there was absolutely no point in travelling thousands of miles in order to encounter an even bigger version of the plague they were seeking to escape. Time and again in the nineteenth century it appears as if economic and political developments were specially designed to arouse expectations among the Welsh which could never be fulfilled in purely Welsh forms: first the concept of individual liberty growing out of religious freedom. Michael D. Jones had his vision of a free Wales. The model would best be constructed in a corner of the world where English influence was least likely to reach. In his view what the Welsh needed more than anything was to recover the self-confidence they had lost through being the inhabitants of territory occupied and administered by a great power. As a population they underestimated their own power and ability and therefore they achieved little. The serf mentality was afraid of exercising self-control. In Patagonia, a vague name for an uncharted region, which at that time had no political significance since it was unclaimed by any country, he and his associates would establish their Welsh settlement and see it eventually grow into a Welsh state where

> . . . a free farmer could tread on his own land and enjoy on his own hearth, the song and the harp and true Welsh fellowship . . . There will be chapel, school, and Parliament and the old language will be the medium of worship, of trade, of science, of education and of government. A strong and self-reliant nation will grow in a Welsh homeland.

The Patagonian adventure became the epic of the ordinary folk in nineteenth-century Wales. The largely working-class settlers endured great privations. Their leader, the printer Lewis Jones, after an uncertain beginning turned into a figure of Arthurian dimension. He had to deal with a difficult climate, with drought and with floods, with the faint-hearted who wanted to return home, with the Indians both hostile and friendly and with a watchful Argentinian government. For ten years the Welsh Patagonians enjoyed a self-government based on the secret ballot. They were probably the first community in the world to give the franchise to everyone over eighteen. Welsh was the language of government, of the law and the law courts, and it could now claim to have given the first demonstration of practical democracy in South America. It was of course too good to last. Lewis Jones was imprisoned more than once for standing up for Welsh rights. Briefly he was made Governor of the region by the Argentinians, the first and last Welshman to hold that office. His spirit was broken when a great flood devastated the valley of the Chubut in 1899. An offshoot settlement was established at the foot of the Andes and they both exist to this day. It is Spanish however that is making even more rapid inroads there than English in the old country.

The Welshness of Michael D. Jones, in spite of his democratic habits and radical turn of mind, was cast in an aristocratic mould. He had no use for the sentimental distortions of a watered-down national pride that sent the Welsh into raptures at the prospect of promotion up an imperial ladder. He could never bring himself to believe that his nation had survived for so long merely to provide a range of colourful leaders for other countries. Like a stern and autocratic shepherd of an erring flock he seized on the language as an instrument that could contain the vaulting ambition he could see emerging. The language and a new responsible patriotism he believed would keep young Welshmen inside the decent boundaries of humanity and duty. As he grew older, he became more convinced that the problem of Welshness was a problem of the Welsh character and that whatever happened overseas, this was the problem that had to be solved in Wales itself.

21 Towards Respectability

By the 1840s the majority of Welsh people were reputed to belong to one or other of the great nonconformist denominations: in the North the Calvinistic Methodists were strongest, in the South the Independents and the Baptists. The established church was very unwilling to recognise this accomplished fact. It still had the ear of the government and could make common cause with an increasingly nervous ruling class. It pushed ahead with a scheme to establish 'National' schools, in spite of the unwillingness of the nonconformists to send their children to them. These stubborn dissenters were beginning to find their feet and would give no ground on religious matters. In 1843 a bill was introduced in the House of Commons that proposed to place the education of children employed in mines and factories under the exclusive control of the established Anglican church. In Wales this caused an immediate outcry. The government sensed that unco-operative nonconformity could make the scheme unworkable. Furthermore there were many nonconformists in Wales who objected in principle to state grants for education because they believed still that any form of public education was essentially part of religious training. This did not necessarily mean that nonconformists were theocratic in the sense of a modern Marxist state. Their objection to state finance was an extension of their objection to the state control of religion. At the same time in Wales in spite of their high principles the nonconformist bodies were too poor to bear the initial burdens of building and maintaining schools in the manner recommended by the London based 'British Society'. The bill was eventually withdrawn, but in that same year, 1843, Hugh Owen, an Anglesey Calvinistic Methodist who served as a clerk with the Poor Law Commission in London, composed 'A Letter to the Welsh People' in which he urged nonconformists to accept state grants towards a system of secular education. This was in effect the first salvo in a lifelong campaign. Hugh Owen was to become the chief architect of a comprehensive educational system which by the year of his knighthood and his death, 1881, was poised to take over from the denominational network as the custodian of the inner sanctuary of the Welsh spirit.

In March 1846 William Williams, M.P. for Coventry, moved a resolution in the House of Commons demanding that a commission be set up to enquire into 'the state of Education in the Principality of Wales, especially into the means afforded to the labouring classes of acquiring a knowledge of the English tongue'. Williams himself was a shining example of what a humble Welshman could achieve once he had acquired 'a knowledge of the English tongue'. He had made a fortune as a wholesaler of cotton and linen goods. He was an Anglican who tended to favour the disestablishment of the church: a capitalist, noted in the House of Commons for his radical views; a reformer dedicated to the inevitability of gradualism. In the course of his speech he made a memorable appeal to balance-sheet pragmatism which won approval on all sides of the House.

> It should be borne in mind, that an ill-educated and undisciplined population, like that existing amongst the mines in South Wales, is one that may be found most dangerous to the neighbourhood in which it dwells, and that a band of efficient schoolmasters is kept up at a much less expense than a body of police or soldiery.

The government reaction was swift. A commission was created and came down to Wales. It was led by three young and able barristers with impeccable Anglican credentials named Lingen, Symons, and Vaughan Johnson. None of them spoke Welsh or had any connection with the leaders of Welsh nonconformity. They and their team relied on the parochial assistance of the clergy of the established church, the Church of England. Their industry was astonishing. Within a year in 1847 they published a detailed report in three large volumes which Saunders Lewis could describe as late as 1962 as 'the most important nineteenth-century historical documents we possess . . . they contain a store of information that has not yet been used.'

The cool style of the report, its assumption of effortless superiority and patronising judicial objectivity, offers a fascinating contrast with the outraged indignation and emotional eloquence of the Welsh response. Nothing could illustrate more vividly or more accurately the ancient antipathy towards each other inherent in the two languages: or the fundamental incompatibility of two cultures and the responses they engendered to the very nature of human existence. The report of the Blue Books, as they were called, drew a dark picture of ignorance and, what was much worse, immorality. And these conclusions were drawn from what appeared to be a detailed mass of evidence drawn up in the latest scientific manner. In the case of Anglesey for example it was stated that in an area of 173,440 acres the number of inhabitants amounted to 50,891. There were thirty-six parishes on the island without any school at all. The future of the only two efficient schools, the National (church) School at Beaumaris and the new British (nonconformist) School at Llanrhuddlad, looked bleak because they were wholly unsupported by public funds. This thorough approach, with detailed comments on every school visited, was backed up by impressive sociological surveys. R.W. Lingen wrote with particular brilliance and perception. He has some claim to being the first to understand the nature of the mass migration from the marginal land to those areas where the smelters and miners could 'wanton in plenty', and the effect this had on Welsh society.

> Yet the families which are daily passing from the one scene to the other do not thereby change their relative position in society. A new field is opened to them, but not a wider. They are never masters . . . It is the same people. Whether in the country or among the furnaces, the Welsh element is never found at the top of the social scale . . . Equally in his new as in his old home, his language keeps him under the hatches . . . He is left to live in an under-world of his own, and the march of society goes . . . completely over his head.'

'Under-world' has a saving hyphen. It does not refer to a criminal class, only to a sub-culture of the dispossessed. The report paraded alarming evidence of conditions which the nonconformists would have preferred to believe did not exist. It was incontrovertibly true that most of the people and all of the children did not speak English. It had not occurred to them before that a stigma was attached to the inability to speak English. From now on this deficiency ranked with being unwashed or going without shoes as a conspicuous mark of poverty and worse still a source of depravation. A lack of English also blocked a reasonable access to the rewards of respectability: above all it retarded the progress of Progress, that element of Hegelian philosophy that so much appealed to the bourgeois age which was gradually insinuating itself into the forms of liberal theology that would in due course dominate noncon-formist thinking in Wales and make it possible for the son of the Principal of the Calvinistic Methodist Theological College in Bala to become the first Principal of the new University of Wales at Aberyst-wyth.

The underlying assumption of the report was that 'ignorance' and 'ignorance of the English language' were synonymous. This the Welsh, with varying degrees of reluctance, could eventually bring themselves to accept. What they could not stomach, on any account was the equating of this state of ignorance with immorality. It was altogether intolerable that the *gwerin*, that simple model of virtue and unpretenti-ous excellence, so often extolled from eisteddfod platforms in the fashion set by that impartial and impeccable Anglican Carnhuanawc, should be pronounced by one of the upstart commissioners as 'almost universally' immoral. By this stage in their development the Welsh were extremely articulate and literate people, and all their papers and magazines bristled with prolonged and elaborate refutations to disprove the shameful accusations made by the commissioners. National reputations were made by the men who made the most effective replies, and a new form of nationalism came into existence, based not so much upon any consistent philosophy as on the touchy pride that Shakespeare portrayed so well in its Tudor form in the character of the Welsh soldier Fluellen. The English public of course understood nothing of this. Sir Thomas Phillips, the lifelong enemy of John Frost and gallant defender of Newport, went to the trouble of writing a book, *Wales: the Language, Social Condition, Moral Character and Religious Opinions of the People*, in which the lack of qualifications of the young commissioners and the inaccuracies and inadequacies of their Report were pointed out. But by that time the attention of the commissioners and the government had moved on to more important matters, and the Welsh were left to mutter among themselves and lick their own psychological wounds.

Welsh journalism gave currency to a phrase '*Brad y Llyfrau Gleision*' (The Treachery of the Blue Books) which is still in general use to describe this crucial turning point in modern Welsh history. The terminology is significant. It refers back to '*Brad y Cyllyll Hirion*' (The Treachery of the Long Knives) a dramatic episode in Theophilus Evans's *Drych y Prifoesoedd* (A Mirror of Past Ages) which describes how the Anglo-Saxon villain, Hengist, instructed his deputation to a peace conference and friendly feast with the Britons to carry knives hidden in their boots to kill off the best leaders in Vortigern's army. This mythical incident in the ancient struggle between the Saxons and the British was still alive in the folk-memory of the Welsh. This latest insult gave it a fresh currency.

In 1850, thanks to industrialism and the expansion of chapels, there were far more Welsh-speaking Welsh than had existed in 1800 and they represented a far higher percentage of the existing population of Wales than had been the case in 1800. Furthermore they had spread abroad and taken their language and their religion with them. They had the capacity to become a formidable political force in their own right without necessarily making any fundamental change in their own nature. They became a force. But they also changed and the main agent of change was the kind of educational system that sprang from a total but unspoken acceptance of the policies recommended by the Blue Books. In the controversy which raged between the most respected nonconformist leaders and the few people who dared to defend the Report, it would seem, in Cardiff Arms Park parlance, that the English were hammered into the ground, and that the Welsh leaders like Henry Richard and Dr. Lewis Edwards and Ieuan Gwynedd deserved to be carried shoulder-high off the field by their triumphant supporters. The subsequent history of Wales shows clearly enough that it was the commission that had won the day.

The process of change in the attitude of nonconformists towards education began when the leadership of the Calvinistic Methodists passed quietly from the strong hands of John Elias to the more supple but no less stubborn grip of Lewis Edwards. As befitted an evangelical movement, John Elias's power flowed from his extraordinary prowess in the pulpit. But the Methodist Connexion in Wales was resolutely Presbyterian in its structure and the manipulation of committees became more important as the organisation grew more widespread and commanded ever greater resources. It was a committee that sent Henry Rees to America, and financed the trip; and there were committees responsible for a wide variety of denominational activities. Lewis Edwards became the editor of the influential monthly magazine *Y Traethodydd* (The Essayist), and held sway as Principal of Bala Theological College for fifty years. John Elias considered himself a 'High Calvinist' and in politics he was certainly a High Tory and viewed all forms of secular education with the deepest suspicion. The young Lewis Edwards was rebuked by the great man for his insatiable appetite for scholarship and knowledge, but he persisted in his quest for higher education and found what he wanted in the University of Edinburgh. There he found access not only to modified forms of Calvinism but also the German intellectual tradition. His *Traethodydd* was modelled on *Blackwood's Magazine* and *The Edinburgh Review* and there can be no doubt that he fashioned it into a substantial intellectual force in Welsh life. There was at all times a conscious rivalry between the larger nonconformist bodies that was in effect a surrogate outlet for political energy and each one took a special pride in the quality of its products, whether they were chapel buildings, hymn books, preachers, choirs, newspapers or magazines. It was the outside pressure of economics and the more pressing social aspects of politics that slowly brought them round to concerted action and eventually what could be described as consensus philosophy. Edwards's *Traethodydd* played a notable part in this process.

There were policies to debate and principles to be argued on vital topics that did not necessarily run along denominational lines. The three issues with the greatest practical consequences for the future of the Welsh people in the first phase of nonconformist supremacy were education, the more effective exercise of political power, and the expression of national consciousness. They were intimately related and an advance or a retreat on one front invariably had repercussions on another. It was a characteristic of this increasingly bourgeois nonconformist world that these debates should be conducted in public on what appears to a twentieth-century reader a surprisingly high level.

Throughout Wales there was an avid readership for these debates, which suggests a general level of intelligence rather higher than that which prevails at the present time. (If this is the case, it is in itself a somewhat ironic comment on the efficacy of one hundred years of free English state education.)

Hugh Owen and the advocates of state aid for education had a great deal of opposition to contend with, especially among the older nonconformist bodies. The redoubtable David Rees of Llanelli, the erstwhile champion of moral force Chartism, in his magazine *Y Diwygiwr*, thundered out his opposition, 'I do not hesitate to say that any system of general education under the patronage of government is as certain to prove a curse in the future as the existence of the Church of England is a curse at the present day'. There would appear to be an undertone of national spirit as well as religious principle, and the cause of the state educationalists was not helped by an element of anti-English as well as anti-government feeling in the wave of resentment that followed in the wake of the Treachery of the Blue Books.

But Hugh Owen was not a man to be deterred. He was an able administrator and by 1853 had been appointed Chief Clerk at the Poor Law Commission. He was influenced to the point of awe by the utilitarian doctrines of Jeremy Bentham and James Mill. Whatever he heard in chapel on Sundays, for a Poor Law commissioner it was very good news to learn that an action was moral to the degree that it was useful. As a weekday ethos for a bourgeois world it was extremely convenient to believe that what was useful was almost bound to be virtuous. For an administrator the processes of bureaucracy were positively beautified by the notion of conveying 'the greatest happiness to the greatest number'. It was a utilitarian rocket fuel that sent Hugh Owen zooming through the proliferating committees of Wales. A more homely metaphor would envisage him a weaver's shuttle intent with mechanistic concentration on weaving an educational pattern that would keep the greatest number of his countrymen warm for ever in the weekday world. He formed a working alliance with men like Lewis Edwards and it would not be completely unfair to say that they divided the Welsh week between them. Sunday and a minimum of three evenings would continue to belong to the chapel; what was left would be devoted to the establishment of a system of secular education that would guarantee to every Welsh youth (and later every Welsh maiden) the opportunity of getting on in the world. To the remnant of a 'chosen people' in the throes of a paroxysm of self-awareness and yet conscious too that they formed less than seven per cent of the total population of a Great Britain which controlled a world-wide empire, men like Hugh Owen and Lewis Edwards were setting out the prospectus of an offer they could not refuse.

To observe the activities of Hugh Owen at close quarters has the fascination that belongs to the study of the amazing industry of the smaller creatures of the natural world. He never gives up. His presence flits through the minutes of innumerable committees, and by sheer persistence he wears down all opposition and attains a position of immense influence in Wales. He began by becoming Honorary Secretary of the Cambrian Educational Society. From this key position he gradually convinced the nonconformist bodies that it was in their best interests to support the establishment of state-aided British Schools in Wales. The bait he hung out was the prospect of getting them up before the Church of England got in with their National Schools. His efforts were interrupted by the Crimean War and it was not until 1863 that he enjoyed his first triumph when the Bangor Normal College was opened for the training of teachers. Symbolic of the alliance between Hugh Owen and Lewis Edwards was the appointment of John Phillips, Edwards's friend and companion in Edinburgh, an ordained Calvinistic Methodist minister, and the first representative in Wales of the British Schools Society, as Principal.

The desire to exercise political power was born from the seed of national consciousness taking root in the stubborn soil of the older nonconformity. Henry Rees's younger brother William (Gwilym Hiraethog) found the Independents a more congenial denomination in which to exercise his talents. His career followed a characteristic pattern in nineteenth-century Wales and offers a good example of the sterling qualities of the *gwerinwr*. As a youth he worked as a shepherd on the slopes of Hiraethog Mountain in Denbighshire and later earned his living as a farm labourer. Nevertheless, as was almost invariably the case, he had that pride of pedigree characteristic of a mountain race and inherent in the very lifestream of the Welsh language. At one time his family lived in Cae Du, the old home of the Renaissance scholar William Salesbury, and the pseudonym he adopted as a writer, Gwilym Hiraethog, was a clear echo of Gruffydd Hiraethog, Salesbury's friend and link with the last of the great mediaeval poets, Tudur Aled.

Gwilym first came to public notice as an eisteddfod poet but he was a man of great versatility and in 1843, from Liverpool where he was minister of a large Welsh Congregationalist church, he launched his radical newspaper *Yr Amserau* (The Times). This was the first really successful Welsh weekly newspaper and in it the literate Welsh peasant had his first chance of being led (by the hand) through the labyrinth of European politics. Gwilym Hiraethog knew Mazzini and corresponded with him. National liberation movements were his special interest. Kossuth sent a deputation from Hungary to thank Gwilym Hiraethog for his support. Like all the Welsh nonconformists he was an ardent advocate of the abolition of slavery in the USA. The most popular feature in the paper he wrote himself, '*Llythyrau'r Hen Ffarmwr*' (The Old Farmer's Letters) written in the racy dialect of upland Denbighshire, and dealing with such subjects as the abolition of the Corn Laws, anti-tithe legislation, disestablishment, education, the shortcomings of the Oxford Movement and the Papacy, and politics in general. Apart from anything else, the chapel-going reader was made to realise that life in the outside world, in spite of its wickedness, could be a lot of fun.

In the middle of the century a sequence of changes took place which ensured that politics would occupy a position in Welsh life that had previously been taken up by the preoccupation of the nonconformist bodies with doctrinal disputation. Whereas in the beginning of the century the Welsh were invariably engaged in heated arguments about Baptism, the doctrine of Atonement, and the true nature of church government, by the end their energy and enthusiasm was absorbed in the minutiae of the Welsh corner of British party politics. In 1862 the English Society for the Liberation of Religion from State Control made a discreet move into the promising arena of Welsh dissent. Reforms of the franchise were in the offing and the Welsh needed to be taught how to run a political campaign. The chief messenger of the society was Henry Richard, a former Congregational minister in London, and now secretary of the Peace Society. He was anxious to interpret Wales to the English and itching to get into parliament. Out of the activities of the Liberation Society came the South Wales Liberal Association. In 1867 the Representation of the People Act extended the franchise and for the first time a potent working-class element was included in the electorate of the industrial parliamentary boroughs. Henry Richard stood as a Liberal candidate at Merthyr Tydfil, where the electorate had been increased tenfold, against the sitting member, H.A. Bruce, later the first Lord Aberdare. With working-class support he was elected by a great majority and from that time forward became the voice of Wales and of Welsh nonconformity in the House of Commons. It is of some interest to note that Thomas Stephens supported H.A. Bruce. This was perfectly consistent. Bruce took the same kind of interest in Welsh antiquities. He had even translated the somewhat pedestrian verses of Taliesin ap Iolo into English. And later Bruce and his son the second Lord Aberdare were to play significant roles in the establishment of permanent intermediate and higher educational systems in Wales. Bruce served in Gladstone's cabinet as Home Secretary and Lord President of the Council and, as a family, they had the kind of connections in government circles that facilitated the changes advocated by men like Hugh Owen, Lewis Edwards and indeed Henry Richard himself. It was by such collaboration, seen and unseen, that the path of progress took on something of the aura of the ways of providence in the Welsh nonconformist mind.

Victory for the nonconformist interest in North Wales did not come so easily. The chosen battlefield was the widespread Denbigh County constituency. There was still no secret ballot and the choice of the rural voter was only too visible to his master or his landlord. A key figure in the campaign for the radical candidate was Thomas Gee, the publisher and newspaper proprietor. Gee was the son of an English printing publisher who had been persuaded to set up business in Denbigh at the turn of the century by Thomas Jones, the Calvinistic Methodist leader. Gee the elder had been so impressed by Thomas Jones that he eventually became a Welsh Calvinistic Methodist himself. When Thomas Gee inherited the business in 1845 he began to publish *Y Traethodydd* and in 1854 he began the publication of the monumental *Gwyddoniadur*, an encyclopaedia which took twenty-four years to complete. A second edition in ten volumes was published in 1896. But is was through his newspaper, *Y Faner*, which he started in 1857, that he exercised his great influence on the political and social life of Wales, for the rest of his long life. The election of 1868 gave him the chance to flex his political muscle. His candidate was elected, but once again Tory landowners took their revenge and either evicted their tenants who had dared to vote for the radical or raised their rents. This had become a pattern at election time in North and West Wales. Evicted tenants suffered great hardship and many were forced to emigrate. These were often the people who responded most readily to the call of men like S.R., B. Chidlaw, Evan Evans Nant-y-Glo, and even of Michael D. Jones. (A harsh life in a settlement in far away South America with freedom would be preferable to a harsh life in Wales with injustice.) Thomas Gee's *Faner* had a circulation of over 50,000. He found little difficulty in arousing the country to a state of intense indignation. Even among the pliant and peaceable Calvinistic Methodists he established a constituency of protest. Henry Richard brought the matter up in parliament and it was largely through his efforts that the Ballot Act of 1872 was passed. From that time forward men could vote in secret and in safety, and political careers became an even more attractive possibility to ambitious and respectable young Welshmen than ascending the steps of a nonconformist pulpit.

22 The Benthamite Train

Eisteddfodau, like public games, are convenient outlets for the apparently ineradicable human instinct to compete. It has been argued that the inhabitants of hilly countries are naturally individualistic and contentious, and the Greeks, ancient and modern, are usually paraded as the outstanding example. In fact this aspect of human nature dominates the sports and games that are now universally accepted as an essential form of relaxation in any large-scale industrial conurbation. But in the Welsh experience the eisteddfod preceded sport as a popular recreation. In contrast to the benevolent but stern regimen of the chapel it offered endless opportunities for competitive activities from singing solos and writing poetry to knitting stockings and writing a treatise on the relative merits of hydraulic engines. By the sixth decade of the nineteenth century, the eisteddfod and all it offered had become an integral part of the Welsh way of life. In industrial centres as far apart as Merthyr Tydfil and Pittsburgh or Llanelli and Liverpool, Utica, Manchester, Middlesbrough, there were families devoted to competing in eisteddfodau to whom the habit became a way of life. Ap Nathan, for example, Jonathan Reynolds, a wheelwright of Merthyr Tydfil, won over a hundred prizes for *englynion* (strict metre epigrams) and *tribannau* (Glamorganshire topical folk-verses). He was noted for his taste for archaic forms, and he indulged this to some extent by translating several of Shakespeare's plays into Welsh. His eldest son, Llywarch Reynolds, edited Thomas Stephens's celebrated essay on Madoc for publication in 1893 and carried on the family tradition into the higher reaches of Celtic scholarship.

In the aftermath of the scandals of the great eisteddfod of 1858 in Llangollen, the word reform was in the air. In 1860 the festival was held in Denbigh under the watchful Calvinistic Methodist eye of Thomas Gee. The irrational enthusiasms of Cymric clergymen, whether in Yorkshire or Meirioneth, were in disgrace. The need for a better order was agreed upon: a decent balance between the bards who, as one writer complained, were getting to be as thick on the ground as blackberries, and 'men of more practical business habits' who had made their way in the world by their skill in manipulating organisations. It was inconceivable that a Benthamite beaver such as Hugh Owen could let slip such a golden opportunity to exercise his talents. In spite of his vaunted friendship with Matthew Arnold there never was a man with less poetry in his make-up. At Aberdare in 1861 he moved in, and with remarkable speed persuaded the appropriate committees to take up his notion of a Social Science section. When it came into operation its declared intent was 'the discussion of subjects calculated to elevate the moral and social character of the Welsh people'. As always the pattern for his endeavours was drawn from his London experience. This was his version of Lord Brougham's Association for the Promotion of Social Science and his innovations were welcomed with particular warmth in Thomas Gee's *Faner*. John Griffiths, S.R.'s cousin and an indefatigable roving reporter who travelled in America to report on the Civil War, wrote enthusiastically in *Y Faner*: 'This is an utilitarian age and all things have to be put to good use . . . the motto of the age is 'Move On' and not 'Stand Still', and the 'move on' of the Eisteddfod is the Social Science Section on the fourth day.'

The 'move on' was in fact no more than a fresh chapter in the struggle for the control of an institution which was generally accepted to be the most outward and visible sign of an amorphous but increasingly potent entity referred to as 'the national soul'. At least four distinct forces can be seen at work contending for supremacy: the bards with their own convocation which Iolo had blessed with the resounding title *Gorsedd Beirdd Ynys Prydain* wrapped up in the splendour of a mythical past; the nonconformist leaders with literary inclinations; the musicians as ever in pursuit of bigger and better platforms; and that element of the well-do-do classes lusting after social and political limelight rather than any mystical eye of light. Hugh Owen showed considerable skill in playing off these elements against each other, and in no time at all it seemed as if his Social Science section would take control. By 1865 it was staging an Industrial Exhibition and Hugh Owen seems to have decreed that all its proceedings should be conducted in the English language in order to demonstrate to a sceptical world – which for him of course meant the main organs of English authority and opinion – that the Welsh were not 'incapable of progress' and that the new eisteddfod, having been thoroughly sterilised and homogenised, was now worthy of the support of nothing less than the very 'best people'.

Alas, as is so often the case in this vale of tears, the dedicated reformer received little thanks for his pains. By introducing so much English, he had opened the door that had once been locked, and revealed for open inspection rites and customs hitherto half-hidden from the cold enquiring Saxon eye. *The Times* was particularly brutal. It took a fiendish delight in pouring scorn on the Industrial Exhibition. And then like a tiger that has tasted blood proceeded to tear the whole cherished institution to pieces. Its essential worthlessness resided with its mindless worship of the vatic outpourings of a language that should have been dead and buried centuries ago.

> The Welsh language is the curse of Wales . . . An Eisteddfod is one of the most mischievous and selfish pieces of sentimentalism which could possibly be perpetrated. It is simply a foolish interference with the natural progress of civilisation and prosperity . . . Not only the energy and power, but the intelligence and music of Europe have come mainly from Teutonic sources, and this glorification of everything Celtic, if it were not pedantry, would be sheer ignorance. The sooner all Welsh specialities disappear from the face of the earth the better.

Owen's response was that of a royal servant who redoubles his efforts to please each time the monarch kicks him downstairs. He worked harder in his self-appointed task of anglicising the eisteddfod and tried to link what he was doing with his crusade for education in Wales. It was at this point that Matthew Arnold made an unexpected and possibly unintended intervention. Unintended or not, it was to have far reaching effects both on Welsh institutions and on the Welsh character.

In 1866 he chose as the subject of his four lectures from the Chair of Poetry at the University of Oxford 'The Study of Celtic Literature'. His reign as the leading literary critic of the English-speaking world had already begun. He was the son of the celebrated Dr. Thomas Arnold of Rugby, and he was also one of Her Majesty's most influential inspectors of schools. To the whole of the Celtic fringe, whatever he had to say would be of great importance; but the full force was directed at Wales, that Celtic country closest to England which nevertheless clung most tenaciously to its separate language and culture. Already Mr. Arnold, HMI, had made a preliminary pronouncement on the problem. As early as 1852, in an official report he had written:

> It must always be the desire of a Government to render its dominions, as far as possible, homogeneous . . . Sooner or later, the difference of language between Wales and England will probably be effaced . . . an event which is socially and politically so desirable.

Since that date he had spent a holiday in Llandudno with his brother Tom, which from his letters we may judge to have been a landmark, in every sense of that word, in his poetic career. After a period of spiritual drought, the visionary gleam was returning. And he attributed this fresh surge of inspiration, not so much to any spark from heaven that fell, but to the mystic landscape he saw around him. He wrote to his mother:

> The poetry of the Celtic race and its names of places quite overpowers me

and it will be long before Tom forgets the line, 'Hear from thy grave, great Taliesin, hear', from Gray's 'Bard', since I have repeated it a hundred times a day on our excursions.

The underlying theme of his lectures was an attempt to reconcile the role of an inspector of schools, a loyal servant of the state, and that of a poet who believed in the capacity of poetry to offer a moral interpretation of man and the world. As a poet he had a mission which was not so far removed from the druidical obsessions of Iolo Morganwg and his even more extravagant followers.

In an age when orthodox religion was visibly failing to control or direct the development of civilisation, and particularly the civilisation of the English-speaking world, it would be a combination of enlightened education and elevated culture that would take its place as the guiding hand. In England he was prepared to do battle with the Philistines, whose appalling vulgarity and materialism and utter lack of sensitivity in their elephantine pursuit of profit threatened everything a poet should hold dear: the glories of the English past, the intrinsic beauty of the language and its literary heritage, and an abiding concern for the good, the true and the beautiful. In Wales, as an agent of the state, he realised that he was required to go against his own nature as a poet and play the rôle of the Philistine, intent on the removal of any obstacles that lay in the road of uniformity, homogeneity, and material progress. The solution he offered was ingenious: dispose of the language, but preserve its essence, bury the body, but bottle the soul. What he advocated was a characteristic Victorian gothic operation that fell neatly half-way between the experiments of Dr. Frankenstein and Dr. Jekyll. Take a victim or a patient and extract from him the vital juices that would cost him his life but which could be used to revive the flagging spirit of an ailing giant with an elixir of life which Arnold labelled 'Celtic Magic'.

Hugh Owen, and the increasing number of influential Welshmen who thought like him, were beside themselves with delight when they read the lectures. England's leading critic and a Professor of Poetry at Oxford was treading down the fences of radical prejudice and refuting the gross libels of those English newspapers which took so much delight in denigrating, in the words of the *Daily Telegraph* . . .

a small country, unfavourably situated . . . with an indifferent soil and inhabited by an unenterprising people . . . a sensible Welshman would direct all his endeavours towards inducing his countrymen to appreciate their neighbours instead of themselves.

Arnold's solution to what was largely his personal problem appeared in their eyes like a sign from heaven written right across the firmament.

All that the Welsh had to do was to anglicise themselves as rapidly as possible and bring to the foot of the throne the essence of their own being, 'Celtic Magic', to be used judiciously from time to time to offset any threatened imbalance in the metabolism of the imperial body politic. Professor Arnold had had some very nice things to say about Celtic literature. He had no knowledge of Welsh or of any Celtic language but he had read Renan's *La poésie des races celtiques* so that he knew that Celtic poetry was characterised by spirituality, melancholy and a heightened awareness of nature. What could be more respectable? His elegant cadences were full of praise of the delicate beauty and charm of *The Mabinogion*. This too was very reassuring. It meant that young ladies could now read it, at least in Lady Charlotte Guest's translation. And to crown the benevolence of his attitude, he was strongly in favour of the creation of a Chair of Celtic in the University at Oxford. This in itself would give fresh ammunition to Hugh Owen in his continuing battle for higher education in Wales.

Hugh Owen begged the great man to visit the national eisteddfod at Chester and use the platform to deliver an address on some fresh aspect of Celtic genius. He did not necessarily have to be at a loss to discover one. He himself had pointed out that Cumbria was his spiritual home, and that his mother was Cornish, a fact which in itself offset his father's unbending Teutonism.

> When I was young, I was taught to think of Celt as separated by an impassable gulf from Teuton; my father in particular was never weary of contrasting them; he insisted much oftener on the separation between us and them than on the separation between us and any other race in the world.

Like so many intellectuals of his time Arnold was fascinated with the notion of a science of origins – 'a science which is at the bottom of all real knowledge of the actual world and which is every day growing in interest and importance'. At this stage cultural uniformity and racialism were close to their common source; but the dangerous habit of labelling what were no more than speculative poetic fancies (for the most part with considerably less substance to them than Iolo's) with the term 'science' or 'scientific' was already well under way.

In the event, Arnold declined the invitation, but the letter he sent, which was for publication, was full of deliberate praise for what he termed the 'spirituality' of the Celtic people.

> When I see the enthusiasm these Eisteddfods can awaken in your whole people, and then think of the tastes, the literature, the amusements, of our own lower middle class, I am filled with admiration for you. It is a consoling thought and one which history allows us to entertain, that

nations disinherited of political success may yet leave their mark on the world's progress, and contribute powerfully to the civilisation of mankind . . . Now, then, is the moment for the greater delicacy and spirituality of the Celtic peoples who are blended with us . . . to make itself felt, prized and honoured. In a certain measure the children of Taliesin and Ossian have now the opportunity for renewing the famous feat of the Greeks, and conquering their conquerors. No service England can render the Celts by giving you a share in her many good qualities can surpass what the Celts can at this moment do for England by communicating to us some of theirs.

This was more than *The Times* and most of the English newspapers could bear. They returned to their attack on the eisteddfod and the shortcomings of the Welsh in general, using racialist terms that were a vivid foretaste of the style of *Völkischer Beobachter*. Everybody joined in the fun and the object of the exercise was to make Matthew Arnold appear the last word in soft-headed liberalism. Arnold was obliged to spell out his message and the terms of the Faust-bargain he was offering the Welsh in simple terms that even the readers of *The Times* could understand: in return for sacrificing their language and their separate identity, the Welsh would be allowed to place their unsteady feet on the first rungs of the ladder that would lead them to the first circle in the evolutionary process that was so closely linked with imperial success.

I must say I quite share the opinion of my brother Saxons as to the practical inconvenience of perpetuating the speaking of Welsh . . . The sooner the Welsh language disappears . . . the better; the better for England, the better for Wales itself.

Poor Hugh Owen was fighting his battles on so many fronts. An unlikely Galahad of anglicisation and education, he scurried about Wales, a familiar figure at railway junctions carrying his little black travelling bag and waiting for yet another connection. He had to reassure the powers that be that there would be absolutely no possibility of his projected University of Wales becoming a hotbed of Fenianism. And on the other hand he had to convince nonconformist leaders in particular that the *gwerin* would never lose its unswerving allegiance to the denomination of its choice if it accepted the Greek gift of an English education. In the 1860s and 1870s the messages of Hugh Owen were not what the Welsh peasants and workers wanted to hear. At the eisteddfod, for example, the great occasions were often impeded by the mass audience's insistence on being spoken to in Welsh. Despite the Prince of Wales's feathers, the Union Jack, and lavish visual demonstrations of loyalty to the throne, if a great man like Henry Richard came down from London with some urgent message, whatever the press reported, the oratorical pill had to be thickly coated in the best possible Welsh and the most flattering references to the inestimable virtues inherent in the character of the Welsh people. As an audience at any eisteddfod, the Welsh working classes were proud enough to demand being wooed. It took some courage on the part of David Davies, Llandinam, in spite of his great wealth, to make his speech at the Aberystwyth eisteddfod in favour of learning English.

> I am a great admirer of the old Welsh language and I have no sympathy with those who revile it. Still I have seen enough of the world to know that the best medium to make money by is the English language. I want to advise every one of my countrymen to master it perfectly; if you are content with brown bread, you can, of course, remain where you are. If you wish to enjoy the luxuries of life with white bread to boot, the only way to do so is by learning English well. I know what it is to eat both.

What Davies imagined were blunt home truths were still not a palatable message to the majority of his listeners. His attitude may well have cost him an early election to that exclusive club at Westminster that he so longed to join. As probably the richest layman in the Connexion he was able to throw his weight about in the assemblies of the Calvinistic Methodists for most of his long life, but he did not get into parliament until 1874. (He lasted there twelve years until he disagreed with Mr. Gladstone over Home Rule for Ireland and lost his Cardigan seat.) Davies never had the popular touch of a man like Mabon (William Abraham) the miners' leader, also a Calvinistic Methodist. Mabon learnt the art of manipulating an audience in the small eisteddfodau around his home in Aberafan, and the eisteddfod and all it stood for was a weapon he was able to use for most of his public life. It is not a coincidence that Mabon entered parliament by defeating a coal-owning collaborator of David Davies in the business of exploiting the Rhondda valleys, and managed to stay there for thirty-seven years. He got on far better with Mr. Gladstone, and Mrs. Gladstone, who was inclined to be Welsh in the tradition of Lady Llanover, gave Mabon a silver leek to wear on his first St. David's Day in the House of Commons. Mabon anticipated Lloyd George in the skilful use he made of the eisteddfod and the shaping of national sentiment for political ends. He also seems to have been the first Member of Parliament in modern times to make use of the Welsh language in the House.

However the cause of English education in Wales did not call for the blood of any martyrs. Hugh Owen loomed as large as the figure of the driver of a model railway whose efforts were open to some criticism from the uncomfortable passengers from time to time. The journey was never as smooth as the first class passengers would have liked, but since the track had already been laid there could hardly be any doubt that sooner or later they would all arrive at the desired destination. The first landmark on the journey was Forster's Education Act of 1870. Mr. Forster was Matthew Arnold's brother-in-law and his Act had the effect of carrying out almost literally the inspector of schools' recommendation that English should be hammered in to the heads of Welsh children. In this system of elementary education Welsh was excluded not only in the classroom but also in the playground. Throughout Wales, if a pupil was heard speaking a word of Welsh in school a piece of wood with the words 'Welsh Not' carved on it was hung about his neck. The child who was wearing it at the end of the school day was thrashed. The system encouraged an atmosphere of tale-telling and betrayal that was in a negative way character forming. But for every schoolboy Lloyd George ready to rebel, there were always more ready to sink deeper into habits of slyness and servility. Many of the new schoolmasters were imported, but there were soon more than enough Welsh volunteers to swell the ranks of this expeditionary force. Even a character like Beriah Gwynfe Evans, who was so ardent a Welshman as to be virtually in a permanent state of incandescence, used the 'Welsh Not' with memorable effectiveness when he was a schoolmaster in the 1880s on the monoglot children of Carmarthenshire. Like the majority of parents he acquiesced in the system because he sincerely believed that it was ultimately in the children's best interest.

Only a small minority of Welshmen dared to suggest that Wales was selling a birthright for a mess of pottage. The Calvinistic Methodist minister Emrys ap Iwan (1851-1906) wrote that the Jews had only worshipped one calf; the Welsh, with their customary versatility, were now worshipping two, *y llo aur a'r llo Seisnig*' (the golden calf and the English calf). Emrys had a horror of what he called 'English fever', the latest manifestation of what Michael D. Jones had termed the lack of backbone and fundamental self-respect. The Welsh were allowing themselves to be brain-washed into underrating their own achievements. What other peasantry and working class had achieved so much in so short a time? If the Welsh were to remain in control of their own destiny they had to do this through the institutions that they had created for themselves and through their own language. Whereas Michael D. Jones, the Independent minister, had looked to the New World, North and South, for inspiration and a means whereby Welsh self-confidence could be restored and balance brought in to the somewhat tortured condition of the national psyche, Emrys ap Iwan, the Calvinistic Methodist minister, looked to Europe and European culture to counter the danger of suffocation from the overwhelming influence of England. Emrys had studied under Lewis Edwards at Bala, one of a generation of particularly brilliant students. He had spent some years in Germany and Switzerland as a tutor. He became a journalist before being ordained and his writing never lost the sharp edge of French influence. Somewhat uncharacteristically for his time he had no political ambition and he was prepared to confine himself to the more difficult task of trying to teach his own people to think.

Hugh Owen was intent on completing his great educational edifice and clamping it down firmly on the mass of people who were now more convinced than ever that they constituted a nation. This was by no means an easy task. In London he was a highly respected civil servant, but there were powerful influences among the English who disapproved strongly of particularism in any shape or form. They saw no reason at all why Wales should have its own colleges and its own university. This was no more than Irish Fenianism creeping around in pious nonconformist disguise. They saw no good reason why Owen and his committees should not be content with a training college for male teachers in the north of Wales and for women in the south. That would service elementary education, and elementary education would service industry's needs for a steady flow of literate labour capable of looking after the ever increasing amount of machinery. For the wheels of profit to keep turning it was necessary for a good worker to be able to read basic instruction manuals in the language of the machine and the rules and regulations that had to be laid down with increasing frequency to assure the smooth working of industry and society in general. Talk of universities drew attention to dangerous glints of greediness in the Welsh eye: it meant that the slippery bounders were either after the more tasty bits of the great and growing imperial capitalist cake, or that they were nursing dangerous dreams of Home Rule and even secession, like the unruly Irish.

The salvation of Hugh Owen's schemes was the strength of his power base among the Welsh Calvinistic Methodists. This denomination had developed as the century progressed into the most firmly bourgeois of all the nonconformist bodies in Wales. It was also far and away the best organised. The connections of the Lewis Edwards faction with Scotland had given them the image of a national kirk to which to aspire. In the political arena they had espoused the cause of disestablishment, and this gave them the appearance of supporting the radical wing of the Liberal party. Their sustained practice of industry and frugality gave meaning to the word Calvinist and from the Methodist inheritance they preserved a steady stream of emotional power which found regular social expression through the revivals which occurred at crucial moments throughout the century.

The denomination also set the pace in embellishing the peculiarly Welsh vision of the self-made man – usually the son of a struggling smallholder who, by dint of a combination of industry and genius, manages to amass a fortune. He demonstrates his loyalty to his people by taking his seat in the *Sêt Fawr* (the Deacon's pew) every Sunday and contributing handsomely to the building of chapels and the denominational coffers. To which was added the quarryman's pence, the farm labourer's farthings and the unstinting generosity of the coal-miner. It was these two sources, which had always provided the complex network of nonconformist institutions with their financial life-blood, that Hugh Owen tapped to establish and maintain the University of Wales at Aberystwyth. In 1872 he resigned from his lucrative London post in order to devote all his energies to promote the interests of what he had come to regard as his crowning achievement. Forty years on George Bernard Shaw was to cause some offence to Aberystwyth sensibilities by calling the place a Methodist academy. It is of course a petty bourgeois characteristic to be ashamed of one's origins and it is doubtful whether Shaw would ever have been capable of distinguishing between the different varieties of Methodists if they were lined up in front of his nose in an intellectual identity parade. Nevertheless he had understood something of the essence of the place and its origin. When it opened it was singularly appropriate that it should be housed in a building on the seafront that had been intended as a railway hotel. Many Calvinistic Methodists, including the mighty David Davies of Llandinam, had made money in the railway boom. There was no place for the Welsh language in the prospectus of the new university. Hegel was in residence for some time before Taliesin slipped in through the back door. Possibly to improve the collection of coal-miners' and quarrymen's pence, a place was found for Welsh. The place in fact consisted of a room that was compared by the incumbent, a learned Anglican cleric, to a cupboard under the stairs. Fortunately because of the growing importance of the Chair of Celtic at Oxford, the subject soon gained an aura of academic significance. But it had to wait until the 1920s to become 'Cymraeg' instead of 'Welsh', and the medium of instruction concerning itself, its own existence, essence and being.

23 Chosen Persons

It may appear strange that a people taking so much pride in their own culture and institutions, and indeed in anything that could be held up as laudable evidence of their particular identity, could bring themselves with such apparent ease to embrace an educational system which rigorously excluded their most conspicuous asset. They were a people conscious of the stern pressures of necessity to the point of self-denial and hunger and well beyond. They were also engaged in continuous debate and no step in any direction was ever taken lightly. The consensus answer with which they presented themselves to this question of education was simple enough. The national language, rather like Hebrew, would be elevated to semi-sacred status and reserved for religion – which was, after all, the most important thing in life – and those aspects of culture that best flourished under the shadow of the chapel, such as Sunday School learning and the more uplifting aspects of poetry and music. English was essential for improving the standard of living and that in essence was what day schools and secular education were good for. Even at the end of the century there could be no real cause for alarm when there were still eight Sunday School teachers in the Welsh world for every one day school teacher. From the eye level of the average intelligence and between the blinkers of wishful thinking, in spite of sweeping social and economic changes and the pressure of immigration on the South Wales valleys, in 1900 the twin plagues of secularisation and anglicisation were still below the horizon.

A good Welshman should never be hindered in making his way in the world. He should be loaded with all the tools that would help him finish that job, and thus bring credit and renown to his family, his neighbours, his chapel, his denomination and, if he went high enough up the ladder, to his entire nation. *'Dyrchafiad arall i Gymro!'* (Another Welshman promoted!) became the order of the day. When Gladstone created the Open Examination for the Civil Service, the sons of Wales who could write English, however humble their origin, provided their parents were prepared to sacrifice on their behalf, had an almost equal opportunity of advancement with the English middle classes. The leaders of Welsh opinion had no great difficulty in convincing themselves that they had obtained an excellent deal when the examination system took over. There was something more ethereal after all in linking the progress of the soul with the progress of the intellect rather than with the progress of industry. Each nonconformist body took to inventing examinations of its own inside the framework of chapel life and the Welsh language, so that the notion of certificates and diplomas became fixed in the Welsh psyche from a very early age.

In a remarkably short time, the examination system produced its own species of folk hero, to be cherished with equal devotion in the miner's or the quarryman's terrace house and the smallholder's parlour. The prototype was Sir John Rhys, born the son of a farm labourer in a tiny wayside cottage in the remote uplands of Cardiganshire. His interest in grammar was said to have been aroused by the local weaver. He became a pupil teacher and eventually found his way to the Normal College at Bangor which had not long been open. From an elementary teaching job in Anglesey, he was rescued by the interest of two literary parsons. He won scholarships to Oxford and became a Fellow of Merton before going to Europe to make an intensive study of comparative philology. When Arnold's dream of an Oxford Chair in Celtic finally materialised in 1877, Rhys was invited to fill it. He was elected Principal of Jesus College in 1895. He was a scholar built in the massive European nineteenth-century style and a pioneer in many branches of Celtic study, from philology to folklore, and he was the first to make possible a thorough-going scientific study of the early history of the Celts in Britain. In Wales he had influence on the imagination of the ordinary people, based on the appeal of his career and the extent of his knowledge. In practical education the Chair of Celtic made him the father figure of a new generation of scholars and writers wholly dedicated to the rehabilitation of Welsh scholarship and literature. It was their influence which brought about the twentieth-century phenomenon which is sometimes described as a literary Renaissance.

Oxford became the Shangri-La of the young Welshman's educational aspirations. This could have been the lingering influence of Matthew Arnold. Cambridge and Aberystwyth were somewhat lacking in dreaming spires, and poor Bala, the scene of epic denominational battles, was much reduced in status even when Thomas Charles Edwards, Lewis Edwards's son and the first Principal of Aberystwyth, returned there in 1891 to succeed his father, seeking some shelter from Aberystwyth storms, and transforming Bala into a purely theological college. It is some measure of the persistence of a rural, almost Arcadian, ideal in the Welsh mind that institutions like Bala and Aberystwyth should have been established so far away from the industrial base of Welsh economy. The modern notion of placing institutions of higher education in the most populated centres was still to take root. It was from the beautiful countryside surrounding Bala lake that two folk heroes emerged like Arthurian knights 'to capture the hearts of their fellow countrymen'.

The two heroes were firm friends. They first met as boys at a sheep dipping on the mountainside. Owen M. Edwards, was the eldest son of Coed-y-Pry, a smallholding near Llanuwchllyn. As a child he had worn the 'Welsh Not' around his neck and he said it was an experience he never forgot. He was intended for the Calvinistic Methodist ministry and studied at Bala College. From there he moved to Aberystwyth, then to Glasgow, and finally to Balliol. His movements suggest those of a man pursued by religious doubts. Like a true child of his age he quietly shifted his devotion from religion to education. He was elected a Fellow of Lincoln College in 1889 and made a considerable reputation for himself as a teacher and a lecturer. In 1907 he was appointed chief Inspector of Schools for Wales where his function eventually became almost the exact opposite of that of Matthew Arnold half a century before. He made it his mission to see that the Welsh language was taught in Welsh schools from which it had been exiled for over a quarter of a century, and to discover ways of injecting into the hardened arteries of an imitation English educational system something of what he considered to be the lifeblood of Welsh culture. In 1891 he had begun publishing on his own account and had set to work with phenomenal industry to place a knowledge of their exciting past history and rich literature within the reach of a wide readership among the peasantry and the working class. He had launched what was virtually a literary revolution among the people and made himself a symbol of a new kind of patriotic awareness.

> *Mae'r oll yn gysegredig* . . . It is all sacred. Every hill and every valley. Our land is a living thing, not a grave of forgetfulness under our feet. Every hill has its history, every locality its own romance, every part of the landscape wears its own particular glory. And to a Welshman, no other country can be like this. A Welshman feels that the struggles of his forefathers have sanctified every field, and the genius of his people has transformed every mountain into hallowed ground. And it is feeling like this that will make him a true citizen.

His childhood friend Tom Ellis was equally patriotic, but with a more pronounced political bias. While still in school at Bala, both these Calvinistic Methodists had dared to listen to the redoubtable Principal of the Independent College, Michael D. Jones, and they had sat at the feet of this Gamaliel of Welsh nationalism along with a group of bright young men that included a lively youth from Criccieth called David Lloyd George. Ellis left Oxford in 1885 to spend a year as tutor in the family of John Cory, of St. Mellons, the nonconformist Cardiff shipowner. His career in Liberal politics was meteoric. At the age of twenty-seven, he was a leader in Welsh life and his first parliamentary achievement was the

Welsh Intermediate and Technical Act of 1889, which laid the foundations of a Welsh secondary and higher education system. It made him a
national hero. As a rising star on the Liberal firmament he made speeches
about the virtues of the Celts which went down equally well outside
Wales. In one of his public addresses called 'The influence of the Celt in
the making of Britain' he begins:

> I desire at the outset to express my gratitude as a student and as a Celt to Mr.
> Matthew Arnold and the band of literary and scientific men who,
> determined to see things as they really are, have endeavoured to understand
> the Celtic peoples and appreciate the Celtic genius.

He proceeds to elaborate an inverted racial argument in which he claims
for the Celts all the virtues ever exhibited by the peoples of Britain since
the beginning of recorded time. Celtic magic could be an intoxicating
brew. As the eloquence reaches its height the reader begins to wonder
whether he is listening to atavistic echoes of Taliesin's hero Urien
Rheged rather than the measured accents of a product of Hugh Owen's
Aberystwyth and Matthew Arnold's Oxford.

> Is it not this very Celticism which gives to Britain that special power and
> genius, that distinctive gift which differentiates Britain from Germany and
> which gives it the pre-eminence!

In 1890 Ellis was given a national testimonial by the people of Wales.
The presentation was at Bala (where his statue now stands) and it was on
this occasion that he set forth, amid scenes of some enthusiasm, his
proposal for a legislative assembly for Wales. This was to replace
disestablishment at the top of the Welsh Liberal programme. Ellis was
disappointed with the response, especially in the South. In two years,
when Gladstone formed his new administration, Ellis accepted office,
much to the disgust of David Lloyd George, who stumped around
Meirionethshire castigating Ellis for breaking his vow and accepting
office in the English government. By this time Ellis was in poor health.
He turned to scholarship for relaxation and became a pioneer of the
movement to secure a National Library for Wales. He died at Cannes in
April 1899.

It could be a tribute to the enduring vitality of dissent among the Welsh
people, both in Wales and across the Atlantic, that the most chosen of
chosen persons should come from the smallest and most rejected if not
actually despised sects: and that they should both avoid the attention of
Oxford-orientated channels of higher education. Frank Lloyd Wright
came out of a distinctly private variety of Welsh Unitarians in Wisconsin
before he entered an architect's office in Chicago. The family of David
Lloyd George belonged to a branch of Baptists who had seceded from the

main body under the leadership of an eccentric genius called J.R. Jones of Ramoth. J.R. Jones was a man of great eloquence who suddenly acquired a revulsion against popular preaching. He wanted his people to study and think and behave as closely as possible to the primitive church. They called themselves *Bedyddwyr Albanaidd* (Scotch Baptists) because of their doctrinal links with Archibald Maclean, although they were known locally as *Bedyddwyr Bara Caws* (Bread and Cheese Baptists) because the members had to travel some distance to the meeting-house and carried their food with them to eat between services. According to Pauline tradition their ministry was unpaid, so Lloyd George's uncle carried on a business as a master cobbler as well as acting as co-pastor of the church at Criccieth.

Uncle Lloyd, through the good offices of his friend, Myrddin Fardd, a blacksmith who was a passionate antiquary and a collector of old manuscripts, managed to place his nephew as an articled clerk in the office of Breeze, Jones and Casson in Portmadoc. Mr. Breeze the senior partner was himself an amateur antiquarian and frequently had dealings with Myrddin Fardd. He was also prominent in Liberal politics. Thus Welsh antiquaries and Liberal politics were the means whereby David Lloyd George was able to take the first step upwards into the ranks of the professional classes. He worked hard, the shoemaker skimped and saved, his mother let rooms to summer visitors, and by 1884 the family was able to join in his triumph when he returned home from London a qualified solicitor.

Matthew Arnold talked about 'the Titanism of the Celt' and there is something awe-inspiring in the magnitude of the ambition that drove on these two men of genius. Again in ancient Celtic fashion, they were men brought up by their mothers' brothers, in the case of Frank Lloyd Wright a whole row of uncles. They were both wonder boys, doted on by the women and cherished by the men, the elected repositories of age-old expectations. Frank Lloyd Wright's mother knew the child she bore would be a great architect and before he was born she had decorated the walls of his room with pictures of cathedrals. Through their families they had access to a magic more potent and more ancient then anything Arnold imagined. The Myrddin (Merlinus) of Nennius's ancient book was a boy skilled in the arts of architecture and understood the relationship between buildings and the landscapes out of which they should grow. Geoffrey of Monmouth's Arthur was a boy born to lead his people through the upheavals of a time of the breaking of the nations. The boy Henry Tudor was schooled by his uncle Jasper for the same imperial purpose. Whatever the mythological element present in their upbringing, in spite of the rigours of rational dissent, there can be no doubt of their sense of destiny as they grew older or of their voluntary cultivation of their chosen roles. They both actively desired the great mass of people to think of them as geniuses, as magicians, as wizards.

They were willing to risk accusations of charlatanry, such was their self-confidence; and they adopted modes of dress that singled them out as artists and figures of priestly power in their chosen professions.

They were not isolated phenomena. The Titanism of the Welsh Celt was particularly noticeable in American life at the turn of the century. D.W. Griffith, the pioneer of motion pictures, somewhat recklessly declared himself to be descended from 'Griffydd King of Wales'. Sam Jones – Golden Rule Jones – mayor of Toledo, Ohio, introduced his own brand of Christian socialism in that city, and his memory remains a startlingly Arthurian episode in American industrial capitalism. Charles Evans Hughes, a descendant of one of Hywel Harris's 'family' of Trevecca, came within an ace of being elected president of the United States in 1917. If that had happened the two great English-speaking empires would have been led by two Welsh-speaking Welshmen and it is alarming to contemplate the paroxysms of joy with which such a divine event would have been greeted in Wales itself. The miner's leader John Llewellyn Lewis, in a manner curiously parallel to Mabon in the home country, began his public career on the eisteddfod platform. He was a product of the Welsh nonconformist tradition. He was equipped with the eloquence of the pulpit, and a man of power in America because of his gift of putting visions into words.

David Lloyd George was imbued with a fierce but highly personal sense of Welsh identity. The sufferings of tenant farmers in the tithe wars of North Wales brought out all his combative instincts. When Michael D. Jones brought the Irish leader Michael Davitt to speak to the quarrymen in Blaenau Ffestiniog, the Liberal establishment was deeply shocked. This was the founder of the Irish Land League, and a man who had served three long prison sentences. There was still deep prejudice in Wales against Irish papists and only one nonconformist minister was present at the meeting, with the exception of course of old Michael D. Jones himself. Lloyd George also spoke and compared the condition of Wales to that of a man lying on the roadside stripped, beaten, and half dead. The priests and the Levites went past on the other side. It was only a Samaritan from Ireland who was moved to pity and was prepared to cross the road to do something about the condition of the oppressed and downtrodden. It was a great oratorical triumph for so young a man and it was also an occasion of even deeper historical significance. For the first time since the Tudor Settlement the two Celtic countries were showing signs of being able to set aside religious prejudice and of being able to collaborate on a political level to their mutual advantage. Davitt was full of praise for the younger orator. He is reputed to have said, 'This is the kind of young man we send to parliament from Ireland these days, and it's the kind that you should be sending from Wales.'

The Irish example fired Lloyd George and more than any of the talented band of Welsh Liberal M.P.s he was committed to Home Rule and a radical populist programme for Wales. The *Cymru Fydd* movement shifted from cultural to political nationalism. Organisers were appointed. Hundreds of branches were formed. Men like Llywelyn Williams of Carmarthen and Herbert Lewis of Flintshire joined him and became more enthusiastic for the cause than Lloyd George himself. In parliament if they stuck together as a Welsh party they could be as powerful as the Irish and Herbert Lewis in particular pressed for a genuine Welsh Home Rule party with an independent organisation. The young enthusiasts were moving too fast, and a visible gap was opening between them and the grass roots of Welsh Liberalism. For Lloyd George the moment of truth occurred in January 1896 in Newport when he made his attempt to unite the Liberal organisations of the North and the South in one national body. An Alderman Bird from Cardiff leapt to his feet and shouted that he had had enough of all this Welsh business. He was an Englishman and he was not going to tolerate Welsh domination. He went on to make a furious personal attack on Lloyd George and swung the whole feeling of the meeting against him. The choice before this rising hope of nonconformist Wales was stark enough. Should he spend the rest of his life sweating to drag an ill-informed and unwilling electorate in the direction of a responsible if limited self-government? Or should he like any other talented politician consider his own career and travel with the prevailing current to see how far he could go? It was a choice between two myths as old as Gildas and history was poised to repeat itself. Lloyd George was a politician of genius; never a mere time-server or opportunist. He made a calculated choice that was even more deliberate than that made by Henry Tudor. The glittering throne reserved for a British Arthur was vacant. Once more there were ancient prophecies to be fulfilled and certainly nothing in the long run would please his uncle more. In the brave new world of the twentieth century a fresh path would open before the feet of the Arthurian Messiah of the Bread and Cheese Baptists. He would also find a way of satisfying the mythological expectations of his people: to survive, mythologies, like politicans, had to be infinitely adaptable. On a more mundane level he only needed to look around the benches of the Westminster eisteddfod to realise that among the competitors there was no one better suited for the chair or the crown than his own self. In the fullness of time A.J.P. Taylor would describe him as 'the greatest ruler of England since Oliver Cromwell'. Other writers have found this parallel useful. That would suggest that he served England well. The influence of his career on Wales and the Welsh character was by no means so beneficial.

24 Heroes of Labour

Unlike established churches, which can afford to be indifferent to indifference for surprisingly long periods of time, dissenting denominations need a fairly constant condition of enthusiastic belief if they are to survive, let alone flourish. For this reason, if for no other, religious revivals were a social necessity in nineteenth-century Wales. The pattern of their recurrence is further tangible evidence on an ideological level of the strength of the links between the 'new' Wales, the Wales which the common people had invented for themselves, with the new nation state of the United States of America. (We have seen that the new eisteddfod had a common source in trends of eighteenth-century thought with the constitution of the United States, and how the small but potent sect of Arians and Unitarians played a vital role in the creation of both institutions.) Revivals tended to originate in America and the spark found no trouble in leaping the Atlantic and igniting fresh fires in the spiritual boiler-rooms of Welsh dissent. Clearly the economic expansion of the two English-speaking empires was closely related. Anglo-British expansion relied on sea-power and colonialism. The main force of American economic manifest destiny was directed towards a sub-Napoleonic opening up of a continental landmass that had never before heard anything louder than 'the stone-age war-cries of noble savages'. As the century wore on it was to their mutual advantage and profit that the dispossessed of increasing areas of the European continent should be transferred across the ocean to take possession of the original romantic Arcadia. This was the large-scale model, but the same process could be seen at work in any corner of the industrial world. Movements of population are of course dictated by economic forces, but in the Welsh and American nineteenth-century experience, as soon as they occur, they are accompanied by the building of largely nonconformist places of worship. At any moment in the westward expansion of the United States the process could be seen at work. What they call churches and what we call chapels spring up to give some semblance of architectural as well as social coherence to the new communities.

The economic exploitation of the Rhondda valleys offers a remarkably well defined image in miniature of the impact of a vast historic
process on a people determined to live as a recognisable community
with as much responsibility as possible for their own destiny. At the
beginning of the nineteenth century, when Wales was a happy hunting
ground for romantic travellers cut off from the continent by the
Napoleonic wars and infected with varying degrees of mild Celtomania,
the Rhondda valleys were singled out both for the glory of their natural
beauty and for the inability of their charming natives to speak English.
For these remarkable qualities they could only be rivalled by the
remoter valleys of Meirioneth. For some time the Rhondda valleys were
left alone, although they formed the geographical centre of the
coalfield, because it was generally believed that the coal lay below the
level of profitable mining. It was as late in the century as the 1860s
before capitalists like David Davies, Llandinam, moved in, sinking
shafts, building railways and docks, so that endless tons of steam coal
could be shifted to Cardiff, Penarth and Barry. By the 1880s it was
acknowledged that this was the best steam coal in Europe. The
prosperity of the future capital of Wales was built on black gold known
as 'cardiff' in the languages of many countries. It only needed one trip in
a train from the Rhondda to Barry to understand that all the visual
evidence of impressive wealth came from the sweat and blood of the
mining community. It is hardly surprising therefore that the life of the
valleys was dominated by the need of the people to hold on to a decent
share of the product of their labour and if possible to increase it.

The organisation of labour in the South Wales coalfield reflects the
rate of change in a people's belief in the nature and purpose of
existence. Whether they appear volatile or tenaciously loyal depends on
the time scale the historian uses. Mabon was elected a miners' agent in
1870. He was miners' Chairman of the Joint Sliding Scale Association,
until that body came to an end in 1903. In spite of his opposition to a
centralised organisation, he was elected first President of the South
Wales Miners' Federation, and even after he had been discredited as a
leader he was allowed to continue as M.P. for the Rhondda until his
death in 1922. This suggests a society with a well developed sense of
community loyalty, a generous spirit towards the loser in what was after
all a power struggle, and something of the ingrained conservatism of a
people nurtured in a traditionalist culture. A stanza in the strict metres
was inscribed on his tombstone. It was composed by his friend the
Archdruid Dyfed, once a coal-miner and now a Calvinistic Methodist
minister.

Great Hero of Labour, live coal of the platform, gifted soul, genial of
nature, brave and beloved, the shield of our rights, honest visionary with

a wide heart. From the tower of his forehead, fire flowed – for the truth, and his eloquence will be remembered by a whole nation.

The stanza itself is an extraordinary memorial to the continuity of tradition. It is a piece of pulpit eloquence concentrated with great skill into one of the more difficult of the strict metre forms. In the act of homage to this working-class leader there remain audible traces of a praise poetry that has survived in an unbroken tradition from the sixth century. It is the ironic and sad comment of twentieth-century realism that records he left a considerable fortune. So big indeed that it finally destroyed what was left of his prestige and popularity.

Nevertheless the period between the 1860s and the 1920s was one of extraordinarily rapid change and this too is amply demonstrated in the life of the people of the Rhondda. As late as 1904 it was shaken by the great religious revival which swept through Wales. This was the last of the Welsh religious revivals and from this distance of time it can be variously interpreted as the last desperate gesture of a people aware in their subconscious mind that their age-old faith was leaving them, or the first of a series of twentieth-century identity crises. It was as if a whole people had become aware of some fatal interruption in the organic process by which the Welsh had been able to recreate themselves throughout the decades of industrial change. Simultaneously their popular religion and their everyday language were running out of the indigenous creativity which had kept them going for so long. It is possible that the regular occurrence of revivals performed the additional service of reaffirming certainties at the points at which the faithful felt most in need of them.

Among a people so fervently emotional in the mass and yet with reserves of cool intelligence and nimble wit, a system of belief was an integral part of the central nervous system. In spite of the apparent strength of the denominations, doubts had been gathering concerning the truth of many of the central tenets of orthodox Christianity. The ministers did not wield any priestly powers and their leadership was based on their ability to convince. This grew weaker with the passage of time, even when successive revivals were apparently adding to the size of their congregations. In far away Llanystumdwy, for example, David Lloyd George in spite of, or possibly because of, the fact that his minister was his doting Uncle Lloyd, seems to have lost his faith in 1875 at the surprisingly early age of twelve. The more intense Owen M. Edwards was beset with doubts early on and settled in the end for a combination of higher education and ethical Christianity.

But long before 1904 the strike had begun to assume a function curiously parallel to the religious revival. It enlarged and then consolidated the power of organised labour: the exact service that the revivals performed for nonconformist religion. The strike was a searing social experience in which the community suffered together, just as they mourned together the frequent accidents and the grim disasters in the mines. These things established standards of human behaviour, of comradeship and courage, which the whole community could admire. It provided them with heroes, with leaders, a sense of solidarity and a capacity to face up to almost anything a hostile world could throw at them. The mining community enjoyed an aggressive pride in its own existence which outshone the dim uncertainties and increasing lack of self-confidence of the growing ranks of the Welsh middle classes. The experience preceded the doctrine. The early strikes were led by chapel men and the call for justice was based on the adaptation of Christian principles. It was still possible for the miners' leaders and the management and even the owners to attend the same chapel. As conditions worsened, the strife intensified. Again, the class war had begun before anybody used that term to describe it. In a sense the 'denomination' of Labour had come into existence before it was equipped with the necessary systems of belief. The struggle for the control of the unions and the leadership of the political life of the coalfield lasted nearly twenty years. In its most polarised form it appeared to be a struggle between Mabon with his Calvinistic Methodism, his eisteddfodic culture and his fondness for compromise, and the new men from the Central Labour College with enough fresh doctrine from Marx and the Syndicalists to fit up a new denomination, complete with socialist Sunday Schools, hymns about a new and better world, sacred texts written almost entirely in English. This is too easy a simplification and anticipates future events. Mabon may have had to struggle with his English when he first arrived in the House of Commons or on the other hand this might have been a convenient legend to make him seem more endearing to his constituents. When he wrote in the *South Wales Daily News* he seemed quite an accomplished journalist in English, in the fashion of that time which can often seem to us to be almost excessively literate.

What seems certain is that the struggle for men's souls had now been replaced by the struggle for their hearts and minds, and that in spite of Mabon and the apparent outward flourishing condition of the nonconformist bodies, they were already in no fit condition to conduct such a struggle. Their superstructures were still impressive. The chapels were full, their publications had wide circulation. (In the early 1900s the Calvinistic Methodists' magazine *Y Drysorfa* (The Treasury) had a monthly circulation of over 45,000. That would mean that the various magazines of the Independents, the Baptists, and the Wesleyans would not have been very far below this figure.) Their colleges had waiting lists of would-be students. A busy social life still revolved around each little complex of buildings, whether in the countryside or in the town, or in the industrial valleys. They were ready for anything except a confrontation with the grim realities of the society in which they lived. For the most part the nonconformist bodies had sold their souls to the Liberal party. One of the first signs of the growing power of Lloyd George, the 'British' politician, was the hold he exerted over every single newspaper and magazine editor in the world of Welsh nonconformity. It became increasingly easy, especially in times of crisis, for the new leaders to convince the miners and the industrial workers that the Liberal party in South Wales was nothing more than the political tool of the owners. If the denominations therefore allowed themselves to be manipulated by the Liberals, they were condoning and perpetuating social injustice. Worse than this, there was an element of betrayal in the arrangement. A network of chapels sustained for the most part by the contribution of the workers had absolutely no right to allow itself to be manipulated by Liberal politicians, no matter how eloquent or how glamorous the upward march of their success.

The advocates of socialism were victorious in debate. The combination of opportunistic Liberalism and a Christianity riddled with inward uncertainties had no weapons to compete with the fresh cutting edge of Marxism and the sharp wits of working-class intellectuals hungry for combat. Nevertheless the victors in debate rarely had things their own way once the crisis was over. Increasingly before 1914, the level of material prosperity also encouraged the forces of inertia. The sponsors of English education may have hoped that it would have made the Welsh worker reach out eagerly towards the riches of Shakespeare and Chaucer. What fell into their hands in fact in increasing numbers, apart from the *South Wales Daily News* and the *Western Mail*, were exotic periodicals like *Answers*, *Titbits* and *John Bull*. All these agents of fantasy presented an imperial vision of the world which was mythical in its essence. They united their readership in contented worship at the same altar, so that the Welsh worker could enjoy a common sense of pride and brotherhood with the loyal members of all classes of the heartland of the greatest empire the world had ever known. In August 1914 the *Western Mail* was happy to report in banner headlines the wave of enthusiasm for the war that swept through the valleys of South Wales. In the Rhondda it was reminiscent of the heady days of the 1904 revival.

25 The Baptist Warlord

To the Welsh themselves, and to the world outside, from 1906 onwards David Lloyd George was the apotheosis of successful Welshness. The bouncing healthy offspring of the love match between Welsh nonconformity and the Liberal party had become the most dazzling performer on the stage of British imperial politics. There may or may not have been fiery shapes on the front of heaven at his birth but everything that had happened subsequently demonstrated that a new Welsh hero had taken the field. The defeated and the downtrodden, the spirits long oppressed could lift up their heads and take heart. Here was a man with the confidence and the capacity to quell the mighty of the earth and to put the oppressor to flight. His career would justify all the fateful choices Welsh nonconformity had made during the nineteenth century. It was for the benefit of the twentieth-century model Welshman, of which he was the shining prototype, that the humble Welsh element had broken out of its monoglot mould. (If only the authors of those treacherous Blue Books could be brought back to life and forced publicly to eat their words like leeks.) Their monoglot hatches had been transformed into a trap-door at the very centre of the political stage, and out of it had sprung an actor in search of the limelight who was capable of playing a whole range of roles from Prince Charming to the Demon King.

He was the living proof of the value of a new Welsh way of life which was already being called traditional in spite of the fact that it was barely a hundred years old. Much to the annoyance of the Anglican minority, militant nonconformity had taken over Welshness and established the habit of behaving as though it was their exclusive property. They had also had the nerve to appropriate the benefits of bilingualism and in the boom conditions of the opening years of the century, they seemed to be all set to receive in regular instalments the very best of both worlds. This man who sat in the cabinet as President of the Board of Trade could also take pride in being elected President of the Welsh Baptist Union and insist that all the proceedings of that annual conference be carried on exclusively in the Welsh language. This was a sweet little triumph for a Bread and Cheese Baptist from the backwoods as he presided over a large denomination which drew its main strength from the thickly populated valleys of South Wales. His whole career seemed a succession of sweet little triumphs. And it was not merely a case of nothing succeeding like success. The speed of his political thinking amounted to genius. He was so many moves ahead of his opponents in the game that his movements seemed tinged with supernatural agility. It gave him special delight to be nicknamed 'the Welsh Wizard'. For him the whole process was basically poetic, an endlessly fascinating combination of art and magic. As the years went on he cultivated the appearance of a Merlin-like character. In his youth he had been an Arthur, but as his power grew he saw the wisdom of fusing the two rôles. The masses of the twentieth century, often frightened and bewildered at the speed of the changes going on all around them, needed reassurance from their leadership: the courage and boldness of an Arthur, but even more important the confident claim of a Merlin, that he was in control of the dangerous machine.

The Whig managers of the Liberal party, men like John Morley, Haldane, Edward Grey and Asquith, had a deep distrust of this intruder and they were right to be nervous. This champion of nonconformity had charm and great intelligence, but hardly any conscience at all in the strict English nonconformist interpretation of that word. He was a force of nature and this explains much of the genuine affection he lavished on the landscape of his boyhood home. Time and again in his speeches the most effective similes and metaphors were drawn from the deep affinity that existed between him and his *bro*. Like the twelfth-century prince-poet Hywel ap Owain Gwynedd, who lived and died in that same area and conducted a tempestuous political career for its possession like a love affair, David Lloyd George 'loved her mountains and her foreshore, the castle near the woods . . . her valleys and her fountains'. Like any ancient Celtic king, he had been married to his territory and his delight in storms was the play of temperament that resulted from his loose interpretation of the bonds of this compact: from any form of marriage he was entitled to be the sole beneficiary. When he died it was his wish to be buried in the woods in sight of the impetuous flow of the river Dwyfor. This would be a pagan burial, in'spite of the Baptist ministers present, when he no longer had any need of the nonconformist vote.

The nonconformist vote in England was the key to his seat in the cabinet. At no other time in English history was that vote to be of so much consequence. From the 1880s it had developed a social conscience and it quickly became the political equivalent of William Booth's newly formed Salvation Army. The nonconformist middle class became aware of the plight of the industrial poor, of the slums, of the rights of working people and their moral responsibility for their welfare. The Welsh Wesleyan Methodist minister, Hugh Price Hughes, was already active in this field and as editor of *The Methodist Times* he was one of the custodians of the nonconformist conscience. The Liberal party could only remain in power with the support of Scotland, Wales, and the English nonconformist vote. Lloyd George was able to exploit this situation brilliantly to his own advantage. It would be unfair however to suggest that he gave the Liberal party nothing in return. It remained wholly or partly in power from the moment he took office in 1906 until he was forced out in 1922. This was due to the skill with which Lloyd George kept the forces of Labour at bay in a period when they were poised to take over power.

He contrived to do this by sleight of hand that would have done credit to a professional conjurer. He borrowed the salient ideas of two unbending imperialists and dressed them up in a way that made them irresistible both to the nonconformist conscience and to the leaders of organised labour. The Prussian Chancellor Bismarck, another admired practitioner of political art and for long the leader of European thought on the subject, had built up the strength of Germany on the basis of fervent nationalism, imperialist expansion and schemes of social reform to ensure the welfare of the industrial workers and thereby provide his empire with a healthy and powerful industrial base. His imitator in England was Joseph Chamberlain, a predecessor of Lloyd George as Liberal President of the Board of Trade. Chamberlain was no less of an imperialist than Bismarck, but he was lacking in his hero's intellectual power and political skill. He allowed his imperialism to drag him into ill-considered adventures in South Africa and ultimately lost the support that he would have gained from his social reforms. Lloyd George made no such mistake. His social measures and his genuine concern for the welfare of working people were the chief weapons that he used to increase his power in the cabinet and maintain the Liberal party's majority share of the popular vote.

From the time of his People's Budget in 1909, his political strategy was based on a brilliant, if sometimes extempore, exploitation of social policies and social legislation. These in reality laid the foundation for the creation of a welfare state a long thirty-five years later. He made the first vital breaks with traditional English oligarchal government and with English laissez-faire economic administration. There could be no doubt that he identified the progress of his own career with far-reaching reforms in both the industrial and the rural communities. Had there been no war, he would in any case have attained supreme power. The choice would have been between the glamorous and experienced Lloyd George, the untried leaders of an untried Labour party, and the unrestrained forces of Tory reaction. This is of course fruitless speculation, since no such situation arose. It was not a choice that arrived but a challenge. The confrontation with the industrial might of

An Arthurian Lloyd George defends the realm against
the Teutonic hordes in 1916, ironically from the battle-
ments of Edward I's Caernarfon Castle, of which he
was Constable. The cartoon appeared in O.M.
Edwards' magazine, Cymru.

Bismarck's German empire transformed a Baptist social reformer into
an Imperial Warlord.

The Welsh response to the call to arms was immediate and enthusiastic: the highest recruitments and the biggest casualty lists in percentage
relation to the total population; top of the league of what rugby
commentators call 'the home countries'. Later statisticians could
readily correlate it to the unemployment figures. From November
1915, when Lloyd George had been appointed Minister of Munitions,
O. M. Edwards' popular illustrated magazine *Cymru* carried a drawing
of the great leader dressed in mediaeval armour, manning the
battlements of Britain and defending the island from invasion by the
barbarian Huns with 'their ten million armed men in the service of the
god of war'. In his magazine O. M. Edwards, himself a hero of the
nonconformist democracy and the gospel of education, calls upon the
young faithful of Welsh nonconformity to offer themselves 'in the
beauty of sacrifice' for the sake of civilisation, the Empire, and 'the
welfare of all mankind'.

In an earlier number, December 1914, a short story written by D. J.

Williams was published: the same D.J. Williams who was to be sent to prison in 1936 for setting fire to R.A.F. installations in Lleyn. It is about a somewhat unreal collier who discovers a sword that has been in the family for generations and decides to go to war. By 1915, in fact, the mining community had lost a great deal of its enthusiasm for the war. The South Wales Miners' Federation was in bad odour with what the press barons had come to describe as the great British public. It had dared to go on strike when the nation was at war and had forced the man now frequently referred to as the greatest Welshman of all time, to introduce the first measures of state control into the coal industry.

The nonconformist networks were much better behaved. They set aside a Peace Society tradition which had been universally accepted in their midst since the days of S.R. and Henry Richard. Their scruples about Home Rule and disestablishment were shelved for the duration in the interests of small nations like 'little Belgium' whose need was so much greater than theirs. Sacrifice was the order of the day and only small adjustments were needed to allow the last generation of pulpit giants, men like John Williams, Brynsiencyn, to tour the country in uniform and wear themselves out addressing recruiting meetings with the fervour of religious revivalists. When Lloyd George was made Minister for War, it seemed as if Wales knew long before anywhere else that it was only a matter of time before he became Prime Minister. Not since Abraham Lincoln had there been a more romantic example of the elevation of a man of humble origin to the position of supreme power. In classical style the hero was given dictatorial powers on condition that he won the struggle with the rival imperial power for control of the world and its markets. On either side, the war machines fuelled by a combination of patriotism and massive economic appetite, churned out a flood of ammunition and propaganda that had to be used. Thanks to trench warfare the actual slaughter was restricted to battlefields in traditional style. It was not so obvious that the bourgeois culture of Europe, of which Welsh nonconformity was a small but not altogether insignificant part, was also being destroyed.

1916 was a fateful and terrible year in Western Europe. The great powers, as they always called themselves, were like dinosaurs with teeth sunk in each other's throats, caught in a trance of mutual destruction. At the point of blood-letting were the young males of either side, laid out in khaki or field grey. Mechanised warfare was intent on its grim task of opening the widest generation gap in the history of Europe. If only in order to keep the thing going, it was described at the time as the war to end all wars. Certainly it ended one kind of war and began another. This was one of the underlying themes in David Jones's epic *In Parenthesis*. This work is modelled on *Y Gododdin* somewhat in the manner in which James Joyce built his *Ulysses* on a structure taken from the Odyssey. But Aneirin performs a more direct cultural service for Jones than Homer does for Joyce. *In Parenthesis* is a sustained elegy, the survivor in his solitude singing his tribute to the fallen, to their agony, their courage and their sacrifice.

...ESPECIALLY PTE. R.A. LEWIS-GUNNER FROM NEWPORT MONMOUTH-SHIRE KILLED IN ACTION IN THE BOESINGHE SECTOR N.W. OF YPRES SOME TIME IN THE WINTER 1916–17 . . .

No one to care there for Aneirin Lewis spilled there
who worshipped his ancestors like a Chink
who sleeps in Arthur's lap
who saw Olwen-trefoils some moonlighted night
on precarious slats at Festubert,
on narrow foothold on le Plantin marsh –
more shaved he is to the bare bone than
Yspaddadan Penkawr.
    Properly organised chemists can let make more riving
power than ever Twrch Trwyth;
more blistered he is than painted Troy Towers
and unwholer, limb from limb, than any of them fallen at
Catraeth . . .

It is a war epic that grows in stature with the passage of time because it is able to relate the exact nature of a personal experience of a crisis in Western civilisation with an abiding vision of the misery and the splendour of the human condition. It has universal reference and yet, like so much of Arthurian literature, it has its deepest tap-root in original, not to say aboriginal, Welsh experience.

The Easter Rising in Dublin, 1916, came as a complete surprise and shock to the loyal Welsh. *Y Faner* reported the events with bemused accuracy. What were the Irish up to? They were little better than the miners. Attempting to snatch private advantage while the British army and its allies were holding back the German horde at untold cost in blood and treasure. Only those who had delved deep into English literature would have recalled the *Faerie Queene* and the 'swarme of gnats . . . out of the fennes of Allan'. The Irish, historically the second of the lesser breeds without the law (the Welsh had almost forgotten that they were the first), were breaking out of the imperial net. A handful led by the visionary Patrick Pearse and the socialist James Connolly declared that they were ready for a blood sacrifice on behalf of their own people and their own class. They had been dispossessed and persecuted for too many centuries to bear it any longer.

The rebellion gave heart to a growing minority in Wales who were full of misgivings about the war. It was from this minority that leaders would emerge to give some shape to the new forms of dissent that were to make themselves felt in Welsh society after the war. Arthur Horner, a young miner from Maerdy in the Rhondda with strong socialist convictions, did not wait to be called up. He decided for himself where and when he was going to fight. He crossed to Ireland to join James Connolly's Citizens' Army. Connolly's ideas of workers' control 'proceeding from the bottom upward' were not far removed from Noah Ablett's, and a workers' republic was something worth fighting for. When he got back to Wales he was promptly clapped in prison. This did not prevent the miners' lodge at Maerdy from electing him checkweigher. The war-fever of the Rhondda had long since subsided.

In other places too socialist and pacifist feeling was making itself felt. At the age of seventeen another David Jones, later to become known as Gwenallt, declared himself to be a Marxist and a conscientious objector. He was imprisoned first in Wormwood Scrubs and then in Dartmoor among the more unbalanced section of the prison population. In his statement of faith, made many years later, he makes it plain that it was Welsh poetry that preserved his sanity; and it is certain that he emerged from his ordeal as a poet of real importance. He describes his youthful feelings in a way that vividly recalls the period.

> Marxism for us was a much better gospel than Methodism. It was a real gospel; a religion, a social religion, and we were ready to live for it, to sacrifice ourselves for it, yes, and to die for it. Who on earth would lift a finger on behalf of Calvinism? To us Capitalism was a living thing. We could see before our eyes the poverty, the starvation and the hunger, the filth of the hovels, mothers growing old before their time, the fierce cruelty of the soldiers and the policemen during strikes, doctors writing 'tuberculosis' on death certificates instead of 'silicosis' to save the company paying compensation to the families, and the bodies carried home after the accidents. They brought my father's body . . . they brought him home burnt to death by the molten metal, an accident that could have been avoided. During the funeral sermon, when the minister said this was the will of God I let loose inside me every haulier's oath I could remember and spat them out at his sermon and his God. And when they sang at the graveside *Bydd myrdd o rhyfeddodau* (There will be a multitude of wonders) I sang in my own heart 'The Red Flag'.

The war had an appetite for poets, and in the languages of all the combatants it is the poets, in both verse and prose, who have left the abiding memorials of the experience. It is only through their voices that we can gain a vision of their life and death and understand, as it were from the inside, the magnitude of the upheaval. Some, like Apollinaire, had already begun to loosen the bonds of inherited techniques as if in preparation for the revolutionary experience to come. Closer to home, from that section of Welsh society that had entered early into the process of anglicisation, men like Wilfred Owen and Edward Thomas made their quiet experiments and unforgettable testimony.

But the Welsh poetic tradition still depended at the core of its being on the strict metres. The influence of scholarship and the new university colleges had been brought to bear in a process of refinement which had been more easily accepted because it seemed to reinforce the respect and veneration due to such ancient and yet living forms. Each year at the national eisteddfod Sir John Morris Jones delivered his criticism with impressive dignity and eloquence. He was not a man to suffer fools gladly and some of the older generation of eisteddfodic bards were frequently piqued by his thinly veiled sarcasms: but the mass of the people listened with awe to the Professor and were happy to renew their pride in their language and the special beauties of the poetic tradition. The poet Thomas Gwyn Jones gained the eisteddfod chair in 1902 for his poem 'Ymadawiad Arthur' (The Passing of Arthur). There were Tennysonian influences in the treatment but the form was a confident repossession of the metres of the fifteenth century and the music was all the poet's own. As if to reflect the new prosperity and confidence of the Welsh people, the poetic tradition was reasserting its pre-eminence as praise poetry. Whatever the subject, the artistry involved in the management of the strict metres turned the thing made into a celebration. In 1910 Gwyn Jones's disciple Robert Williams Parry became virtually a national hero overnight with his *awdl* '*Yr Haf*' (The Summer). The expression of romantic hedonism seems mild enough to us now, but in nonconformist Wales it struck a new note. From one end of the country to the other young men learnt passages off by heart. The achievement of these poets demonstrated that fine poetry could be popular. It gave a new impetus to the central function of the eisteddfod. This was the meeting point of the whole people. It was on the Thursday, the day of the chairing of the bard, that David Lloyd George always chose to renew his compact with his people and immerse himself in the atmosphere of praise, in much the same manner as a prince of the heroic age.

London newspapers had established their grip on the thinking of all the beneficiaries of a universal English elementary education, and they were particularly opposed to fringe activities that made no contribution to the war effort or to mobilising the morale of one united and uniform population. To the press lords a national eisteddfod in wartime seemed a frivolous indulgence in a piece of antiquated nineteenth-century pageantry. It was Lloyd George himself who persuaded the organisers to carry on and make certain that there should be no break in the eisteddfod tradition. This annual affirmation of the existence of a Welsh nation was also a celebration of his own origins. Before the war a book had been published with the title *The Early Life of Lloyd George together with a Short History of the Welsh People*. The implication was clear enough.

No politician in the history of Britain ever had a more captive audience. Lloyd George could study his own qualities in the great mirror of their unstinted admiration. In the national eisteddfodau in London in 1909 and in Wrexham in 1912, suffragettes were almost lynched for interrupting him. A journalist in a Welsh weekly paper reports watching a struggle on the eisteddfod field between rival groups for pieces of a suffragette's coat that had been torn off her back. They wanted them as trophies to take home, in the same way as they took home snatches of Lloyd George's addresses.

Like the poets, he had a way of expressing himself that made his words stick in the memory. More than this, he was the pulpit giant literally to end all pulpit giants. His eloquence was based on one hundred years of development of the art of the spoken word. He spoke as a connoisseur of oratory to a monster convention of 15,000 connoisseurs. But the period of his triumph also signalled the decadence of the art form. Politics had initially detached it from dogma and doctrine. His quick wit and manipulative incantations released it from too close an adherence to accuracy. When the war came the exigencies of propaganda made him rely increasingly on emotion. The blur of sentimentality transformed both the occasion and much of the substance of what he had to say into palatable forms of deception.

The impact of the war on a working-class home is vividly illustrated in Kate Roberts's novel *Traed Mewn Cyffion* (Feet in Chains) first published in 1936.

> And the people who were left at home began to ask themselves and ask each other what it all meant. They understood what hard times meant. They had suffered wrongs and injustices in the quarries: the oppression of the masters and the owners, the oppression of bribery and favouritism. They had seen their children and their friends killed at work, but they had never before seen their sons taken away from them to be killed in war. Since the quarry-cabin was closed, the forum of discussion shifted to the Sunday School where they tried by every means to explain and understand what was happening . . . They no longer believed that the purpose of the war was to protect small nations, or that it was the war to end war, and neither did they believe that one country was to blame more than another . . . In the depths of their being, they believed by this that someone was making money out of it, the same people who exploited them in the quarries and sucked their blood to turn it into gold for their own use. These were the people who desired to delay the return of peace.

The heroine figure of the mother in the latter stages of the novel receives an official letter in a language she cannot read. She knows it's something to do with her son because his name and number are on it. She hurries down to the shop, and that is how she learns that her son has been killed. Again in another novel *Tegwch y Bore* (A Fair Morning), written in the late 1950s, Kate Roberts gives a more detached account of the impact of the war on people at home. At a greater distance the characters are seen with a calm but sympathetic eye to be the prisoners of a large historical fate of which the war is but an isolated but terrible symptom. The heroine, working as a schoolteacher in one of the valleys of South Wales, receives a small parcel containing a few personal belongings left by her brother who has died of wounds in a far away military hospital. His comb, his toothbrush, a brown army-issue handkerchief, with food stains still on it. She decides to burn them instead of sending them home.

A multiplicity of such small sufferings was beyond the poetic eloquence of Lloyd George. But they were the stuff of which true literature was made. Once more in the Welsh experience a question of language was crucial. He never lost his ability to mesmerise a Welsh audience. In the Welsh press sober journalists vied with each other to capture something of the atmosphere of his meetings. In Manchester when 'The Overseer of the Empire' as they called him was due to receive the freedom of the city, the Manchester Welsh, against the wishes of the city fathers, insisted on inviting him to a meeting of their own where they wanted to present him with an illuminated address in a leather binding boldly stamped with a red dragon. Lloyd George accepted. He arrived late as usual. His fellow countrymen had already sung themselves hoarse. There were two hundred Welsh soldiers in the audience, convalescing in a nearby hospital. As he was assuring them that while he admired and respected England, he positively loved Wales, the audience were startled by the explosion of a photographer's flashlight that filled the house with smoke. The old entertainer was more than equal to the occasion. Pointing to the wounded men, he cried out in his musical tenor that had such a vibrant steely core, 'Now don't you imagine a little flash like that is going to have any effect on these fine lads who have stood the test of real fire in France!' When the applause subsided he went on to a lyrical invocation of the river Dwyfor and his childhood home. ('Dwyfor' was the name of one of the hymn tunes printed in the programme.) 'That's where I was brought up, that's where I played as a child, that's where I found everything I treasure most and all the strength that has kept me going under the weight of the world . . . They tell me the old Welsh used to worship their rivers and I'm not surprised: because a river like everything that flows is always pure, always alive, always full of joy . . .' and so on until the great audience lay at his feet, ravished and happily exhausted.

26 Things Fall Apart

The Arthurian vision of history is in many ways a discredited mediaeval concept. It has little relevance to the complexities of political structures in the modern world, and manipulated by propaganda machines lends itself only too easily to dubious dictatorships. But in the Welsh experience, which is where it all began, it has a residual value and is worth contemplating as a continuing historical dynamic. For example, Lloyd George gave up his strictly Welsh Arthurian mission one evening in January 1896. At a meeting of leading South Wales Liberals held in Newport, Monmouthshire, he was howled down for being too Welsh. This influential audience had already decided that active Welshness should be confined to the rugby football field. They had their own version of a tamed Arthur. He was Arthur Gould, the Newport centre-three-quarter who played for Wales twenty-seven times. It was in that same year, 1896, that Arthur Gould made his celebrated after-dinner joke about not knowing what *Cymru am Byth* meant. This was the moment when the boy-wonder from Llanystumdwy took on the mantle of Henry Tudor. The stone that sheathed the sword would be transformed into a stepping-stone to the one seat of power.

The great war and its aftermath left vacant thrones from one end of Europe to the other. The homespun Welsh populist had already demonstrated the most effective formula to produce a political saviour: an heroic and charming young champion capable under pressure of office of becoming an all-wise and all-knowing father figure. In this sense David Lloyd George was a model for the hand-out life history of a whole string of European dictators. However deplorable the consequences we have to accept that his neo-Arthurian ideal is an inevitable human response in a world dominated by the impersonal rhythms of technology, of the superstructures of government and multi-national economics. We have learnt to watch with foreboding when cameras show us the image of a great leader being carried like an icon above a human tide flowing slowly down the main thoroughfare of a capital city. It is more difficult to admit that this could be the only outlet left for the sensibility of the individual in a suffocating social structure.

It remains therefore a matter for quiet rejoicing that the first cracks in Lloyd George's monolithic structure should have appeared in the heartland of Welsh Wales, and be related to the revulsion of Welsh Liberal opinion against his repressive politics in Ireland. The by-election in Cardiganshire in 1921 had an epic quality which has influenced the whole life of that county down to the present day. One of the knights of Lloyd George's Welsh Round Table, the barrister and author Llewelyn Williams, his erstwhile bosom friend, raised the standard of revolt and the ensuing battle raged from one end of the county to the other. Characters direct from the stories of Caradoc Evans were carried on stretchers to the polls, students roamed the countryside in rival flying columns, stately matrons spat at each other and chapels were split permanently between the two rival brands of Welsh Liberalism. Lloyd George's man won; but only just.

In 1922 the Lloyd George empire collapsed and with it a Welsh palace of illusion. It was like the signal for a storm which would destroy the comfortable nonconformist Wales which everyone, including the great leader himself, had been at so much pains to preserve as intact as a nineteenth-century dream cottage on a dateless calendar. Historical necessity was on the march, intent on wiping out the last traces of a recognisable Welsh identity. There were, to begin with, statistics that had been staring the nonconformist leadership in the face for a very long time. In 1871 the percentage of the population speaking Welsh was something over eighty per cent, and this did not include the thriving Welsh nonconformist communities outside Wales. By 1901 a drop of catastrophic proportions had already occurred – the figure was fifty per cent. During the very period which Lloyd George and his generation looked upon as a Golden Age, a veritable Welsh Garden of Eden, the foundation of the whole system was being rapidly eroded. There were a few lonely voices making warning noises. But they were quickly shown the way to the nearest wilderness. Emrys ap Iwan, the boldest of all, was already writing in the 1870s, 'Show me a man who disowns his mother tongue and I will show you a man who will renounce his Christ when the time comes for equally sordid reasons.'

The census held in the penultimate year of the Welsh Caesar Augustus, 1921, revealed that the percentage of speakers of his mother tongue in his native country had sunk to thirty-seven. At last the chapels were worried. It was no longer enough to wallow in vicarious pride at the thought of a Welsh family singing hymns in No. 10 Downing Street; or the language being used as a sleight of hand shorthand in the preparation of cabinet minutes. Ministers began to insert their grave misgivings in their introductions to the chapel's annual report. The faithful were reproved for their lack of zeal. There were continuous complaints about poor attendance at Sunday Schools and week-night meetings. Chapels which less than fifteen years before had resounded with the fervour of the revival, began to show ever increasing rows of empty pews. Religious leaders thundered against the rise of materialism and a whole range of atheistical attitudes: the larger the chapel, the more ominous the reverberations between the bare walls.

The industrial strength of South Wales was the most exposed sector of a British economy which rested on the control exercised by the British Empire on the export markets of the world. When this control was lost the heavy industries of South Wales – coal, steel, tinplate – went into catastrophic decline. The economic history of Wales between the two wars was a record of such unremitting disaster that an apocalyptic note entered the writing and the speech of those people most concerned. What had promised less than a generation ago to be a new dawn for the Welsh people was rapidly transformed into a conglomeration of natural forces out of control that threatened their very existence. The sacrifice of the war was something that had to continue in the bitter fruit of the Great Depression. Unemployment, the weapon of an invisible enemy, drove out more than half a million people, the young and the able-bodied, and what was left in the industrial areas was a derelict society symbolised by the tips and the groups of idle men congregating wearily on drab street corners.

The Union, the Labour party, and industrial strife became the main agencies of the people's spiritual welfare and the expression of the reserves of energy in their communal life. Pride and loyalty and the elements of daily heroism were the legacies of their nineteenth-century past to which they were determined to cling. The Labour party took over the political power enjoyed by the Liberals and the Lib-Labs, and in addition, in the south-east, many of the social functions that had been previously carried out by the hegemonical denomination. Service jobs, such as teaching or local government, became increasingly at a premium. In Glamorgan, for example, it had always been something of an advantage to be a Baptist when applying for this type of job; from this time forward it became much more important to be a member of the Labour party, and to be related to a leading figure in the organisation would be an additional advantage.

It was the South Wales Miners' Federation, the Fed, which provided the people with the degree of organised militancy which they knew was necessary in order for their society to survive. Out of all the invisible forces that were threatening their very existence, the alliance between the government and the owners alone gave shape to an identifiable enemy. Increasingly one confrontation after another took on the lineaments of the class war. Not all the miners' leaders could accept such raw definitions. The older generation were still chapel-goers, Baptists, Calvinistic Methodists, Independents. It was their combination of socialism and old style nonconformity which made the transfer of power in South Wales from Liberal to Labour such a swift and easy process. Throughout the inter-war period, the defining experience, the testing ground, the touchstone of sincerity in the leadership struggle were the series of defensive battles undertaken by the Union against all forms of authority in order to protect what was left of the living standards and the self-respect of a whole community.

By the 1920s English had become the everyday argot of those parts of the South Wales coalfield hardest hit by the depression. The culture shift that had taken place had been all the swifter because it coincided with late waves of immigration and rapid changes in religious and political allegiance. It was an English with its own peculiar character-istics and heavy Welsh undertones, but in educational circles it was frowned on as being unworthy of a great literary language. The English education system was the only route which the brighter children of Welsh-speaking families could take to reach that Nirvana of literary expression which remained a central feature of the great Welsh dream. This background has to be borne in mind as we marvel at the wit and eloquence of, say, a Gwyn Thomas: it is as though Spartacus had expressed himself in boisterous Latin while writing about working-class life in Thrace. An inevitable gap opens between the artist and his most cherished audience, between the manner and the matter.

Of the galaxy of talent which emerged from this transitional situa-tion, it was Idris Davies who made the most strenuous attempts to communicate directly with his own people. He issued a self-denying ordinance and suppressed as much of his native ebullience as he could in order to arrive at an honest and affecting statement that could relate his own personal dilemmas to those of the people to whom he wanted to feel the deepest allegiance. In a sense each of his collections of poems, *Gwalia Deserta*, *The Angry Summer* and *Tonypandy* are about the same thing.

Do you remember 1926? That summer of soups and speeches
The sunlight on the idle wheels and the deserted crossings . . .

'Ay, ay, we remember 1926,' said Dai and Shinkin,
As they stood on the kerb in Charing Cross Road,
'And we shall remember 1926 until our blood is dry.'

He worked in the mines as a boy and experienced the bitterness of unemployment until he found his way by self-tuition to Loughborough Training College and a teaching job in the East End of London. Teaching was the main escape route laid down for Welsh working-class youth and Davies knew this only too well. His work was published by J. M. Dent and Faber and Faber, like that of his more celebrated contemporaries, Dylan Thomas and Vernon Watkins. But teaching in London offered him nothing of the sustenance he was looking for.

Ah, 1926, I will never forget you!
You brought me the long, long strike . . .
And late in your wonderful summer
You led me to Wordsworth and Shakespeare . . .

Grateful as he was for the pleasure of English literature he became increasingly resentful for the loss of his native inheritance.

I lost my native language
For the one the Saxon spake
By going to school by order
For Education's sake . . .

He knew that he was a victim of exploitation, whether as a member of the working class or as a Welshman of the diaspora, cheated of his birthright. He also knew that as a poet he had been placed in an impossible position, trying to sing the songs of his own people in an alien bourgeois culture mode. He hated the pressure towards individualistic exhibitionism that this precarious stance exerted on the poet. He knew the despair that arises from this form of alienation, and had an awareness of his own inability to do much about it.

Aneurin Bevan was the child of a very similar Welsh mining community. He went out to work at eleven and at fourteen, like Idris Davies, he was working underground. He too was brought up in the atmosphere of chapel and eisteddfod. He was named after Aneurin Fardd (Aneurin Jones), a Monmouthshire exponent of the strict metres who edited a Baptist newspaper, emigrated to America where he became Superintendent of Public Parks in New York and Brooklyn and a notable figure in Welsh American eisteddfod circles. Again, like Idris Davies, Aneurin Bevan developed an early thirst for reading. He also had a taste for leadership and a powerful physical presence. Part of the abiding fascination of his character arose from the combination of the sensibilities of a poet and the aggressive daring of an agitator dedicated to the destruction of an inhuman social order 'gone in the teeth', and the construction of a new society based on the Marxist principles taught at the Central Labour College. His chosen instrument for the transformation was the British Labour party. With impressive tactical brilliance he made certain of his power base in South Wales before he entered the first British parliament to be elected on universal suffrage in 1929. The men of the western valleys of Monmouthshire had risen in the cause of universal suffrage in 1839. Bevan's first great cause was the unemployed. During those years more than thirty per cent of the workers of the South Wales coalfield were unemployed. The spearhead of the Unemployed Workers Movement was the Communist party led by men like Arthur Horner, Lewis Jones and Will Paynter. These were the men who presented Bevan with the abiding dilemma of the British Left: the relationship between parliamentary and extra-parliamentary agitation. His association with them must be part of the reason why he never achieved supreme power. Like Lloyd George and Churchill he was deeply distrusted by the apparatchiks of his own party. As an individualist and a Welshman he was built on an heroic scale. As an effective politician he was maimed by the same unresolved and possibly unresolvable conflict that inhibited the muse of Idris Davies: how to reconcile undivided devotion to his own class and his own people with the siren calls of political ambition and much metropolitan adulation.

In establishing the National Health Service, Aneurin Bevan completed the work Lloyd George had begun almost forty years earlier. In this sense the Welfare State is the most enduring contribution of the reforming aspirations of Welsh nonconformity to the British nation state. Indeed Bevan's state of open rebellion and unstinting honesty make him a more sympathetic product of the Welsh nonconformist conscience than Lloyd George. He was not so narrowly concerned with the pursuit of power for its own sake. His generosity of spirit and the manner of his going are sufficient in themselves to ensure his Arthurian status among his own people.

Many Welshmen rose to dominating positions in the British Labour party. Not because they set out like the psalmist's hart for the cooling streams of undeviating service to Wales. In those days of heady internationalism this would have seemed intolerably parochial. Their careers echoed faithfully the progress of Tom Ellis and Lloyd George and their confrères in the not so distant days of the Liberal nonconformist ascendancy. They could be passionately and unmistakably Welsh, like James Griffiths or Arthur Jenkins, so long as these appealing folk qualities did not impede their parliamentary progress in what they all discovered, like Aneurin Bevan, was the abiding home and impregnable bastion of English political, economic and cultural supremacy. James Griffiths had a brother, Amanwy, who was an eisteddfod poet and he was the natural hero of a London film made in the 1940s idealising the stalwart cultural interests of the Welsh miner. Griffiths himself became the first Secretary of State for Wales and, by virtue of his origins and office, was charged with fending off from time to time the growing challenge of a resurgent Welsh national spirit. The first step was always to reaffirm the prior allegiance of the Welsh worker to the British Labour party and by unspoken inference to the British nation state that party aspired to govern and transform by gradual parliamentary processes.

Political awareness on a mass scale reached its high-water mark in

Wales during the 1930s. The sufferings inflicted on the working people and particularly the mining communities by unrestricted capitalism forced their leaders to search desperately and painfully for political and economic theory that would make sense of the agonising processes and offer some remedy. They were never able to do this in comfort or academic seclusion. Twelve months in the Central Labour College was no substitute for a lifetime in the British Museum. The residue of a law-abiding nonconformist tradition discouraged open revolutionary violence. In the course of the day to day struggle events were always in charge and the initiative was inevitably with the well-fed agencies of authority. Leaders of the unemployed would stay up all night to equip themselves with sufficient arguments to conduct the next stage of an endless rearguard action. Men like Arthur Horner, Lewis Jones and Will Paynter suffered imprisonment and persecution. Their reward was the affection and loyalty of the Miners' Union and of the organised unemployed. They seized on international Marxism as a science and a faith which explained the nature of existence and related it to their own struggles. They embraced a vision of an earthly paradise purged of irrational superstition that had to be fought for with the fervour their countrymen reserved for the singing of hymns. In a curious imitation of the Welsh Catholic recusants who travelled to Rome for instruction and refreshment, they made repeated journeys to the curia of a new world religion in Moscow.

Vague forms of pacifism and internationalism coloured the whole of Welsh thinking in the period between the wars. It provided a not unpleasant pink haze that covered the wide landscape of the middle ground between the revolutionary extremes that lingered on the fringes of both the Welsh-speaking and the non-Welsh-speaking communities. The League of Nations Union gained widespread support. Among the native Welsh the old imperial enthusiasms had exhausted themselves on the battlefields of the great war. Nonconformity had reverted to its peace-loving nineteenth-century stance. The Labour party in Wales during this period was committed to semi-permanent opposition to the government in London that still reigned over an increasingly ram-shackle empire. It was not until the 1960s that Welsh Labour leaders would be heard extolling the unique virtues of the British Common-wealth and expressing profound and yet guarded nostalgia for the days of empire. Labour after all owed more to Methodism than to Marx and it was still the secular expression of the voice of the nonconformist conscience in an increasingly naughty world.

27 Poet and Proletariat

Throughout the period of nonconformist ascendancy in any Welsh community the minister occupied a conspicuous position. He was a man set apart and the degree of his authority related to the extent that he had been demonstrably chosen. It was assumed that a divine agency had at some point in his upbringing directed his conscience to his calling. The denomination, after its own processes of deliberation, which attached an increasing emphasis to educational attainment, set a seal of approval on the call to office. An individual church, or a group of churches, then bore the main responsibility for maintaining him and his family. Much therefore depended on the minister's character. He was called upon to lead, but his leadership was hedged about with many restrictions. Whether among the industrial working class or in the rural areas or in the prosperous surburbs, any intelligent child brought up in the manse was aware from an early age of the hazards of leadership, of exercising any form of moral authority and of the strain placed on behaviour by living more than most in the public eye.

Saunders Lewis came from a family highly regarded among the Calvinistic Methodists. His great-grandfather, William Roberts of Amlwch, had been the close friend and confidant of John Elias. His grandfather, Owen Thomas, had been a leader in the denomination and one of its most successful writers. Owen Thomas's ministries had been in London and in Liverpool. Liverpool at the end of the nineteenth century supported a Welsh population of around 100,000 and performed the function of an urban metropolis for most of North Wales. The Calvinistic Methodist leadership was an active element in the creation of a Welsh bourgeois culture. In all the urban areas where they were established – with more of them probably in England than in Wales – their way of life would be discreet and middle-class. Their sons enjoyed the best possible secular education in English: but home life would be governed by the Welsh Bible, the denominational hymn book, and the apparatus of a Welsh-speaking church life. Saunders Lewis came early to the kind of choice that has since become standard for the twentieth-century bright young Welshman, a choice that was the inevitable consequence of all that had gone before, a choice that on one level appeared to be no more than picking out a preferred culture, but on another involved endless questions of family loyalties, of honour, of roots in the past, of obligation to voices from the past and to the survival of an ancient nation and a distinct people.

For many young Welshmen this uncomfortable dilemma masquerading as a choice has been the cause of lifelong unease. In his volumes of autobiography, Goronwy Rees has described how he made his own choice as a young man in Cardiff in the late 1920s. His father, too, was a Calvinistic Methodist minister and a power in the denomination. The Reverend R.J. Rees was a committed supporter of the Lloyd George candidate in the fateful by-election in Cardiganshire in 1921. Goronwy Rees made his choice and achieved a distinguished, if sometimes erratic, career in English letters and academic life. His Welsh connections seem to have caused him more pain than pleasure.

Saunders Lewis made his choice during a war. At twenty years of age he volunteered for military service in 1914 and served throughout as an officer with the South Wales Borderers, mainly in France. His interest at Liverpool University had all been in the direction of literature and drama in English, and the visual arts. He had joined the army eager for experience, 'to be present always at the focus where the greatest number of vital sources unite in their purest energy'. In the trenches he continued to pursue his practice of the philosophy of Walter Pater and became an avid reader of current French literature. In 1916 his brother was killed at Nieuport. In the same year Lewis was wounded at Bourlon Wood.

Where the machinery of death rules, survival is a matter of chance for the individual. In the seventh part of David Jones's *In Parenthesis* there is a compassionate vision of the sacrifice of soldiers:

> Seven minutes to go . . . and seventy times seven times to
> the minute
> this drumming of the diaphragm.
>
> Every one of these, stood, separate, upright, above ground,
> blinkt to the broad light
> risen dry mouthed from the chalk . . .
>
> But sweet sister death has gone debauched today and stalks
> on this high ground with strumpet confidence . . .
>   By one and one the line gaps, where her fancy will . . .

It was the direct intrusion of the machine into the flesh of history. One way to face it was to accept the gamble. Within the lifetime of those who survived, the survival of whole nations would become subject to more powerful engines of destruction by an analogous process. Whoever survived would make their contribution to the continuation of the society which had given them their particular identity.

1916 was a fateful year. The stage was being set for the great drama of our own times. War was becoming the crucible of revolution. Between German trenches Adolf Hitler lay wounded among the bodies of men and horses and began to dream of himself as an artist who would one day become the architect of a new Germany. His future mentor, the Italian socialist Benito Mussolini, also a corporal, had plans for a new Italy which were already much further advanced. In Zurich, Lenin was anxiously watching the progress of the war on the Eastern front and waiting for the first cracks to show themselves in the imposing façade of the Tsar's power. And yet in 1916 it looked for a moment as if the British Empire would be the first of the *anciens régimes* to disintegrate. The leaders of the Easter Rising in Dublin were shot. Lloyd George of Wales became Prime Minister of Great Britain and war leader of a reinvigorated British Empire. It is difficult for us to imagine the traumatic effect these events had on the minds of impressionable and intelligent young people at that time.

Among the books Saunders Lewis read in France was *Le Culte du Moi* by Maurice Barrès, and a few years later he quotes from it a passage which helped him to decide his own future.

> It is by throwing himself into the life of his country and his people that a man can best come to know himself . . . and live as an artist to the limits of his consciousness . . . He who cuts himself off from his own past, his own land, his own people, starves and frustrates his own soul.

There was also the influence of his father and the writings of Emrys ap Iwan and Thomas Gwyn Jones. Although he returned to Liverpool to complete a first class honours in English he had already made up his mind to pursue a literary career in Welsh. This was not an easy choice. The influence of nineteenth-century pulpit oratory which had produced the eloquence of Lloyd George had also extensively muddied the pool of contemporary Welsh literature. Among a people easily intoxicated with words, the most difficult task of all would be to give accurate expression to any form of truth. This task had already begun. Thomas Gwyn Jones sought direct inspiration from the great poetic classics of the fifteenth century. Sir John Morris Jones had completed the first stages of his monumental grammar and the re-establishment of the classical canon of Welsh prose. W.J. Gruffydd was engaged in iconoclastic literary journalism before joining the navy; and after the war he became editor of the most influential literary magazine in Welsh, *Y Llenor*. Scholars like Ifor Williams, Griffith John Williams and Sir John Edward Lloyd, had begun vast projects of which Sir Ifor Williams's inspired detective work on the oldest manuscripts remains the most brilliant example.

In post-war Europe it seemed as if the prospect of proletarian revolution had stimulated the bourgeois world into a final burst of feverish activity. Experiment was the order of the day. Americans like Gertrude Stein, Ernest Hemingway and Ezra Pound sat around in Paris, fraternising with every available art form and telling each other that beauty was only a brief gasp between clichés. Their vocation was 'to resuscitate the dead art of poetry' even though they 'had been born in a half-savage country', where the monstrous machines of profit were already lining up to replace the 'botched civilisation' of Europe, 'the old bitch gone in the teeth'. Inside the quieter purlieus of the Welsh language the problems were the same, but the solutions had to be different. The work of conservation and revolution had to proceed side by side. Whereas bourgeois English literature could be invigorated and even replaced by a younger version from across the Atlantic, there was nothing to replace unsatisfactory or indifferent Welsh except an improved version of itself based on a clearer vision of the most dynamic periods of its own past. Inevitably this had to be in part an academic exercise and the Welsh departments of the university colleges had to give a lead.

Everywhere the processes of experiment and reformation opened up a gap between the artist and his public. Nothing in any form or any language seemed quite as difficult as revolutionary simplicity. To over-simplify was to stumble into the traps of slogan and propaganda: to over-elaborate was to lose your audience. The one advantage the Welsh enjoyed was their poetic tradition. This had centuries of experience of the delicate relation between poetry and politics in an integrated society. Through the eisteddfod many of its forms had maintained their hold on the affections of the common people. Wherever the writ of the language ran, Taliesin was waiting in the shadows and his first lesson was the necessity of re-establishing the close links between literary criticism and political awareness. When a garden was run to seed and choked with weeds the first task would be to clear and clean it.

It was as a literary critic that Saunders Lewis first made his mark. His brisk incisive style was much appreciated by his contemporaries. Like R.T. Jenkins and Ambrose Bebb he was influenced by an enthusiasm for French literature. Everything they wrote was gratefully accepted as a useful counterweight to the smothering effect of English literary fashions that flowed so easily into Wales as a result of the education system. If a Welsh point of view in literature existed at all, it was felt that it needed to be put in a European context if it was to escape the stigma of being irredeemably provincial. Lewis's first play in Welsh was an echo of the theme of Barrès's novel *Colette Baudoche*, the young woman from Metz who stifled her love for a German schoolmaster out of her love for the France which she believed to be her native land. Lewis's heroine makes a similar choice in early nineteenth-century Wales when she refuses to emigrate with her lover in order to avoid arrest:

> 'My roots are here. Even if I were free, I wouldn't wish to turn my back on my own country. I am dust of this earth . . . You attach great value to life. Sometimes we have to learn to throw it away . . . You belong to a new people, forward-looking, living on hope. I belong to a very ancient people. My proper roots stretch back into the remote past. There is small place for hope in my way of living. I don't hope, but neither do I fear. My life shall be an altar where my nation remembers. I shall make it so and live like a nun to do it.'

If the condition of Wales had been anything like as stable as that of England, there is no doubt that Saunders Lewis would have attained quite quickly a position as poet and arbiter of literary taste closely parallel with that occupied by T.S. Eliot. There was a striking similarity between their critical and cultural attitudes and their conviction that drama was a natural outlet for poetry and a poetic tradition in the twentieth century.

In 1923 Lewis published the first act of a poetic drama, *Blodeuwedd*, in W. J. Gruffydd's *Y Llenor*. It was based on the story of the girl made of flowers which occurs in the Fourth Book of *The Mabinogion*, a mythological setting but a modern preoccupation with sex and science. The plot dealt with yet another conflict between honour and desire and appropriately enough the play was not completed until 1947. The author himself was driven to political action by a political awareness inherent in the poetic tradition he wanted to practise. After a long sleep, Taliesin was active again. The times were not auspicious. On the other hand historical necessity, which is visible to ordinary mortals as well as historians, had firmly decreed that since the failure of *Cymru Fydd* in the 1890s, henceforward no time would be auspicious: Welshness was scheduled for indefinite postponement.

At the national eisteddfod held in Pwllheli in August 1925 a group of six men decided to form a Welsh Nationalist party. Tom Ellis and Lloyd George had used this term before. The difference now was the idea of something totally independent from the existing English political parties. Of the six, the quarryman member was elected secretary. The chairman was a Baptist minister. Of the remaining four, one was a university lecturer, Saunders Lewis, one an agricultural adviser, one a carpenter, and one a Welsh Independent minister from Treorci. This new party began its life inside the shrinking frontiers of the Welsh language. By 1926 it was able to publish a monthly paper, *Y*

Ddraig Goch (The Red Dragon). In his first article, Saunders Lewis sets out his political confession of faith.

> Man is a social being. It is only in his social role that he attains dignity. Only in a community can he achieve contentment. The sum total of his achievements, the masterpieces of the mind and the imagination, in utterance, in colour and image, in architecture, was at all times arrived at by co-operation and joint invention with his neighbours and fellows. He is obliged to associate and be social. He is compelled to love his community.

As a writer he understands that the basis of his creativity is the accumulated deposit of literary tradition inside the language that he is using. The language exists for the service of the Welsh community and is a central part of the capital available, in the economic and political sense, for the preservation of the well-being of the whole people. To abandon the language, therefore, or even to stand passively by and allow its destruction, was to assist in the diminution of the precious reserves of the human spirit, of essential capital, at that very moment in time when the people never needed it more. In the first pamphlet published by the new party he sets out a characteristic warning against extremism. He speaks in the measured and moderate tones of a Manawydan restraining a proletarian Pryderi. 'Hot-headed and limitless nationalism is a highly dangerous force. To mark out the limits: to fight only for those things that are indispensable and essential, to use restraint and to resist extremes – this is the soul of wisdom and of justice'.

His literary gifts were not always an advantage to him as a practical politician. In an age when slogans meant more than they have ever done before or since, his adherence to verbal accuracy and rational critical procedures was liable to puzzle his followers and enrage an increasingly large proportion of the Welsh public, nonconformist still, but increasingly committed to one form or another of socialism, who began to see him as a sinister bogey-man threatening to disturb the anaesthetic peace of a people already resigned in their subconscious mind to a programme of painless cultural euthanasia. When he was received into the Catholic church in 1932, this confirmed all their worst fears.

The language of suffering was much easier to understand. In September 1936 Saunders Lewis, together with D. J. Williams and Lewis Valentine, set fire to RAF installations in the Lleyn peninsula. This was the culmination of a year of protest in which the whole of Wales was united. The government had established their bombing school in Lleyn in defiance of the wishes of the Welsh people. The breeding swans of Dorset and the wild life of Holy Island were more important to the English government than the preservation of the integrity of a stronghold of the Welsh language. The three men were seen to be defending part of the heartland of an ancient culture, and when they gave themselves up after their symbolic act the seal of approval on what they had done was given when a Welsh jury refused to convict them. Much to the anger of the ageing Lloyd George who was resting with his second family in the Jamaican sun, the case was transferred to the Old Bailey where an English judge and jury took no time at all in sending the three of them to prison for nine months. Lewis was dismissed from his post at the University College of Swansea in the face of loud but ineffective protests. In the country of the unemployed he joined the ranks of those who suffered most and stayed there for almost fifteen years.

Conservative and moderate as he was by nature, circumstances compelled Saunders Lewis to recognise the fact that only some form of revolution could save the Welsh nation, and the language which he understood to be the *sine qua non* of its identity. Creative writing had driven him towards political thought. He was not the kind of man to allow his political thinking to dissipate itself in rhetoric. Sooner or later the logic of his position would demand that he took action. In this respect alone he was reversing the trend of an oratorical culture in which the word had become a perfectly acceptable substitute for the deed.

It was the age of idealistic youth movements and in the early 'twenties O. M. Edwards's son, Ifan ap Owen, founded his Urdd Gobaith Cymru (The Welsh League of Youth but more literally The Order of the Hope of Wales) amid noises of universal approval. This was a form of childlike patriotism that even the age of internationalism could accept. Its symbol was a triangle with white at the top, green at the base and red in the middle. Each member declared that he would be faithful to Wales, to his fellow-man and to Christ. Forms of heady idealism were propagated beyond the scouting oaths of the pragmatic English; but the movement played an important part in an adaptation of eisteddfod culture to meet the needs of Welsh youth. In the inter-war period it held great athletic events and made much of the cult of the out-of-doors, and a whole range of activities helped to make the Welsh language and Welshness attractive to the young. In retrospect, its influence can be seen to have been limited by two vital factors: the growing attraction of mid-Atlantic Anglo-American culture and the movement's confinement to a pre-adult world. As far as the psychology of the individual Welsh person was concerned, enthusiastic membership of the Urdd in childhood and youth could only serve to intensify a sense of disillusionment on discovering how small a part those ideals and that language and culture played in the adult world.

When the three men who had burned the bombing school in Lleyn came out of prison, they were given a tumultuous welcome by 12,000 people in that old pavilion at Caernarfon which had been the scene of

Lloyd George's oratorical triumphs. For a moment it seemed as if they would succeed to what was left of his political kingdom. During their trial the old man himself had been moved to write angry protests to his daughter Megan:

> I wish I were there, and I certainly wish I were forty years younger. I should be prepared to risk a protest which would be a defiance. If I were Saunders Lewis I would not surrender at the Old Bailey: I would insist on their arresting me, and I am not sure that I would not make it difficult for them to do that . . . It makes my blood boil.

The forty years he wanted back might as well have been four hundred. Indeed in Taliesinic terms they were. It was certainly that long since Welsh poets dared to intervene directly in the political process and challenge the power of the state. Language statistics alone showed how the Lloyd George inheritance in Wales had shrunk immeasurably since the heady days of *Cymru Fydd*.

In the South Wales coalfield the moral and intellectual leadership of the working people had already passed to the more self-sacrificing and disinterested leaders of the community. Here a prison sentence had become the passport to leadership. Part of the vital function of a man like Aneurin Bevan was to keep the lines of communication open between these new folk heroes and the more sober operators of the power-structure of the Labour party. The attention of the Welsh workers in 1936 was riveted on the great drama that was unfolding in Spain. Here was the confrontation between Fascism and Socialism which so many of the more intelligent political commentators had been predicting. Spain was the theatre of the greatest drama of modern times. Here, and nowhere else, the fate of all mankind would be worked out. Here was a cause to restore to a proud working class a sense of its own dignity and importance. The miners and the unemployed of South Wales would show the world that they were more than hunger marchers obliged to sing in the streets of English cities, obliged to hold out their battered enamel mugs like begging bowls to receive the patronising pity of a weak and indecisive central government. Out of what little they had they gave everything they could to the cause of Republican Spain: clothes, food, money, even tinned milk that they could ill spare. South Wales miners formed the largest regional group in the International Brigade. The Communist spearhead of the industrial workers and unemployed was prepared to sacrifice everything for the anti-fascist battle in Spain. Within the limitations of a pacifist tradition, the Welsh-speaking intelligentsia, in more comfortable material circumstances, were equally determined to make sacrifices. Two languages, two faiths, two distinct and positive ways of looking at the world, existed side by side in the same small country: the Welsh language and the nationhood that went with it and the Spanish Republic were both in need of saving. At least it seemed that what they had in common was the fatal attraction of the 'lostness' of lost causes.

This was the period during which Economics became the Queen of the Sciences. The nonconformist legacy of guilt suffered its own peculiar form of trans-substantiation when young people realised that the cheap food they were eating had been made available by the exploitation of less fortunate human beings in far away territories of the Empire. If it was true that the financial supremacy of the City of London was being preserved at the expense of the nation state's industrial base, it had to be admitted that it was this state of affairs that made cheap food possible. For people on the dole it made the difference between subsistence and starvation. For people of good will with an appetite for reform, it pushed them further in the direction of root and branch solutions and revolution. Sympathy for the cause of the Spanish Republic was all the more widespread in Wales because an imaginative people was acutely aware that all the suffering was being endured on their behalf.

In prison and subsequently out of work Saunders Lewis had the leisure to return to the practice of poetry. *Buchedd Garmon* (The Life of Saint Germanus) was a verse drama for radio that went back to the fifth-century origins of the Welsh people in order to look for the seed of a viable future. At that time, too, civilisation had been on the brink of collapse. The comfortable certainties of the long afternoon of Empire were coming to an end. The slogans were on the streets. The placards of every newspaper in Europe announced that we were running out of time. The key word of the 1930s was crisis. In Guernica the dive-bombers had already struck. 'Beloved . . . the foundations of our world are giving way. Nearer and nearer through the eastern forests I see the torches of the Barbarians flicker and in the African dust the Vandal hordes swarm around the walls of Hippo.'

A later poem 'The Deluge' was more specific. It begins: 'The tramways climb from Merthyr to Dowlais, the slime of a snail on the mound of slag . . .' and ends, '. . . the journey was without profit, the zest was in vain, our dark defence is a flood of despair . . . and with the tide the sound of tanks assembling.'

28 Survival

In Spain, probably because General Franco had the support of the world's leading industrial power, it was the Fascist cause which triumphed. In spite of this, when the German dictator launched the second world war, the astute Spaniard contrived to stand aside from the conflict. He had the excuse that his country was already devastated by civil war, but from the beginning he believed that the deciding factor would be the relative productive capacities of the United States and Germany. In June 1941 Germany attacked Russia and in December of the same year Japan attacked the United States. There was no knowing which way the tide would turn in so massive a confrontation. Mechanised warfare was laying down the production lines of industry that continue to dominate the world up to the present day. Franco did well to bide his time. By 1945 for the first time since the Renaissance the fulcrum of power in world politics had moved out of Europe.

The force which sustained Great Britain and its ramshackle Empire throughout these dangerous years was a characteristic combination of righteousness and the abiding instinctive patriotism of the English. This accounts for the unity of all the effective political forces in the state behind a purely nationalist right-wing figure like Winston Churchill. Churchill was an English imperialist with a strong sense of history. He saw the German threat in terms of the Danish Great Army that ravaged England in the ninth century. His chosen hero therefore was Alfred not Arthur. Alfred was the defender of England who possessed 'the sublime power to rise above the whole force of circumstances, to remain unbiassed by extremes of victory or defeat . . . this raises Alfred far above the turmoil of Barbaric wars to his pinnacle of deathless glory.'

In Wales, Labour occupied the position of power that had been held by the Liberals during the long reign of Lloyd George. It was therefore appropriate that the effective mouthpiece of what can only be described as the loyal opposition in the House of Commons should be Aneurin Bevan, a man of the same Arthurian potential as the young Lloyd George who campaigned for Welsh Home Rule and against the Boer War. Bevan was a Welshman less certain of his roots and always ambivalent in his attitude to his native country. The difference between the two men is an interesting measure of the decay of nonconformist power and the transfer of social and ethical concern from the religious sphere to a purely secular body like the Labour party. Because of the influence of men like Bevan, the atmosphere of the Popular Front permeated left-wing politics, and Communists who had previously been isolated, were allowed to come in from the cold to make their contribution to the war effort. Because of the alliance with Russia and the horrific excesses of Hitler's National Socialist totalitarian machine, the war took on the appearance of an international crusade on behalf of international socialist ideals.

The phrase in common use was 'total war' and this process had very little room to accommodate 'Welshness'. Welsh broadcasting for example, which had come into existence as a recognised region of the BBC through the joint exertions of Lloyd George and Saunders Lewis, and in the teeth of strong opposition from Sir John Reith, was put away for the duration. The eisteddfod almost disappeared. Certain Welsh-language newspapers were suspected of varying degrees of disloyalty. All aspects of Welsh national aspirations were regarded with disfavour unless they were prefaced with protestations of unlimited devotion to the Allied cause in general and English institutions in particular. A voluntary body with the respectable but cumbersome name *Pwyllgor Diogelu Diwylliant Cymru*, (The Committee for the Safeguarding of Welsh Culture) came into existence, and its chief achievement was a newsletter for distribution among the Welsh-speaking members of the armed forces.

Between the wars it is possible to outline a struggle for the hearts and minds of the Welsh people which could be crudely and even mislead-ingly described as a battle between the Red Dragon and the Red Flag. Within the shrinking confines of the national language, from 1930 onwards, the overwhelming majority of creative writers became mem-bers or associates of the Welsh Nationalist party which in the post-war period came to call itself *Plaid Cymru*. In an age of mass communica-tions this can hardly be considered of much statistical importance; and it is only an act of faith to assume that it will have any long term significance. Throughout the 'twenties and 'thirties and up to the end of the second world war, the Marxists and the Communist party fared much better in terms of political influence. In South Wales they set the pace, and whenever the going was rough they were to be found in the forefront of the struggle. But they were never allowed to offer a serious challenge to Labour as a party of government on any level. Their influence withered with the first blast of the Cold War. In all the proliferating communication systems of the West, Stalin was given the rôle of threatening monster left vacant by the suicide of Hitler. The revelations of Khrushchev in the twentieth congress of the Communist party of the Soviet Union in February 1956 set a seal on the portrait of tyrannical wickedness and put an end to a phase of internationalism that had dominated the imagination of Welsh socialists for almost three decades.

The sentiment of internationalism in South Wales was replaced by an unswerving loyalty to the British Labour party. This phenomenon had many curious aspects. Former Communists and fellow-travellers became fervent adherents of the last vestiges of imperial glory. In a behaviour pattern curiously reminiscent of the devotion of the aristocracy to the house of Tudor, they formed a deep attachment to the monarchy and the elaborate ceremonial surrounding the institution. Once again the dominant section of Welsh political and social life could believe that it had virtually invented a new 'Britishness' and added the concept of a Welfare State as an additional jewel in a glittering crown. Along with this neo-royalist spirit went an increasingly suspicious dislike of European entanglements, and an even sterner disapproval of the heresy of separatism that the Labour establishment began to detect in too much concern for the fate of the Welsh language. The ultimate ironic twist came on March 1st, 1979 when the Referendum stage-managed by a minority Labour government appeared to prove that Wales was in fact not Wales at all but the last bastion of Little England, lightly disguised as 'Little Britain'.

The creation of any viable form of Welsh nationhood, and the conditions for a new stability in the Welsh character that would go with it, clearly becomes more difficult with the falling away of a sense of Welsh allegiance among ever increasing sections of the population. The experience of the last sixty years offers a stark contrast to that remarkable resurgence of the Welsh identity which took place in the nineteenth century. Then all the omens were favourable: a strong economic base, a vigorous and aggressive working class, religious organisations that were also powerful social structures and in many ways alternative structures of political autonomy. It was a country then in a dynamic condition of expansion where a variety of forms of moral imperatives and religiously based altruism could combine private welfare with larger loyalties, and provide a reputable balance between personal ambition and national pride. It is not without reason therefore that we measure the acuteness of the present crisis both in the general decline of British economic and political power and the statistical decline of the Welsh language.

In the post-war period, at the very moment when there were more members of Parliament of Welsh origin sitting in Westminster than at any other time in history, Wales itself was obliged to endure one encroachment after another on its well-being, its identity, and even its territorial integrity. In economic terms its position was that of a client colony totally dependent on the hand-outs from central government and too weak even to think of developing any techniques of self-help or self-reliance. Great English cities were allowed to help themselves to Welsh water and sell it back to the natives at a profit. Many of the valleys of the industrial South remained crippled communities emasculated by rapid economic change and paralysed by power-structures that were socialist in name but inflexibly conservative in practice. The Welsh railway system was torn up by a government-controlled corporation with the minimum of consultation and a total disregard for the needs of the local population. The whole of Britain, of course, suffered and continues to suffer, from industrial emasculation and the break up of the railways. But the more marginal the society, the more acute the loss, and in the case of Wales, the remnants of a national identity were, and are, at stake. Increasingly Wales did not exist in the bureaucratic mind as anything more than a geographical expression. In the 1950s the country itself was considered long overdue for economic dismemberment. It was an ideal site for a vast recreation area to meet the needs of the overcrowded English conurbations. An efficient educational machine could be relied on to cream off the last generations of bright pupils and post them to comfortable situations and the membership of gramophone clubs in the suburbs of the south-east of England. What little was left of Welsh industry could be tacked on to those planners' dreams called Severnside in the South and extended Merseyside in the North. There was no need for the Welsh to have any control over the systems of mass communication, radio, television, the popular press, because the prognosis for their continued existence was so unpromising. In North American terms the whole place could be converted into an Adirondack park stretching from Pontypridd to Penygroes with a couple of emaciated Jersey shores hanging on like seaweed to the north and south coasts.

It was understandable that the declining numbers of Welsh-speaking Welsh should feel themselves threatened and their way of life under siege. What is less obvious is the sense of disorientation prevailing among the majority who have been deprived of the language and the opportunity of inheriting the history and traditions that go with it. The consolations of history are never to be lightly discarded. At the most simple level it is they alone who offer the clues and keys to the meaning and the magic of a landscape in which a man must live and work. One of the encouraging elements that emerges from even the most superficial contemplation of Welsh history is the capacity of such a marginal society to generate and perpetuate so large a body of myth. The myths of the Welsh were closely bound up with a living poetic tradition. This meant a degree of discipline in their formal arrangement and a social and political significance attached to their correct propagation. Myth-making is a recognised activity among defeated peoples. It is not only a source of consolation. Properly understood and used it is a most potent weapon in the struggle for survival. In a world which is hostile, both to the society in which he was born and to those aspects of his own personality which he owes to that society and from which he cannot easily be parted, how else is a sensitive young person able to find his way through the labyrinth without clutching more tightly to the thread which connects him to an honourable past? He must know both consciously and unconsciously that his own dignity as a human being is linked with the dignity of the national entity to which he belongs. He knows that this is a destiny from which he cannot escape and the mark of the hero in any myth is the degree of readiness with which he embraces his destiny.

In the early 'sixties Saunders Lewis received an unexpectedly ardent response to a memorable and sombre broadcast that he made on the future prospects for the language. A new generation of young people formed Cymdeithas yr Iaith Gymraeg (The Welsh Language Society), dedicated to the defence of the language by campaigns that involved carefully calculated degrees of militancy and civil disobedience. It is this numerically small society of young people which has set the pace in Welsh politics for the past twelve years or more. The course of action which made the greatest impact in the early stages was concerned with road-signs. New road-signs in Welsh became a symbol of the spirit of the language reaffirming its privileged relationship both with the landscape of the country and the historic past of the human settlements within it.

In 1966 Gwynfor Evans was returned to Parliament as the first Plaid Cymru member. By-election results indicated that many hitherto safe Labour seats were in danger. This swing in electoral opinion combined with the partial success of the Cymdeithas campaigns induced the Labour government to stage an Investiture of the Prince of Wales in Caernarfon Castle in order to turn the rising tide of Welsh national sentiment into more manageable channels. The Investiture provided a brilliant lesson in the fine art of manipulating the mass media. It also demonstrated their overwhelming power, and the rigidly centralised nature of their control. If the Welsh language and Welsh culture were to have a sporting chance to survive, it would inevitably involve a battle for an adequate place in the television channels. This became the main objective of the Cymdeithas campaigns in the 'seventies which involved a prolonged series of civil disobedience, fines and imprisonments and culminated in Gwynfor Evans's proposed hunger strike in September 1980.

Unless a people are certain of their identity and its values, they are fatally inhibited from exercising that degree of creativity which is necessary to reaffirm civilised values in the corner of the globe that they inhabit. In the course of history the Welsh experience demonstrates the unhappy effects that occur when a class is persuaded for one reason or another to turn its back on its natural inheritance. When a language is abandoned for example, either by Tudor aristocrats on the make or an industrial working class, the first reaction is one of guilt. This is followed in due course by an identifiable phenomenon called 'culture shame'. Children become ashamed of their parents and begin to display towards the old language attitudes inculcated by the education of the conqueror. Hard upon this phase develops a kind of 'culture hatred' in which the victims of the process happily operate the apparatus of extinction on behalf of a distant and invisible authority. It is only after these painful phases have been endured that a population can reach the numb but comfortable condition of indifference. Indifference is fundamentally uncreative. It produces a people ideally conditioned for manipulation by mechanised superstructures operating for either profit or power or a judicious mixture of both. Such a people can be sufficiently sustained on synthetic substitutes for their own history; a nice balance of sedative and convenience food that can be controlled and adjusted to keep the masses in a state of complaisant lassitude. Too abrupt a change to the mother's milk of unadulterated history always entails the risk of a rash and a fever of activity.

Nations incline to look at the past like young persons who never miss the opportunity of a surreptitious glance in the mirror to measure the degree of their own attractions. There are always warts and blemishes, but there must also be things to admire, otherwise the adolescent will succumb to suicidal panic. Ordinary folk must have responded to all those Celtic saints as eagerly as they did to Howel Harris and Pantycelyn, or to Mabon, or to the Communists in the 1930s. There is always a chance they will listen to those who take the trouble to speak to them.

A people cannot lose altogether the capacity to appreciate effort and sacrifice. History accumulates for them evidence through the centuries of dedicated minorities prepared to bend their entire life energies towards the salvation of the whole nation. A living society never loses the ability to relate the quality of the sacrifice and the prospect of survival. In Wales, both myth and history record the responses to this unceasing challenge. They both exist primarily in order to convince a beleaguered remnant that they are a fragment of humanity scheduled, in spite of everything, for ultimate preservation.

A small nation has a more active relationship with both the prophet and the poet because each category is obliged to live on a war footing with the same enemy. Each conducts an unending campaign against historical necessity. It is a war on two fronts: the first in the conscience and sensibility of the individual; the other that sector of common effort that has the adhesive power to preserve the society under siege, clutching its proper share of the benefits of the civilisation to which it belongs.

There has to be an abrasive element in the relationship. Gildas knew from the Old Testament that he would not sustain the morale of his people merely by singing them to sleep. At all times the society has the right to put the individual to the test; and the individual in his turn has the right to put the society to the test. The tests are painful. If the society is uncontrollably totalitarian he can be put to death. If it is monolithic in the East European socialist mould, the artist just as much as the prophet can experience banishment, imprisonment or exile; or he can sit in his *dacha* and drown his sorrow in the local liquor. There his situation is oddly parallel with a campus poet in the richest country in the world suffering from the same paralysis. Political and market forces in an otherwise comfortable world can have the same effect on the artist, making him feel an irrelevant outsider and parasite.

Viewed from this standpoint the Welsh situation doesn't look so hopeless. Taliesin and his more worldly alter ego, Merlin, are European prototypes. The Welsh tradition offers a whole range of alternative heroes who have not lost the gift of shape-shifting inside the confines of the tribal language. It is true they are condemned to be encompassed and encumbered with a thick cloud of witnesses; to be cut off from the untold riches of international recognition; to be weighed down with marches and protests, imprisonments and social responsibilities that most artists avoid in more privileged cultural milieux. Nevertheless they are anchored in historical reality by their language, their land-scape, their history. They can practise their art under conditions of spiritual freedom that are a direct reward of their honourable servitude. And what they have to say, like the music of J.S. Bach or Dafydd ap Gwilym, will eventually reverberate on that level outside the restrictions of time and place that is an abiding consolation of the human condition.

Afterword

The writing of history is a process that is condemned never to catch up with itself. In the decade since this extended essay on the Welsh identity was first mooted the civilisation of the western world has come to appear even more precariously balanced between destructive and regenerative powers. The emergence of peristroika and the promise of gradual nuclear disarmament give grounds for the kind of hopeful prognosis that would not have been possible in the nineteen seventies. On the other hand we are expected to deal with incontrovertible evidence that our world is on the brink of environmental catastrophe. This condition offers perfect material to the myth-making processes of the mass media. Nothing gives a better edge to the dramatic presentation of news and current affairs than a flow of conjecture and information, cunningly mixed, that alternates between a doomsday scenario and the imminent arrival of the earthly paradise. The journalist like the historian is allowed to cast off the shackles of professional calm and bend and buckle his language into the lurid shapes of folk tale and fiction.

It is instructive to observe the manner in which our defining British state has responded to these world-wide challenges both to its essential identity and to its powers. Throughout this decade the political party in power has used existing systems or devised new ones in order to enhance, and further entrench and fortify the grip of Westminster on the lives of all its subjects, irrespective of class, colour, culture, or primary nationality. The thrust of its legislation has been towards making British politics the plaything of the rich and the opium of the poor. It has been able to do this with comparative ease because of its overwhelming majority in the House of Commons and because it interprets its political mandate as a licence to re-enforce its own identity at the heart of a socio-political complex traditionally designated to guard the heart and soul of what can only be designated as Anglo-British nationalism. This is the cave of the Minotaur and in terms of folk-lore, and that quasi mythological element which sober historians find so suspect, it is appropriate that the mouth of the cave, so to speak, should be a woman, whom the myth-making mass media can describe as Fairy Godmother or Wicked Witch on alternate days of the week.

The Anglo-British identity is described everywhere outside these islands as English, plain and simple. I use the term Anglo-British in the interests of accuracy in order to include the devoted services to the state, which are far from inconsiderable, of the peripheral nationalities. If the Scots and the Welsh and the Irish were removed from the House of Commons, the strength of that institution as a bulwark of English nationalism and first line defence of the English identity would be seriously weakened.

Throughout this decade while the industrial and manufacturing base has weakened to the point of collapse, the power of the state and its apparatus has increased. As in Kinder-und Hausmärchen, internal and external bogies have been deployed to frighten the children and make them seek the shelter of state-mother's skirts: fierce red-haired and black-hearted union leaders; tin-pot South American dictators; rampant inflation; Russian missiles and missions; coloured immigrants; Irish terrorists; drug traffickers; litterbugs and strikers. The list is long and variable. The mandate for the state's manipulation of its population's consciousness is not merely a parliamentary majority. The abiding power rests on the rock of the defence of the realm: and the defence of the realm is licensed to operate as a vital part of a system which justifies its existence by perpetuating and celebrating the virtues of Englishness as perceived by the English themselves: a love of their language, of their Shakespeare and their Common Law; a love of the ritual of monarchy and parliamentary institutions; an equal love of liberty and privacy, of good humour, fair play, decency and respectability, sweet reason, pragmatic judgements and the unshakeable conviction that most things English and particularly the English language, can only be described as 'best in the world'. The confidence trick, in the literal sense, performed by the Tory party and its present leader, is to convince its public that all these things held so privately precious are being publicly defended by a vigilant government against threats from every point of the compass: from Europeans and the European community, from Brussel sprouts, from the greenhouse effect, from socialist malcontents and from terrorists at home and abroad; even, at rarer moments, from the baser elements of United States culture, and their impudent misuse of the glorious restraint inherent in the English language.

These are the defining political parameters inside which the Welsh identity has to live and breathe and regularly reassure itself of a continuing existence. The wild despairing note in the last line of the most comprehensive and brilliant history of the Welsh written in this decade becomes readily understandable . . . 'My people and no mean people, who have for a millenium and a half lived as Welsh people, are now nothing but a naked people under an acid rain.' Allowing for a tradition of rhetorical hyperbole that has flourished in South-East Wales long before the chapels or the pits were opened and closed down, there is no disguising the cry from the heart of an historian who is a people's remembrancer in the tradition of the poets, – The Taliesin Tradition. Gwyn A. Williams has sensed that the hunger and depression of earlier periods – the last one late enough to be still painfully alive in his memory – has now shifted decisively from the belly to the head.

This is a strange reversal. The great Marxist poet Berthold Brecht decreed in one of his most famous lines, 'Erst kommt das Fressen, dann kommt die Moral,' which establishes that first you eat and then you think. The word 'Fressen', 'devour' or 'stuff', suggests a more ironic translation, 'First you stuff and then you moralise'. But the order of precedence remains. The economic well-being of a people has to be established before they can turn their attention to things of the mind or 'Higher Things', in the sense that the head is always higher than the belly if a man has the strength to stand on his feet. What enables a man to hold his head up high and stand on his own feet is an inner conviction about his own identity which is normally crystallized in the language he has inherited. His identity is threatened when his language is under threat. It is a matter of instinct as well as resolve and honour that he should wish to defend and preserve and perpetuate both identity and language. Historically in the English experience this has been the business of politicians and soldiers rather than historians. Our case is different. The responsibility of defence has long rested on poets, or poets disguised as preachers or historians. Without being over-fanciful this condition can be traced back to a prehistorical oral tradition where the prime function of praise poetry in the Celtic world was to celebrate a social order that was otherwise resistant to any form of political unity.

Poets, as ordinary mortals unversed in the arcane rubrics of academic history, are well aware that there is more to the business than the relentless 'March of Time'. They can imagine the 20th Century as a train-load of humanity scheduled for a journey to an unknown destination that need not and probably will not be a new Garden of Eden or the ultimate Holocaust. Reputable historians gallop along the platform, clutching their expertise like hand-luggage and longing to board the train in order to reassure passengers about the nature of the journey. Alas, like the messenger sent by Prince Pwyll of Dyfed to overtake the mysterious veiled one on her pale horse, the greater the turn of speed and verbal dexterity, the further ahead of them the mystery moves without in any way increasing its pace.

In spite of Marx and Engels, or for that matter Trotsky, Stalin,

Mao Tse Tung, Pol Pot, or Deng Chai Ping, history is still not a guided missile, and thus far at any rate, no amount of plotting its past course or theorising about a 'Scientific world-view' can ascertain its future trajectory. Aboard the last compartments of the 20th Century train, the word 'ideology' has earned itself a bad name. Few of the occupants of these seats expect to arrive in an undiscovered country where socialism in all its purity has been put into practice, or even a supermarket metropolis where capitalism like the sphinx has acquired the mask of a thoughtful human face. Certainly there is no one left on board who sits up expecting to witness the awesome spectacle of the state withering away.

The most terrifying memory the 20th Century leaves with the passengers still alive on the train is the spectre of the increasing power of the centralised state. It was this sinister machinery that made it possible for dictators like Stalin and Hitler to dispose of millions of their helpless subjects with barely a murmur of protest. All over the world there are tribes and nations and inconvenient categories of peoples being shunted about, transferred, incarcerated, liquidated to suit the convenience of one kind of state machine or other fuelled by a noxious mixture of lethal ideologies. In my own back garden as I write with the freedom guaranteed by hearsay and legal tradition rather than a Bill of Rights, the State, using the Central Electricity Generating Board as a stalking-horse, intends to build a second nuclear power station. When we murmur nervously about the mistakes made at Three Mile Island and Chernobyl we are assured that the Anglo-British state and its utilities have attained such transcedent perfection that they are incapable of error. But should the unthinkable come to pass the sixty thousand odd inhabitants of the island should be prepared to make a sacrifice and become expendable in the interests of the energy needs of the majority who under our perfected democratic system keep the government in power.

As early in this essay as page 58 it was established that the Welsh were an endangered species. Gwyn A. Williams maintains that we have survived as an historical people in spite of a condition of permanent emergency. 'The Welsh as a people were born disinherited' ends the second chapter of his 'When was Wales?' (Even in the title there is a question mark.) This is oddly reassuring. It suggests that the Welsh condition mirrors the human condition with a degree of accuracy that should make us feel privileged. Aside from the theological overtones, in the context of natural history and the environment, shape-shifting has something to contribute and is certainly preferable to the spine-chilling mutations of the science fiction scenario of the future. The mere act of presuming to write our own history would suggest that in spite of Engel's brand of materialism, our continuing existence is more than a modified continuation of natural history.

We are not only here because we are here; we are a subjective species, we have departments of Welsh History and a national university and they both exist as much to determine the frontier of our identity as the frontier of knowledge.

The processes of education should give a people the confidence to take over the extent of political and economic leadership necessary to allow their identity to flourish. Many of the foregoing pages have been at pains to explain why this never happened in Wales. The more urgent question that remains is how can it take place now in a country where economic power rests in multinational hands – chiefly Japanese and American – in clandestine consort with a Westminster apparatus of government desperately seeking allies from any quarter of the globe to fend off the encroachments of European community authority on its ancient powers, prerogatives and privileges. It is under such daunting conditions that a 'disinherited people' has somehow to generate a revolution that will give it sufficient power to protect its essential identity from either annihilation or assimilation.

It is unlikely that any such revolution could emerge from technical exercises in conventional party politics. Representation in the House of Commons was never intended to accommodate let alone protect Welshness or the Welsh identity. In our case the Act of Union was intended to be an act of submission and submersion. Such identity as was left was directed to abolish itself by acts of the House of Commons passed four centuries ago, and it says something for the capacity of hope to spring eternal in the Welsh breast that we should continue to cherish great expectations from this institution that has, more often than not, done all it could to expunge the last traces of our separate existence with the moral fervour of reformers bent on stamping out some intolerable social evil.

Any political revolution in Wales must entail an awakening in the population of desire for liberation and an intellectual maturity capable of facing the formidable power of Westminster and Brussels. This awakening has to take precedence over attempts to take responsibility for the machinery of government. It pre-supposes a process of spiritual emancipation in which the language of the country, and indeed the Taliesin tradition, has a central part to play. The fight for the language has been the most striking and immediately recognisable source of inspiration in Welsh life over the last three decades. It is this struggle above all others that has shown a capacity to sustain and direct forms of non-violent revolutionary protest which remain the most effective weapon left to any minority who wish to be creative while in unrelenting opposition to the worst effects of the bureaucratic centralism of the Anglo-British nation state. An initial concern for the language of their fathers obliged the young protesters of the sixties and seventies to take into account the economic and social welfare of the land of their fathers. They have made the language a key issue in Wales because it is so closely bound up with the wellbeing of the whole community. These are the unacknowledged legislators of an ecology which is both cultural and environmental. For a naked people in the acid rain they offer a coat of many colours and a cleaner air. They have taken upon themselves the heavy responsibility of leadership and it was the prison cells that gave them time to think.

A Personal Postscript

The mass media have poured torrents of words and pictures over our heads in order to convince us that a new millenium brings with it an acceleration of technical progress which will send us spinning into a thrilling but unpredictable future. If we are allowed to stop and think we can discern a deep contradiction in this popular proposition. Technological progress means an increased control over the forces of nature. If that is the case why must we expect to be swept off our feet like so many Judy Garlands caught up in a tornado? Who in the end are the servants and the victims and where exactly dwells that invisible wizard we are all to accept as master?

As I write we are reassured, between outbreaks of genocidal savagery that no leading state on earth is bent on military conquest, and authoritarian regimes are once and for all discredited. Human aggression can be combined with human ingenuity and conveniently diverted into space exploration. This should give our capacity problem solving time to concentrate on improving life on earth. Our formidable brain power will be extended by computer technology to make progress in every conceivable sphere. Already progress in microbiology and genetics holds out the prospect of better health and longer life for billions. Digital technology will be harnessed to an education that will teach us to control the earth's resources properly, tame the population explosion and even replace unbridled capitalism with intelligent economic planning.

With such a delectable prospect before us, the temptation is of course to turn our backs on the past. The dynamic of an advanced industrial society is more than forward looking. Technology evenly applied, worldwide, is capable of reducing the entire species to a condition of uniformity and equality beyond any previous imagining of a brave new world. Separate societies cease to exist and individuals take on the characteristics of tiny light bulbs responding gratefully to an omnipotent planetary electric circuit. In the face of such awesome progress, what can our small Welsh concerns matter?

It is reasonable to hope that in Wales, as well as world-wide, millennial euphoria will eventually give way to a period of deeper reflection. We have a National Assembly for example, but will this institution become a stronghold of national identity and will it safe-guard the language of Taliesin for the free use of future generations? To be of enduring value institutions, just like abstract concepts, must be seen to contribute to that creative process that makes the life of a people richer and more fulfilling. In literature, and particularly the literary tradition outlined in this book, it must be assumed that words are taken seriously. At the very least they are the distilled experience of our ancestors available to add depth and resonance to the life of succeeding generations. It is the busi-ness of a literary tradition to ensure that language does not deteriorate into an anodyne mulch of cliché and received opinion. A tradition remains of enduring value when it preserves the ability of words to possess the power of meaning more than they say.

Let me take as an example an unfamiliar word that I encountered for the first time sixty years ago. I was struggling with the aid of a dictionary to understand a sonnet by Robert Williams Parry addressed to 'J.S.L.', namely John Saunders Lewis. The word was *petryal*. I was intrigued to discover that this word had hardly been used since the story of *Branwen Ferch Llyr* in the *Pedair Cainc*: that would be in effect, since the twelfth century. It was Branwen who died of grief because two great islands had been ruined on her account, ...*a gwneuthur bed petrual idi, a'e chladdu yno yglan Alaw*... "and they made for her a four-sided [petryal] grave and buried her there on the bank of the Alaw". The manner in which the survivors set about making a four sided grave for the dead queen sets a seal on the sequence of calamitous misfortunes. When we turn to recognise the word in the final couplet of the sonnet composed in 1937 we are compelled to hear it resonate with a bitter irony: *Gan bwyll y bwytawn, o dafell i dafell betryal / Yr academig dost. Mwynha dithau'r grual.* "With caution we eat, [munch, nibble] from slice to four-sided slice / The academic toast. You – enjoy your [prison] gruel."

Lewis had been imprisoned for his part in starting a symbolic fire in Llyn. He had been dismissed from his post as lecturer in Welsh literature at Swansea. The poem is a tribute to Lewis's courage: it is also a disciplined but savage satire which is given an enduring emotional charge by the poet's own guilt and self reproach. The key to our understanding is that word *petryal*. Williams Parry had failed to persuade his colleagues to do something on behalf of his hero at a time when Lewis was being subjected to a sequence of injustices, because he was prepared to sacrifice himself in defence of the language and the values that they all professed to love.

The 'academic toast' was in fact a cosy ritual enjoyed in the professor's room on Monday afternoons. The same professor and head of department whose celebrated edition of the *Pedair Cainc* expounded the original and full meaning of the word *petryal*. He more than anyone else would recognise the reference. Robert Williams Parry was a man of particularly nervous and sensitive disposition. For fear of giving offence and perhaps of putting his own job in jeopardy he delayed publishing the sonnet. He cursed himself for his cowardice and tried to make amends by writing more brilliant poems in praise of his hero. It seemed to me all those years ago that there was an underlying relationship between the two extracts using the word *petryal*: in eating those four sided pieces of toast the complacent academics were miming the process of digging a grave for Branwen's language.

Even at the start of a new millennium the words of the sonnet still disturb as much as they delight. There are some situations in the human condition that are liable to recur. By now, to an ear enriched with bilingual impurities *petryal* rhymes dangerously close to *betrayal*. Loyalty as well as freedom requires eternal vigilance. Poets like Robert Williams Parry never start revolutions: but poets like Saunders Lewis do. This man continued to be reviled by influential quarters in Wales right up to his death at ninety two in 1985, and indeed well beyond it. Nevertheless it is reasonable to argue that without his sacrifice and unwavering witness such nationality as remains to us would have sunk long ago to the level of a deflated rugby ball. Without his example such trappings of nationhood as we now enjoy would never have come into being. As for that poem, it is there to remind us whatever the future, that without an apostolic succession of cultural heroes there is small chance of preserving a civilised way of life in this 'world of Wales'. The struggle continues.

Index